THE SMELL OF RISK

The Smell of Risk

Environmental Disparities and Olfactory Aesthetics

Hsuan L. Hsu

NEW YORK UNIVERSITY PRESS
New York

NEW YORK UNIVERSITY PRESS
New York
www.nyupress.org

References to Internet websites (URLs) were accurate at the time of writing. Neither the author nor New York University Press is responsible for URLs that may have expired or changed since the manuscript was prepared.

Library of Congress Cataloging-in-Publication Data
Names: Hsu, Hsuan L., 1976– author.
Title: The smell of risk : environmental disparities and olfactory aesthetics / Hsuan L. Hsu.
Description: New York : New York University Press, [2020] | Includes bibliographical references and index.
Identifiers: LCCN 2020016693 (print) | LCCN 2020016694 (ebook) | ISBN 9781479807215 (hardback) | ISBN 9781479810093 (paperback) | ISBN 9781479805372 (ebook) | ISBN 9781479808144 (ebook)
Subjects: LCSH: Deodorization—History. | Odors—Social aspects—History. | Environmental health—History. | Health risk assessment—History.
Classification: LCC RA576 .H78 2020 (print) | LCC RA576 (ebook) | DDC 613/.1—dc23
LC record available at https://lccn.loc.gov/2020016693
LC ebook record available at https://lccn.loc.gov/2020016694

New York University Press books are printed on acid-free paper, and their binding materials are chosen for strength and durability. We strive to use environmentally responsible suppliers and materials to the greatest extent possible in publishing our books.

Manufactured in the United States of America

10 9 8 7 6 5 4 3 2 1

Also available as an ebook

CONTENTS

Introduction: Deodorization and Its Discontents   1

1. "Every Crime Has Its Peculiar Odor": Detection,
   Deodorization, and Intoxication   27

2. Naturalist Smellscapes and Environmental Justice   56

3. Olfactory Art and Museum Ecologies   85

4. Atmo-Orientalism: Olfactory Racialization and
   Environmental Health   113

5. Decolonizing Smell   152

   Epilogue: Reshaping Olfactory Ecologies   193

   Acknowledgments   203

   Notes   207

   Index   247

   About the Author   261

Introduction

Deodorization and Its Discontents

Richard Powers's epic novel *Gain* (1998) chronicles the intertwined growth of the United States, the corporation, and the deodorized body. Tracing a soap manufacturing firm's growth into a multinational conglomerate, Powers charts how the corporation interfaces with everyday, multifaceted relationships ranging from the molecular to the global scale. A pivotal moment in the two centuries of corporate history spanned by the novel occurs when the botanist Benjamin Clare, having shipped with the United States Exploring Expedition (1838–42), is stranded near the South Pole. After spending a few minutes struggling to pull the ship around, Clare realizes that the air has relieved his fear of death: "All terror over the disintegrating *Peacock* vanished, like the visions of an opiate dream. A perfumed thread entered Clare's nostrils: an old, life-long friend. Yet he had never smelled its like. A scent wafted upon him, a redolence for all the world like the smell of a forgotten existence. . . . Fetid fragrance had so ruled his every inhalation [aboard ship] that the thing he smelled, out on the ice, was the sachet of scentlessness: air before the employment of lungs."[1] Fresh, scentless air after a lifetime lived in the closed spaces of cities, dormitories, factories, and ships has the calming effect of an "opiate." There is something uncanny about this inodorate scent, at once unprecedented and evocative of a "forgotten existence" or old friend. "Air before the employment of lungs" is air that can't be sensed at all—it enables Clare to breathe without the consciousness of breathing. Surmising that the cold polar air caused heavy odorant molecules—"those smells that otherwise relentlessly bombarded human nostrils"—to drop away, Clare finds that both his own position as the ship's botanist and the fate of the ship itself have become "a matter of indifference" (*G*, 61). His life is changed not by the ship's miraculous deliverance from the polar maze of ice but by the existential shift triggered by "his first whiff of nothing" (*G*, 61).

Clare's olfactory revelation conveys a paradoxical "sense of the senses' lie" (*G*, 61). The smell of nothing gives material expression to a modern sensorium premised on the suppression of the embodied senses of touch, taste, and (especially) smell. Months after this scene, Clare encounters another, similar smell when exchanging botanical knowledge with the High King of Fiji. The king introduces Clare to a rhizomatous tuber that "possessed a faraway smell, an astringency that Clare would not have been able to detect until a few months before" (*G*, 65). This root—which Clare carries back to New York and names *Utilis clarea*—becomes the key ingredient in Clare & Company's leading nineteenth-century product, Native Balm Soap. By translating polar scentlessness into a subtly scented product, the soap manufacturer renders deodorization—along with its associated ideas of individual responsibility and self-care—into a highly profitable "opiate" of the masses.

Native Balm draws its appeal from the myth of the "ecological Indian," as well as early white ethnographers' representations of "Indians' innate sweetness of odor."[2] As Powers puts it, "The age of steam produced certain unprecedented shocks to the skin unknown to earlier ways and races. Live as the natives once did, and these shocks might disappear. Unnatural skin needed a natural cure, a cure whose formulas machine progress had somehow mislaid" (*G*, 132–33). Smelling almost—but not quite—like nothing at all, *Utilis clarea* promises sensory relief from the ambient environmental "shocks" associated with modern technologies. Clare & Company literally deracinates the root, detaching it from any reference to the iTaukei (Fijian) people in the course of renaming it and stamping "the profile of a noble Brave" on each bar of soap (*G*, 134). Although Clare is initially "as interested in the plant's fictive attributes as in any real properties" when the king of Fiji tells him about the root, this very distinction derecognizes iTaukei botanical knowledge—along with any medical or spiritual properties that may have been attributed to the root—as "fictive" (*G*, 65). Even the name *Utilis clarea* dismisses an entire range of attributes: whereas "The King called the root by a name that meant either *strength* or *use*," Clare's naming highlights its utility (*utilis*) while associating it with both the light of enlightenment (*clarea*) and his own significance as its putative "discoverer."

Utilis clarea channels both Indigenous botanical knowledge and US stereotypes about Indigeneity into a product that promises to ameliorate modernity's ever-increasing risks. As Clare's brother realizes, "they could solve the needs of progress by selling the very condition that the need remedied" (*G*, 133). This insight about risk's capacity for generating new markets echoes sociologist Ulrich Beck's observation that, as opposed to the finite demands of hunger and need, "*civilization* risks are a *bottomless barrel of demands*, unsatisfiable, infinite, self-producible."[3] Its Native American associations and its subtle scent ("it smelled like the liniment that the angels applied in God's own sickroom") are sufficient to make Native Balm a nationwide "health" sensation—the product on whose profits Clare & Company's future enterprises are founded (*G*, 132). Yet, as Powers points out, in the 1840s there was no government agency of business regulation to determine whether Native Balm was indeed "restorative" in its health effects or whether it was a toxic product "pack[ing] a delayed punch more poisonous than henbane" (*G*, 133).

A century and a half later the corporation's ongoing failure to investigate and disclose risks associated with its products—which by the 1990s encompass a vast range of synthetic products including pesticides, cosmetics, pharmaceuticals, and plastics—is juxtaposed with the illness narrative of Laura Body, a middle-class neighbor of Clare & Company's Midwestern headquarters who is slowly dying of ovarian cancer. Powers sets the stage for Clare's revelatory encounter with the scent of scentlessness by cataloguing the outdoor smells that flow in when Laura opens the window to air out her stuffy hospital room:

> The breeze that flushes these rooms imports its own aromas: stubborn lilacs and stultifying magnolias. Ozone from dry lightning, forty miles distant. Swiss almond decaf from the new coffee shop, half an hour from its red-eye opening. Organophosphates wafting in from the south farms. Undigested adhesives slipping up Clare's smokeless stacks. The neighbors' gerbil food and scoopable cat litter wafting over her fence in two parts per billion.
>
> But mixed together in the air's cross-breeze, these smells sum to a shorthand for freshness. The day's background radiation. (*G*, 53)

In contrast with Clare's "whiff of nothing" in the polar regions, the outdoor air of Lacewood, Illinois, is no purer than the hospital's "unpleasant odors" (*G*, 53). Whether or not Laura herself detects them, the narrator catalogues a motley mix of smells that includes the natural and the synthetic, the local and the imported, domestic and everyday objects, as well as the sublime lightning storm and the dystopian image of invisible emissions emanating from the Clare chemical plant. How many of those synthetic scents were fabricated by the Clare corporation or one of its many subsidiaries? The overall effect pulls in two directions: on the one hand, a "shorthand for freshness" that could easily pass as fresh air for a long-acclimatized local like Laura; on the other hand, a looming "background radiation" suggesting that those airborne adhesives, organophosphates, and cat litter particulates may have contributed to the onset of Laura's cancer.

In charting this trajectory from an industrially produced, chemically engineered soap that associates Indigeneity with deodorization to Laura's illness and a class-action lawsuit against the corporation, *Gain* provokes many of the questions explored in this book. How did deodorization become conflated with middle-class ideas of health and morality, and how was it mobilized as a putative antidote to modernity's pervasive and unpredictable health risks? How did the ideology of deodorization intersect with ideas about racial difference—whether the racial "innocence" attributed to Native Americans or the racial depravity and dystopian hypermodernity attributed to Black and Asiatic bodies? How do nineteenth-century beliefs about noxious miasmas—along with techniques of atmospheric manipulation designed to address those miasmas—persist in the present? And how did proponents of deodorization smooth over the contradiction between the ideal of pure air and synthetic deodorizing products like Native Balm? Or the contradiction between the doctrine of deodorization and the real atmospheric disparities necessitated by capital expansion—for example, the carcinogenic fumes disseminated by Clare & Company's suppliers, factories, and products not only in Laura's hometown of Lacewood, but increasingly in sites of extraction and subcontracted manufacture located throughout the Global South? And how might the suppressed potentialities of scent—the unspecified "strength" of the *Utilis clarea* root that Clare obscures in favor of its "utility"—be excavated and reactivated in the interest of redressing capitalism's unevenly distributed atmospheres?

These questions emerge from a set of aesthetic problems arising at the intersection of olfaction and environmental risk. Commonly mobilized as a tool of "citizen science," the sense of smell is a widely available resource for detecting unfamiliar and potentially dangerous materials in the atmosphere: in the words of the psychophysiologist G. Neil Martin, smell is "the first chemosensory custodian of survival."[4] Although olfaction often occurs on an unconscious level (particularly in societies where it is devalued as a source of knowledge), a recent study of odor mixture discrimination found that humans can discriminate among more than one trillion olfactory stimuli.[5] Because olfaction is physiologically connected to the limbic system (a key neurological site of emotion and memory),[6] descriptions of unwelcome smells exert immense rhetorical force. In the early stages of local struggles over toxic exposure, olfaction often plays a "starring role."[7] As historian Joy Parr explains, "Smell has a history as warning of contamination linked to practices of self-preservation; its interiority . . . is historically often a ground for authoritative truth-telling."[8] For example, the activist Lois Gibbs reports that even before she was fully aware of its chemical risks she was disturbed by the smell of Love Canal: "The closer I got to the canal, the more I could smell it. I could *feel* it, too, it was so humid. The odor seemed to hang in the thick air. My nose began to run, and my eyes were watering."[9] Although such olfactory descriptions underscore smell's insidious effects on the breather's body, they also register how atmospheric toxins settle and recirculate—their "agitations, suspensions, and sedimentations"[10] throughout the more-than-human world, flowing in and out of water, soil, plants, and nonhuman animals. Smell's viscerality and chemical vulnerability make it a powerful tool for communicating about atmospheric toxins even when some of those toxins are scentless: although some of the more than two hundred organic chemical compounds found at Love Canal may be undetectable by smell, they are all metonymically indexed by Gibbs's unsettling account of the air's thick odor.

Yet smell is also notoriously difficult to discern, describe, and recall—at least for subjects of Western modernity who are trained to neglect it. These difficulties are compounded by the socially constructed nature of olfactory experience, which superimposes cultural significations upon the chemical characteristics of odorants: thus, Native Balm has both materially cleansing (emulsifying) properties and a slightly astringent scent that, for many Americans, signifies "freshness." The social construction of smell informs—and is informed by—the social construction of environmental risk perception, such that smells thought to be unpleasant (for example, the smells of an ethnic restaurant) may be perceived to be more harmful than inodorate or pleasant-smelling substances (e.g., a perfume or scented pesticide).[11] Thus, the human body's most sensitive tool for detecting invisible chemical threats across space is also deeply ambiguous, fraught with uncertainty, socially constructed, culturally neglected, and resistant to representation.

These problems with olfactory epistemology and representation have contributed to the denigration of smell in Western aesthetics. At least since the Enlightenment, smell has been framed as too immersive, imprecise, subjective, interactive, involuntary, material, promiscuous, and ineffable to convey aesthetic experience: as Kant puts it, smell is a vehicle of sensual "enjoyment" rather than "beauty."[12] The Smell of Risk grows out of my conviction that these very qualities of olfaction make it an especially effective vehicle for staging and thinking about problems of environmental risk. For risk, too, is immersive, imprecise, subjective, interactive, involuntary, material, and resistant to representation. A sense that is at once materially embodied and spatially extensive, olfaction offers writers, artists, and activists a powerful tool for exploring modernity's stratified geographies of risk.

My own investment in the kinds of knowledge and intimacy made available by smell can be traced back to an experience of toxic exposure. Years ago, when I was moving away from Berkeley to take up my first full-time position, I slept in my apartment shortly after it had been repainted. There was a faint odor of paint fumes in the bedroom, but a combination of exhaustion, nostalgia, and trust (the paint had had several days to dry, I told myself) made me decide to spend one more night in the apartment that had been my home for the last six years. I woke with a headache, a mild case of asthma, and an attenuated sense of smell. For weeks after that I could barely detect familiar scents of cooking, plants, body products, or loved ones. Fifteen years later, my olfactory sensitivity has improved somewhat, but it's impossible to know whether it has recovered fully. What had I lost? Only years later, when I initiated this research project, did I come to understand the profound stakes of this partial anosmia: it eroded a sense with powerful connections to the neurological seat of memory and emotion, as well as an important tool for detecting environmental risks. The smell of paint fumes was not just a sign of toxicity—the smell was itself an intoxicating airborne substance whose long-term effect was, ironically, to consign me to a partially deodorized experience of the world. On the other hand, this experience with anosmia has made me acutely aware of the richness of olfactory chemosensation, not only as a tool for sensing unevenly distributed toxins but also as a pathway to ecological and social intimacies that, like scents, often refuse to be contained.

This introductory chapter develops a framework for approaching smell as a contested—though often overlooked—tool for sensing the dynamics of atmospheric differentiation that have been vital to capitalism's processes of colonization, racialization, extraction, industrialization, urbanization, uneven development, and environmental depredation. The following sections consider how the recent turn toward interdisciplinary research on atmospheres nuances accounts of modernization as a teleological history of "deodorization": instead, framing the cultural suppression of smell as a process of *differential deodorization* draws attention to the insidious ways in which atmospheric disparities literally get into people's bodies. I then suggest that scholarship in materialist ecocriticism—informed by recent research on olfaction in the fields of sensory studies and environmental history—can help us better understand how aesthetic projects have variously sustained, contested, and presented alternatives to differential deodorization.

The Atmospheric Turn

In *Foams* (2004), the third book in his *Spheres* trilogy on the phenomenology of anthropogenic spaces, philosopher Peter Sloterdijk identifies the deployment of mustard gas during World War I as the beginning of a contemporary era marked by "the principle of air conditioning."[13] *Air conditioning* encompasses techniques of atmospheric manipulation across multiple scales (e.g., filter masks, air-conditioned buildings, gas warfare, the offshoring of toxic industries), as well as the profound and little-understood ways in which these manipulated atmospheres condition human being. Sloterdijk's concept reframes the human as a breather whose being is contingent on the condition of the surrounding air; but it also reframes the air itself as a medium for differentiating human populations through the "microclimatic 'splintering of the atmosphere'" into compartmentalized and stratified breathing spaces.[14] This differentiation goes far beyond the discursive stigmatization of working-class and racialized communities as malodorous: disproportionate and prolonged exposures to risky atmospheres biochemically transform people's bodies, minds, and moods.

Sloterdijk's work has been pivotal for a broader "atmospheric turn" that has animated provocative interdisciplinary spatial research in the social sciences and humanities. As Peter Adey has observed, "human geography suddenly seems afloat with airs and winds, fogs and aerial fluids, with volumes, verticals and objects in the air."[15] The turn to atmosphere brings the insights of new materialism to bear on the elusive yet vital medium of air: rather than focusing exclusively on the "vibrant" qualities of objects,[16] scholars of atmosphere shift attention to our material interchanges with the air. This work brings a materialist perspective to the study of atmosphere—a term that has long circulated as a metaphor for the "emotional tone" or distinctive mood of an aesthetic work.[17] Geographers have investigated atmospheric phenomenologies exemplified by contemporary art, nineteenth-century novels, olfactory walking tours, and public deployments of balloons and tear gas.[18] Other scholars of architecture, anthropology, geography, and feminist theory have illuminated the affective qualities of atmosphere: as Ben Anderson explains, "Affective atmospheres are a class of experience that occur *before* and *alongside* the formation of subjectivity, *across* human and non-human materialities, and *in-between* subject/object distinctions."[19] Along with geographer Derek McCormack and environmental anthropologist Tim Ingold, literary critic Jesse Oak Taylor has illuminated how atmospheric perception can conjoin lived, affective experience with an (often technologically mediated) awareness of meteorological transformations.[20]

In *Spatial Justice: Body, Lawscape, Atmosphere* (2015), legal geographer Andreas Philippopoulos-Mihalopoulos draws suggestive connections between the affective appeal of engineered atmospheres and the perpetuation of power relations. According to Philippopoulos-Mihalopoulos, the physical and affective comforts of atmosphere prevent us from apprehending that the law is immanent throughout everyday spaces (in property law, safety regulations, trademarks, etc.). Whether in a shopping mall, a museum, or a bourgeois sitting room, we are held in an "atmospheric captivity" whereby "our needs are converted into one foundational need: the need of the atmosphere to carry on existing."[21] Because atmospheric comfort immerses and suffuses us as we breathe, Philippopoulos-Mihalopoulos argues that the air itself is an insidious, little-noticed agent of interpellation: "In a time of intense atmospheric engineering, Althusser's interpellation is atmospherically diffused. No one needs to call us anymore. We do it ourselves . . . being interpellated not through ideology (this has been suffused in atmospherics) but [through] a constructed, furious desire to perpetuate the atmosphere."[22] Whereas Philippopoulos-Mihalopoulos underscores the need for atmospheric ruptures and ethical decisions to withdraw from atmosphere's affective enticements, scholars in critical race studies, Indigenous studies, and queer studies have drawn attention to the debilitating and, for many, fatal effects of atmospheres mobilized against Indigenous and racialized populations. Their interventions—which include provocative concepts such as "racial atmospheres," "settler atmospherics," and the reframing of antiblackness as "the weather"[23]—describe conditions of violence (rather than "interpellation") in which atmospheric "withdrawal" is not a viable option. Instead, capitalism's dependence on varied practices of *racial atmospherics* underscores the problem of how to transform or abolish the apparatuses of "air conditioning." What would an equitable and/or decolonial practice of air conditioning look like—or, perhaps more importantly, what would it smell like?

Insofar as it addresses the effects of intentional and unintended atmospheric manipulations, air conditioning intersects with the systemic atmospheric transformations commonly designated by the term "Anthropocene"—or by more historically precise terms such as "Capitalocene" and "Plantationocene."[24] By approaching these transformations from the perspective of local, multifarious, and fragmented atmospheres, the framework of air conditioning challenges the tendency, in many scholarly and public conversations about the Anthropocene, to privilege the totalizing scales of the species and planet. Planetary climate change cannot be disentangled from the uneven distribution of airborne materials in the lowest sections of the troposphere (the layer of the atmosphere closest to Earth's surface, which carries between 75 and 80 percent of atmospheric mass). As critics have noted, emphasizing the vast scales of deep geological time and the planetary atmosphere frames the Anthropocene as a crisis generated by all humans and one that threatens all humans equally; in reality, nearly all greenhouse gases have been generated in connection with racial capitalism's cycles of extraction and accumulation, and the effects of climate change disproportionately harm vulnerable racialized, Indigenous, and postcolonial populations in places such as Syria, New Orleans, Oceania, and coastal Indigenous settlements in Alaska.[25] Insofar as it maintains pleasant atmospheres for those with the most influence on environmental and economic policy, air conditioning sustains unsustainable practices of production and consumption. Thus, air conditioning is a multiscalar phenomenon not only because the local atmospheres whose molecules enter breathers' bodies are frequently affected by the forces of global capital accumulation and the transnational offshoring of environmental externalities but also because these unevenly distributed local atmospheres reduce the sensory urgency of the (colonial, racial) Capitalocene's emissions for those who benefit most from air conditioning. Thus, feminist philosopher Val Plumwood argues that in order to manifest the "shadow places" whose disavowed exploitation sustains culturally and materially privileged places, "we must smell a bit of wrecked Ogoniland in the exhaust fumes from the air-conditioner, the ultimate remoteness, put-it-somewhere-else-machine."[26]

By filtering and manipulating atmospheres—or simply moving them around—air conditioning generates and maintains comfortable, breathable spaces for some while unevenly exposing the bodies of the poor and vulnerable to risky inhalations. As McCormack puts it, "Processes of envelopment are differently implicated in an infrastructural politics of immersion, awareness, and exposure that draws some bodies in and excludes others."[27] On an everyday level, these differential effects play out in what Elias Canetti calls "the defenselessness of breathing."[28] Breath is the most continuous site of bodily porosity or "trans-corporeality"—to invoke feminist critic Stacy Alaimo's term for "the material interconnections of human corporeality with the more-than-human world."[29] Whereas geographers tend to think of bodies as being "in" space, breathing foregrounds how atmosphere gets into bodies: "Even as we breathe in and out, the air mingles with our bodily tissues, filling the lungs and oxygenating the blood, and in this metabolic mingling we are constituted."[30] The Latin *animus* associates breath with life and soul, underscoring air's vitality as "that which animates the flesh and makes it move."[31] Even before they reach the lungs and blood, inhaled molecules directly access the brain's limbic system through the olfactory bulbs, whose receptors "are the only neurons that are . . . directly exposed to the environment."[32] Through our differently composed breaths—modulated by factors such as air filters, fragrances, access to green space, industrial emissions, and synthetic chemicals—atmosphere materially differentiates bodies, minds, and moods. To invoke Timothy Morton, the air we breathe is a "hyperobject"—"massively distributed in time and space relative to humans," composed by anthropogenic processes sedimented through time and dispersed across space in the form of deforestation, factories, intensive agriculture, carbon exhaust, and trajectories of waste disposal.[33] Under such conditions, breath becomes "an important spatiality through which to critique contemporary relations of power and to imagine a better world."[34] And as Patrick Süskind explains in his classic olfactory crime novel *Perfume*, scent represents a powerful mechanism for leveraging breath's fragility: "Scent was a brother of breath. Together with breath it entered human beings, who could not defend themselves against it, not if they wanted to live. And scent entered their very core, went directly to their hearts, and decided for good and all between affection and contempt, disgust and lust, love and hate. He who ruled scent ruled the hearts of men."[35]

Air pollution is the world's leading environmental contributor to disease, causing an estimated seven million premature deaths per year.[36] In addition to premature deaths and accretive effects such as endocrine disruption, atmospheric disparities contribute to a multitude of ambient, everyday modes of debilitation ranging from lowered educational outcomes, diminished capacity to perform complex tasks, and increased suicide mortality to changes in mood including feelings of lethargy, brain fog, and chronic stress.[37] Many of these effects are gendered and racialized: toxins increase breast cancer risk and disproportionately affect women's reproductive health, and activism around asthma and other threats to children's health in the United States tends to be led by Black and brown mothers.[38] While not all airborne toxins can be perceived through smell, odors are a common medium through which risk becomes perceptible. Smells themselves frequently take the form of (or indicate the copresence of) volatile organic compounds, which have been associated with a range of short- and long-term health effects.

The consequences of air conditioning frequently manifest as shifts in affect, minor debilitations that may or may not build toward chronic or terminal health conditions. These instances of atmospheric debilitation do not conform to the common framing of disability as an identity category, or to what Jasbir Puar has called the "living/dying pendulum that forms most discussions of biopolitics."[39] Instead, they call for an understanding of debilitation as a potential outcome—"becoming disabled"— that is unevenly distributed across spaces and atmospheres.[40] As Jina Kim writes, "Diverging from the theories of minority identity that have come to define the category of disability, disability functions here as atmosphere, as ambience, as an event that unfolds through the interpenetration of human and environment."[41] Building on these and other scholars working at the intersection of disability studies and critical ethnic studies, I approach atmospheric violence as a mode of proliferating toxic debilitation without forgetting that debility can give rise to transformative, even intoxicating modes of knowledge, experience, and community.

Atmospheric violence frequently overlaps with—and amplifies— patterns of racial violence, as attested by Eric Garner's suffocation at the hands of police and the subsequent taking up of his last words (repeated eleven times), "I can't breathe," by Black Lives Matter activists drawing attention to the collusion between direct modes of police violence and slower, environmentally induced forms of debilitation such as Garner's asthma.[42] Both the uneven distribution of air and its insidious effects on breathers pose obstacles to representation: atmospheric differentiation is a form of "slow violence," to quote Rob Nixon's term for "a violence that occurs gradually and out of sight, a violence of delayed destruction that is dispersed across time and space, an attritional violence that is typically not viewed as violence at all."[43]

Differential Deodorization

In a 2016 *Los Angeles Times* article, "'We Cannot Breathe': A Poor Alabama Town Has Lived with the Rotten Egg Stench of Gas for 8 Years," Ivan Penn contrasts the promptness of relocations and remediation in the wake of the 2015 Aliso Canyon methane leak near a wealthy, predominantly white neighborhood outside Los Angeles with a similar incident in the low-income, predominantly Black neighborhood of Eight Mile, Alabama. Although Eight Mile residents had endured the "stifling rotten egg stench" of mercaptan (a chemical used to add odor to natural gas) resulting from an estimated five hundred gallons of spilled natural gas for over eight years, "there have been no relocations to hotels or rented homes. No transfers to schools out of harm's way. No US Cabinet members swooping in to investigate. No national media hordes."[44] In both locations residents alleged that the odor was not just obnoxious but physically debilitating, "describing symptoms such as nosebleeds, respiratory distress, nausea, vomiting, seizures, vision problems and hypertension."[45] The different responses to these two leaks on the part of media, politicians, and Sempra Energy (a San Diego–based corporation that owned both facilities) illustrate how economic, political, and discursive forces shape the dynamics of differential deodorization. In addition to disparities in income and political representation, long-standing stereotypes about race, purity, and hygiene inform the decision to deprioritize calls to clean up noxious odors in a poor, predominantly Black neighborhood. How could odor complaints in Eight Mile register as worthy of sustained media attention in a culture steeped in racist beliefs about deodorized whiteness and Black "odor"?[46]

Eight Mile's eight-year exposure to noxious fumes exemplifies a glaring problem with accounts of modernization as a process of progressive deodorization. As Mark Jenner observes, historians tend to assume that modernity is deodorized, focusing their olfactory inquiries on the unpleasant odors of past eras.[47] Like beliefs in the universality of breathing, atmosphere, and even the human species (which is biochemically differentiated by chemical and radioactive body burdens), the notion of deodorization as a teleological process is belied by ongoing and increasingly complex techniques of air conditioning. The historical period covered in this book begins in the late nineteenth century, when industrialization—a process entangled with both air pollution and vast waves of immigration and rural-to-urban migration—dramatically transformed the atmosphere of many US cities and towns. Before the adoption of the germ theory of disease in the later part of the century, health authorities attributed disease to "miasma" or polluted air. London sanitary reformer Edwin Chadwick's assertion that "all smell is disease" captures the essential role that smell played in detecting nineteenth-century health risks.[48] Miasma theory made deodorization and other modes of olfactory regulation a central goal for urban planners and public health officials in Europe and the United States: as art historian Caroline Jones puts it, "Bureaucracies found smells imperative to organize; in turn, smells called further bureaucracies into being."[49] Even after miasma theory gave way to germ theory, deodorized spaces have continued to be associated with Enlightenment conceptions of "civilization," health, and the transcendence of the body.

But deodorization was not evenly realized across space: rather, it was a partial and differential project of air conditioning. While efforts to deodorize public and private space claim to improve public health, they frequently focus on semiotic and cosmetic forms of deodorization (covering up unpleasant smells or moving them around) rather than equitably reducing atmospheric risks. Alongside these processes of atmospheric engineering—which have disproportionately exposed industrial, agricultural, and domestic laborers; poor and/or racialized communities; military personnel and communities located near military sites; and colonized and postcolonial populations to noxious air—discourses associating the health of individuals, races, and nations with pure air have blamed atmospheric pollution on these very populations by representing them as "ecological others," Sarah Jaquette Ray's term for groups that are stigmatized as environmentally impure, careless, or disengaged.[50] Thus, differential deodorization simultaneously produces atmospheric disparities (from the scale of the individual body to the transnational impacts of heavy industry in the Global South) and discursively stigmatizes the populations targeted by those disparities by representing deodorization as either an individual hygienic responsibility or a racial characteristic. Reframing the history of modernity's atmospheres through the concept of differential deodorization emphasizes how the sense of smell has been entangled with contested understandings of environmental health over the past two centuries. Whether through unpleasant smells, mood-enhancing smells, or the putative absence of smells, olfactory aesthetics stages the political and ethical implications of atmospheric differentiation from the Progressive Era to contemporary contexts of environmental injustice and colonization.

The Perfumed Handkerchief

"The man who pulls his perfumed handkerchief from his pocket treats all around to it whether they like it or not, and compels them, if they want to breathe at all, to be parties to the enjoyment."[51] This example from a foundational text of modern aesthetics—Kant's *Critique of Judgment* (1790)—disqualifies smell as a medium of aesthetic judgment because it infringes on the perceiver's body and mind. Rather than judging smells from a position of disinterestedness and autonomy, bystanders are unwittingly immersed, their bodies penetrated by odor. Kant's aversion to the "chemical" senses of smell and taste stems from his acute awareness of their affective power and their trans-corporeal materiality: "In the case of smelling and tasting, the components of the smell and the salts of the fluids of the body are first dissolved and then absorbed by the organs, and only then do they produce their effect."[52] Ironically, Kant's example of the difficulty of containing smell is itself a deodorizing instrument of olfactory mitigation: although its purpose is to protect its user against unpleasant smells, the perfumed handkerchief itself imposes on the autonomy of others. This instrument of personal deodorization intended to mask unpleasant odors enacts a sort of atmospheric violence, "compel[ling]" any living, breathing person in its range to "enjoy" its heady scent by taking it in as both sensory stimulus and chemical composition.

Kant was not alone in denigrating olfaction's subjective, passive, and chemical properties: "The philosophers and scientists of [the eighteenth and nineteenth centuries] decided that, while sight was the preeminent sense of reason and civilization, smell was the sense of madness and savagery."[53] This "philosophical abjection" of smell in Western thought has continued into the twentieth century,[54] when Max Nordau identified "smellers" as "degenerates" whose atavism goes back "to an epoch anterior to man," Sigmund Freud postulated that smell lost its significance as humans evolved to stand erect in a way that exposed their genitals to sight, and Adorno and Horkheimer wrote that "when we see we remain what we are; but when we smell we are taken over by otherness. Hence the sense of smell is considered a disgrace in civilization, the sign of lower social strata, lesser races and base animals."[55] The consequences of this osmophobic (smell-fearing) tradition include not only the deodorization of Western aesthetics and criticism but also the equation of the modern subject with both an inodorate body and an attenuated sense of smell. Elaborating on the connections between deodorization and the sensory requirements of capitalism, Jones writes,

> Various interlocking, subjectivating regimes (Enlightenment science, positivist philosophy, professional specialization, colonial politics, capitalist market developments, aesthetic formalism, et al.) worked together to produce a profound bureaucratization of the senses throughout the nineteenth and twentieth centuries. . . . No amount of sniffing and snuffling can remove the evidence of that long process; the modern subject emerged precisely via these various regulations of the disorganized mammal . . . this segmenting of the human sensorium for industrial and epistemological use.[56]

In addition to sustaining this "bureaucratization of the senses," claims to inodorateness also disavow differential deodorization as an ongoing—indeed, increasingly pronounced—means of reproducing social, environmental, and embodied disparities. Having removed smell from the proper domain of critical thinking, the subject of deodorization (a term that denotes both a subject who values deodorization and someone subjectified through deodorization's rituals, products, and aversions) is ill equipped to produce or analyze olfactory knowledge and thus lacks robust archives, methods, and concepts for engaging with this vital mode of embodied ecological experience.

If philosophers and critics have had relatively little to say about the aesthetics of smell, marketing experts have long known that olfactory air conditioning can enhance the appeal of French fries, new car interiors, casinos, and even beer-scented darts.[57] As a recent *Harvard Business Review* article notes, "Scented environments have been shown to reduce typos made by office workers; improve the perception of product quality; increase purchase intent, average unit sales, and duration of a retail visit or stay among consumers; and boost the willingness of consumers to pay more for a product."[58] Research on the chemical senses has been dominated by corporate interests and the search for new markets: in a discussion that pertains to both flavor and scent research, Sarah Tracy writes, "The molecularization of taste and smell extends expert understanding of chemosensation throughout the body, such that the eater's body-mind is more accessible to the goals of corporate capital."[59] In addition to olfactory marketers, mood enhancement therapists, crowd control weapon manufacturers, memory researchers, and activists wielding stink bombs have found diverse applications for olfaction.

Precisely because it's so seldom the object of sustained attention, smell is a powerful medium for orienting and communicating our affective predispositions: in her influential theorization of the atmospheric transmission of affect, Teresa Brennan writes that "[the] process whereby one person's or one group's nervous and hormonal systems are brought into alignment with another's . . . works mainly by smell; that is to say, unconscious olfaction."[60] Thus, affect is communicated not only when "[people] observe each other but also because they imbibe each other via smell."[61] Psychologist Silvan Tomkins coined the term "dissmell" to identify an innate affect modeled on the way in which humans register and communicate a defensive response to a noxious odor: "the upper lip and nose are raised and the head is drawn away from the apparent source of the offending odor."[62] Geographers and environmental studies scholars have also noted the importance of smell as both an integral affective component of the sense of place and a tool for detecting invisible environmental changes—including potential threats. In theorizing the concept of "smellscape," geographer J. Douglas Porteous draws attention to the immersive and emotive force of smell as a dimension of spatial experience.[63] Insofar as it attunes us to spatial distinctiveness, olfaction is also particularly well equipped for the task of sensing—and orienting our visceral responses to—geographic disparities.

Despite its marginalization from Western philosophy, smell has recently emerged as a powerful medium for communicating risk perceptions in literature, olfactory art, and environmental justice discourses.

Experiments with smell as a formal and thematic element range from the literary detective's hypersensitive nose to the naturalist novel's obsessive descriptions of bad smells, from stink bombs deployed by environmental activists to the illness narratives of people with multiple chemical sensitivity, from multimedia artworks that incorporate smell to diasporic and Indigenous works that challenge racial and colonial smellscapes. These experiments in olfactory aesthetics enrich our language for describing and communicating smells while strengthening our capacities of olfactory distinction and recall. For, as Bruno Latour details in his discussion of the odor kits used to train professional "noses" for the perfume industry, the capacity to "be affected" by "a richer odoriferous world" is not based on innate ability but acquired through practice.[64] Olfactory researcher George Dodd explains that approaching smell through language "strengthen[s] the neural pathways in the brain itself and, in turn, that helps you to become better at smelling things."[65] In her illuminating study of literary engagements with psychophysics, Erica Fretwell suggests that literature may also function as "a sensitizing mechanism, a 'kit' not simply for differentiating feeling but more broadly for *learning to be affected*."[66] Olfactory aesthetics matters not just because it represents how we smell but, more importantly, because it modulates—and, in many cases, sharpens—our (deodorized) sensitivity to odors and their intoxicating chemical intimacies. Refusing Kant's aesthetic values of autonomy and disinterestedness, smell foregrounds the entanglement of bodies and environments: because breathing is necessary to living, olfactory aesthetics is critically situated at the intersection of *air conditioning* and biopolitics.

The Smell of Risk builds on work in the growing field of olfactory literary and cultural studies, which has illuminated understandings of both smell and deodorization across a range of genres and historical eras. Hans Rindisbacher, Janice Carlisle, Emily Friedman, and Catherine Maxwell have detailed how British and European authors mobilized and reshaped historical understandings of olfactory differences as well as the transformative force of specific olfactory objects such as tobacco, sulfur, and perfume.[67] Scholars of US literature such as Christopher Looby, Stephen Casmier, Daniela Babilon, and Erica Fretwell have interrogated olfaction's complex entanglements with race, gender, sexuality, and power relations.[68] Beyond the US context, Indigenous studies scholars such as Warren Cariou and Vicente Diaz have posed vital questions about decolonial approaches to olfaction inherent in practices such as sweetgrass smudging and Chamorro navigational techniques. The following chapters are also indebted to studies of olfaction in art criticism and cultural studies, such as notably Jones's work on art and the senses and Jim Drobnick's wide-ranging publications on olfactory art.[69]

While these contributions have significantly advanced our understanding of how olfactory perception inflects ideas about social identities, memory, and place, research on olfactory aesthetics has seldom considered smell as a vehicle for sensing and conveying environmental risk. The critical tendency has been to focus on the semiotic dimensions of smell while downplaying its material dimensions. To contextualize smell's environmental and health implications, I turn to scholars of environmental history and sensory studies. In his foundational study *The Foul and the Fragrant: Odor and the French Social Imagination* (1982), Alain Corbin tracks the profound transformations in health, governance, urban planning, architecture, and culture brought about by miasma theory and deodorization initiatives in eighteenth- and nineteenth-century France.[70] Building on Corbin's work, Melanie Kiechle's *Smell Detectives: An Olfactory History of Nineteenth-Century Urban America* (2017) demonstrates how olfactory framings of environmental health in the nineteenth-century United States extended from public health campaigns and city planning to everyday interactions with scented products, household manuals, and domestic architecture.[71] Sensory historians and anthropologists have documented how olfactory rhetoric has been mobilized to control and exclude Black, Asian diasporic, Indigenous, and Dalit populations in ways that subject racialized bodies to environmental violence and often also misrepresent the effects of those environmental disparities as innate racial characteristics.[72] These studies illuminate olfaction as a sense fraught with uncertainty and ambiguity insofar as it blends representational and material modes of communication.

As the fields of sound studies, food studies, and haptics have expanded our understanding of sensory aesthetics well beyond its traditional focus on visual form, olfaction has remained largely neglected by cultural critics. Given the ways in which vision prioritizes a liberal model of putatively disembodied perception, olfactory aesthetics demands a nearly unthinkable shift in what Jacques Rancière calls "the distribution of the sensible," or "the system of self-evident facts of sense perception that simultaneously discloses the existence of something in common and the delimitations that define the respective parts and positions within it."[73] Deodorized spaces, bodies, and ways of thinking orient our common culture, but deodorization also requires the aesthetic suppression of those who inhabit pungent spaces or bodies, or those who indulge in smell as a mode of embodied environmental perception. Both the devaluation of smell and the removal of (some) noxious smells deploy the sensorium in the service of sustaining a *sensus communis*[74]—the shared sensory order that in turn delineates the limits of community. For Rancière, a political aesthetics always involves "a certain recasting of the distribution of the sensible"—a process he nevertheless explains in visual terms: "a spectacle does not fit within the sensible framework[,] an expression does not find its meaning in the system of visible coordinates where it appears."[75] To think with smell is not only to redistribute the sensible but to develop a sensory alternative to the system of Western aesthetics and its tendency to downplay invisible, environmental slow violence by framing the atmosphere as an empty space between (ocularcentric) subject and object rather than apprehending it as a material, biopolitical medium.

Olfactory Ecocriticism

In an effort to understand the physical, affective, and social implications of breathing in the Anthropocene, this book brings together concepts, lines of inquiry, and incipient literary and nonliterary archives for doing olfactory ecocriticism—a mode of cultural analysis attuned to both the trans-corporeal transformations wrought by airborne chemicals and the representational challenges posed by the sense of smell. Environmental humanities scholars have demonstrated how cultural analysis can enhance our understanding of material entanglements between differentiated environments and the human and nonhuman bodies that inhabit them.[76] This materialist turn in ecocriticism has drawn attention to molecular, cellular, and radioactive scales of "intra-action"[77]—to invoke feminist materialist philosopher Karen Barad's term for "*the mutual constitution of entangled agencies*"[78]—that frequently resist visual representation. Not only do trans-corporeal relations involve scales of matter too small to be seen; they also call for nonrepresentational approaches to aesthetics attuned to transformations of embodiment and affect. As Dana Luciano has suggested, "The most compelling contribution of the new materialisms is not conceptual or analytic, strictly speaking, but sensory. The attempt to attend to the force of liveliness of matter will entail not just a reawakening or redirection of critical attention, but a reorganization of the senses."[79] Smell is inherently trans-corporeal, but (unlike taste) its perceptual range is both intimate and extended across space: thus, it is well adapted to the task of sensing how differentiated atmospheres get into bodies and populations.

Of course, the interpretive challenges presented by olfaction must be taken seriously. Smell's subjectively variable, flitting, immersive, spatially dispersed, and hybrid (mixed with other smells or atmospheric conditions) qualities seem to defy the very concept of form—a concept that, even in literary studies, is frequently modeled on the visual arts (figured in terms of shapes, diagrams, and well-wrought urns). At the same time, the weak olfactory lexicon characteristic of many languages—which is at least partially the outcome of a studied lack of practice—makes smell difficult to communicate directly. Moreover, the combination of socially constructed and molecular components that informs olfactory perception frequently gives rise to *material ambiguity*—the impossibility of fully disentangling the cultural and chemical meanings of olfactory experience. If smell, like atmosphere, comprises an inchoate medium "in between" subject and object, it nevertheless takes shape in formal conventions and distortions, in vague yet elaborate descriptions, and in multimedia artworks that deploy smell as a complement or threat to visual and spatial perception. Although smell often floats in the background of texts and art galleries, it is nevertheless bound up with breathers' bodies, minds, feelings, and actions. Olfactory reading thus blends the "atmospheric reading" practice modeled by Jesse Oak Taylor—which prioritizes aesthetic elements that hover in the background rather than plots of subject formation in an effort to "materialize the climates of history"[80]—with an attentiveness to the trans-corporeal and, in many cases, debilitating effects attributed to smells. It requires reading for olfactory references and descriptions that (like our awareness of unfamiliar smells) quietly blend into the background, while also attending to the ambiguous ways in which smell corporealizes both environmental materials and culturally constructed expectations. Beyond exposing the debilitating effects of bad air, reading for smell can attune us to the potentialities of altered mood, perception, and intimacy accessed through trans-corporeal intoxication. In both literature and visual art, olfactory reading does not just attune us to the presence and meaning of smells but also intervenes in the distribution of the sensible by challenging hegemonic practices of air conditioning and (putatively) disembodied perception.

The Smell of Risk covers literary and olfactory art focusing on the United States—not only one of the nations with the highest levels of carbon emissions but one whose culture has profoundly influenced global patterns of consumption and atmospheric differentiation. The nation's outsized role in generating air pollution both within and well beyond US borders belies its exceptionally deodorized public culture: as anthropologist Edward Twitchell Hall notes, "In the use of the olfactory apparatus Americans are culturally underdeveloped."[81] To understand the transnational scope of air conditioning, I also consider texts concerned with extranational spaces—such as Cuba and Oceania—that have been affected by US-based practices of air conditioning. My archive juxtaposes literary texts oriented by olfaction with olfactory maps, artworks, nuisance complaints, public health investigations, crowd control weapons, and Indigenous accounts of smudging ceremonies. I center works of olfactory literature and conceptual art because they embrace the very difficulties—such as its resistance to description, recall, isolation, archiving, and objectivity—that have led the sense of smell to be marginalized in assessments of environmental risk. By embracing smell as a lived, embodied experience, the literary genres and olfactory artworks I analyze invite us to rethink how personhood is constituted through material association with engineered atmospheres. There are also productive differences between literary and nonrepresentational engagements with olfaction: whereas literary works leverage olfactory experience to critically represent and reframe practices of atmospheric engineering, olfactory artworks and practices are themselves performances of atmospheric engineering that can reinforce, critique, or enact alternatives to differential deodorization. In an effort to underscore the persistence of these aesthetic engagements with olfaction—as well as their transformations across time—this book (and several of its individual chapters) spans a history of industrial and postindustrial differential deodorization that begins with intersecting anxieties about miasma and race precipitated by industrialization and urbanization in the late nineteenth century and extends to the new miasmas introduced by twentieth- and twenty-first-century synthetic chemicals, urban redevelopment, and intensive agriculture.

The Smell of Risk is divided into two parts. The book's structure—moving from literary forms to olfactory art, then to the olfactory dynamics of racialization and colonialism—blends a roughly chronological progression with a conceptual arc moving from specific olfactory forms to later chapters that cover a range of antiracist and decolonial olfactory practices. The first three chapters consider the stakes of smell's emergence into the deodorized field of Western aesthetics by analyzing aesthetic forms that foreground olfaction. Detective fiction, naturalist novels, and artworks that incorporate smell have all been marginalized for their "sensationalism";[82] yet these forms experiment with smell as a medium for deciphering and choreographing relations between bodies, populations, and atmospheres. Given the deodorized state of most nineteenth-century literary works and twentieth-century museums, why does smell emerge as a central element in these genres, and what aesthetic and political work does it do? The first two chapters consider the emergence and afterlives of the most prominent olfactory literary forms, emphasizing how detective fiction and naturalism model different approaches to smell as an index of environmental risk. Taking an ambient approach to the formal concerns that have been at the center of recent debates in literary studies,[83] these chapters consider how olfaction manifests formally in genres that seem particularly sensitized to smell. Chapter 1, "'Every Crime Has Its Peculiar Odor': Detection, Deodorization, and Intoxication," considers two forms—detective fiction and narratives by people with multiple chemical sensitivity (MCS)—that deploy hyperosmia (an extraordinary sense of smell) to detect, interpret, and resolve modernity's proliferating risks. Whereas the deodorization plots that pervade nineteenth-century detective fiction tend to reassert social boundaries, Rudolph Fisher, Raymond Chandler, Chester Himes, and Sara Paretsky unsettle the figure of the deodorizing detective by representing hyperosmic detectives who are increasingly compromised by modernity's racially and socioeconomically stratified atmospheres. This shift from policing crime to a more atmospheric and ontologically oriented *environmental detection* extends into MCS memoirs, which mobilize conventions of olfactory detection to manifest scientifically derecognized forms of embodied experience and environmental violence. Chapter 2, "Naturalist Smellscapes and Environmental Justice," assesses literary naturalism's thick descriptions of smell through an atmospheric reading of Frank Norris's novel of lycanthropic transformation, *Vandover and the Brute* (1914). Unlike hyperosmic narratives—which frame olfaction as a mode of environmental perception—naturalist fiction depicts hypo-osmic characters who are hardly aware of the smells that envelop and debilitate them. Naturalism's fascination with smell as an uncertain and hardly acknowledged index of debilitating urban atmospheres, I argue, has made it an invaluable resource for twentieth-century authors—like Ann Petry and Helena María Viramontes—whose works dramatize the everyday experiences of "breathers" traversing racially stratified urban and agricultural smellscapes in Harlem, East Los Angeles, and Central California. Chapter 3, "Olfactory Art and Museum Ecologies," argues that the modern, air-conditioned "white cube" art gallery has been designed to conserve not only artworks but the deodorized sensorium of Western aesthetics. This account of the gallery as an architecture of deodorization illuminates the significance of olfactory art practices, which activate the gallery's air as a material medium of sensation, affect, and potential threat. I focus on the intervention of artists—such as Boris Raux, Sean Raspet, Peter de Cupere, and Anicka Yi—who deploy nonrepresentational, olfactory elements to stage trans-corporeal interactions with modernity's differentiated atmospheres.

The book's concluding chapters shift focus from formal configurations of smell to the ways in which atmospheric manipulation contributes to racialization and colonization. Racial atmospherics spans a range of discourses and practices, from law, public health, and colonial education to architecture and olfactory weapons; it encompasses both the racializing dynamics of risk perception and differential exposures to material toxins. Aesthetic challenges to racial and colonial atmospherics have likewise experimented with a range of forms and strategies: thus, rather than focusing on specific forms, I consider how Asian diasporic and Indigenous writers, artists, and botanists have incorporated critical perspectives on olfaction into fiction, poetry, memoir, plant science, and the cultivation of nonhuman species. While some of these texts deploy olfaction to underscore atmospheric disparities among humans, others move beyond the anthropocentric frame that frequently constrains research on health disparities: in their work, olfactory ecologies encompass companion species such as ants, bacteria, maile, and sweetgrass. Chapter 4, "Atmo-Orientalism: Olfactory Racialization and Environmental Health," considers how literary and public health discourses have racialized Asiatic bodies and spaces in olfactory terms. Instead of addressing the social and infrastructural determinants of environmental health in Chinese settlements, atmo-orientalism constructs the Chinese as a population plagued by risky, malodorous behaviors. In addition to provoking questions about how racialization works through olfaction and trans-corporeal atmospheres (rather than primarily through vision and the ascription of innate biological characteristics), this pattern of stigmatizing Asian immigrants as an atmospheric threat provides context for understanding olfactory and atmospheric language in the writings of Edith Maude Eaton / Sui Sin Far, as well as intoxicating olfactory encounters orchestrated by contemporary artist Anicka Yi. Chapter 5, "Decolonizing Smell," argues that colonization disrupts Indigenous cosmologies, cultural practices, and health by simultaneously derecognizing olfactory epistemologies and materially reshaping atmospheric ecologies. After documenting how colonization manipulates the smellscape by selectively deodorizing, transforming, polluting, and weaponizing atmospheres, I turn to the work of three Indigenous authors—Albert Wendt (Samoa), Haunani-Kay Trask (Kanaka Maoli), and Robin Wall Kimmerer (Potawatomi)—who address the challenges of decolonizing smell at the levels of the sensorium and material ecologies. In a brief epilogue I consider how the olfactory narratives, artworks, and poems traced in this book might reframe our understanding of everyday olfactory interventions such as "fragrance-free" advocacy, stink bombs, and smudging. While advocacy for fragrance-free products and spaces has made important contributions by exposing everyday toxic exposures in particular contexts, I argue that this deodorizing thread of olfactory politics should be supplemented by a renewed sensitivity to olfaction as a powerful tool for thinking, feeling, and producing ecological relations across spatial and temporal scales.

1

"Every Crime Has Its Peculiar Odor"

Detection, Deodorization, and Intoxication

In Spider Robinson's Hugo Award–winning speculative narrative "By Any Other Name" (1976), an environmentalist who has become disillusioned with industrial modernity designs a virus that radically enhances humans' olfactory sensitivity, leaving humanity with "a sense of smell approximately a hundred times more efficient than that of any wolf."[1] This "hyperosmic plague" ("BA," 29) brings about the end of industrial civilization: a fifth of the world's population is killed (or self-immolates) as a result of sensory overstimulation concentrated in cities and industrial sites; others survive by emigrating to rural settlements and developing advanced nose plugs. The novella's hyperosmic humans experience olfaction as both capacity and debility: on the one hand, they can use it to track the scent trails of human and nonhuman creatures, including hitherto unperceived atmospheric entities called "muskies" ("BA," 31); on the other hand, the sensory overstimulation can devastate their minds, and synthetic cleaning chemicals become deadly weapons.

Robinson's novella draws together an eclectic range of influences: his own experiment with living in the woods as a young man, his job as a night watchman guarding New York City's pungent sewers in 1971, the synergies between 1960s counterculture and environmentalism, and the 1970 Clean Air Act spearheaded by Maine senator Edmund Muskie.[2] Hyperosmia connects all these threads, precipitating a massive worldwide decline in anthropogenic emissions that have suddenly become unbearable. Enhanced olfaction also attunes the novella's characters to the differential distribution of noxious smells in dense urban communities like Harlem, where the African American narrator's mother and brother die almost instantly. Robinson's work exemplifies the critical potential of hyperosmic narratives: in addition to zeroing in on airborne particles that usually float near—if not below—the thresholds of sensation, attention, and cultural value, a heightened sense of smell amplifies patterns of premature death already present in differentiated atmospheric geographies. Hyperosmic narratives experiment with a radical redistribution of the sensible, simultaneously inverting the hierarchy of the senses and drawing attention to the visceral, trans-corporeal environmental exchanges inherent in olfactory perception. In the novella, this reorganization of the human sensorium has immediate and radically transformative effects on nearly every aspect of political, economic, social, and environmental activity.

"By Any Other Name" also exemplifies the *material ambiguity* of olfactory perception, which blends cultural associations with biochemical materiality. Robinson's hyperosmic humans are not directly harmed by airborne toxins: they self-immolate when their olfactory bulbs are overwhelmed by urban and industrial smells. If this implies a vital distinction between industrial odors and putatively natural ones, it also suggests that the difference may have to do more with cultural perceptions of smell than with the chemicals that compose those smells. After all, why should the scent of bleach or asphalt be more overwhelming to a hyperosmic than the scent of the rose invoked by the novella's title? In the course of imagining olfaction as a site of trans-corporeal vulnerability, Robinson paradoxically privileges smell's semiotic dimensions. In his hyperosmic narrative, industrial odors are not unpleasant because they're harmful: they're harmful because they're unpleasant. As one of the hyperosmic plague's inventors puts it, "All the undesirable by-products of twentieth-century living . . . quite literally *stink*" ("BA," 25, emphasis original). Paradoxically, Robinson's engagement with olfaction functions both to dramatize geographies of atmospheric violence and to translate them into the moralizing, dematerialized language of pleasant and unpleasant sensations, fragrance and "stink."

To the extent that they mobilize the sense of smell as a tool of risk perception, hyperosmic narratives must negotiate the tensions between olfaction's cultural and biochemical components. To what extent can cultural and moral discourses about smell—frequently oriented by imperatives of deodorization—be disarticulated from chemical toxicity? This chapter explores how two genres in which hyperosmia has played an integral role—detective fiction and multiple chemical sensitivity (MCS) narratives—engage with the cultural and chemical components of olfactory risk perception. Positioned as agents of deodorization, hyperosmic detectives endeavor to stigmatize and eradicate odors perceived to be culturally and morally deviant; yet their very dependence on smell renders detectives vulnerable to olfactory intoxication and the uneven dynamics of differential deodorization. I move from the figure of the deodorizing detective established in nineteenth-century narratives to later works that juxtapose the sniffing out of clues and culprits with what I call *environmental detection*, or the detection of unevenly distributed material presences. Finally, I consider how narratives of chemical injury leverage tropes of detection to chart the chemical pathways of olfactory risks from their environmental manifestations to their embodied effects. Both these genres are shaped by olfaction's material ambiguity: detectives find themselves unwittingly intoxicated by smell, and people living with MCS struggle to recode scents associated with freshness and modernity in terms of chemical toxicity.

Detective Fiction and Deodorization

In an incisive reflection on the sniffer dog as an instrument of state surveillance, political theorist Mark Neocleous asks, "Why, with a critical intellectual culture saturated with analyses of biopolitics, biosecurity, biosurveillance and biometrics, has so little been said about the smell of power? Why is the state's 'nosiness' still understood almost solely through the ocular and the aural?"[3] Like biosurveillance more broadly, the genre of detective fiction is commonly associated with visual surveillance and ratiocination. In Edgar Allan Poe's formative detective tales "Murders in the Rue Morgue" (1841) and "The Purloined Letter" (1844), C. Auguste Dupin intersperses his detective work with improvised lectures on ratiocination and optics that draw analogies between his methods and the judicious employment of sidelong glances by astronomers as well as the perspectival shift required to discern a word stretched across the surface of a map in an "excessively obvious" fashion.[4] But "Rue Morgue" juxtaposes vision and ratiocination with another influential motif: the figuration of the detective as a sniffer dog. When Dupin boasts that "the scent had never for an instant been lost,"[5] he initiates a mode of olfactory detection that at once positions the detective as an agent of deodorization and undercuts the notion of the detective as a disembodied mind or "private eye." This motif of the deodorizing detective extends across nearly two centuries of detective fiction, from the olfactory methods staged by Arthur Conan Doyle and Rudolph Fisher (both discussed below) to the olfactory hypersensitivity of contemporary characters like Rudolfo Anaya's Sonny Baca, Thomas Pynchon's Conkling Speedwell, and Artyom Litvinenko's "Sniffer." Although it has received little critical attention, the trope of the "nosy" detective is so well established within the genre as to have inspired devices such as Conkling Speedwell's olfactory laser or "Naser,"[6] and punishments such as the slitting of Jake's nostrils in Roman Polanski's *Chinatown* (1974).[7]

The sense of smell—one of the most pervasive metaphors and methods for the detective's virtuosity—is also a site where bodily, mental, and affective integrity gives way to chemical intoxication. Thus, the deodorizing detective is a deeply ambivalent figure that renders one of the most prominent cultural icons of rational deduction dependent upon olfaction—a sense that is inherently trans-corporeal, immersive, and (for post-Enlightenment Westerners) notoriously difficult to describe. While nineteenth-century detective fiction acknowledges the presence of intoxicating atmospheres (for example, the "curling eddies of smoke that oppressed the atmosphere of [Dupin's] chamber,"[8] the "opalescent London reek" described outside the windows of Sherlock Holmes's apartment in "The Adventure of the Abbey Grange,"[9] or the psychoactive drugs that animate the thinking of both these detectives), its plots underscore the detective's role as an agent of deodorization who sniffs out and expunges deviant odors. Legal scholar Sarah Marusek aptly characterizes smell's normalizing function in detective plots: "Through smell, law normalizes bodies, place, and expectations through the exclusion of the deviant, the noncompliant, and the disempowered."[10]

Arthur Conan Doyle's Sherlock Holmes stories build on Poe's metaphor of detection as "scenting." In Holmes's debut novel, *A Study in Scarlet* (1887), Watson describes the detective at work as "a pure-blooded, well-trained foxhound, as it dashes backward and forward through the covert, whining in its eagerness, until it comes across the lost scent" (*OI*, 22). Elsewhere in the story Doyle literalizes this metaphor when Holmes deduces the use of poison from the "slightly sour smell" of a dead man's lips (*OI*, 61). *The Sign of the Four* (1890) introduces Toby the dog, whom

Holmes employs to track the faint scent of creosote tar from the scene of the crime. Holmes refers to Toby as "a queer mongrel, with a most amazing power of scent. I would rather have Toby's help than that of the whole detective force of London" (*OI*, 83). In "The Adventure of the Creeping Man" Holmes reports that "I have serious thoughts of writing a small monograph upon the uses of dogs in the work of the detective"—a monograph that would presumably dwell on the dog's olfactory capacities (*OI*, 65). Holmes's olfactory virtuosity in *The Hound of the Baskervilles* (1902) suggests a connection between the detective and the titular hound: "I held it within a few inches of my eyes, and was conscious of a faint smell of the scent known as white Jessamine. There are seventy-five perfumes, which it is very necessary that a criminal expert should be able to distinguish from each other, and cases have more than once within my own experience depended upon their prompt recognition" (*OI*, 550). Olfaction plays a crucial role in a later story, "The Adventure of the Retired Colourman" (1926), where the killer attempts to cover up the smell of gas used to murder his wife and her lover by repainting his house (*OI*, 1095–1106). In Doyle's work, scent is both a metaphor and a sensory method of detective work—a powerful tool for policing the boundaries of class, religion, race, and nation.

In his influential study of literary engagements with the London Fog, the ecocritic Jesse Oak Taylor reads Holmes as a sort of amateur meteorologist perfectly attuned to variations in London's thick, anthropogenic atmosphere. Taylor explains that the "opalescent" fog that suffuses the Sherlock Holmes stories is not an obstruction to vision but the very medium of detection in the Anthropocene's irrevocably transformed atmospheres: "Holmes sits 'amidst the teeming millions, with his filaments stretching out and running through them' ('The Cardboard Box,' 1113). Those filaments exist in a more 'prosaic and material' form in the patterns and curling wreaths of the fog outside the windows, infiltrating all of London, its alleys and byways, the crevices of its windows and the bodies of its inhabitants. Sherlock Holmes gains access to this pervasive climate of interconnection by manufacturing a malodorous and disordered atmosphere of his own."[11] Thus conceived as a hypersensitive atmospheric instrument, Holmes deploys his hyperosmic sensitivity as a tool for identifying and expunging deviant odors. In the course of doing so, he both navigates London's dramatically differentiated atmospheres and obscures them by targeting deviant bodies rather than disparities. In "The Adventure of the Three Gables" (1926), Holmes claps his hand to his pocket upon seeing a "grim and menacing" negro prizefighter named Steve Dixie, who asks, "Lookin' for your gun, Masser Holmes?" Holmes's reply: "No, for my scent bottle, Steve" (*OI*, 1063). Instead of physical violence, Holmes protects himself by using his personal air freshener to ward off Dixie's supposedly intolerable odor. In "The Adventure of the Devil's Foot" (1910), Doyle stages a material confrontation between Holmes and a toxic West African root whose powder produces both "a thick musky odour, subtle and nauseous" and a fatal sense of terror in anyone who inhales it. As Watson and Holmes learn firsthand, the root's odor is a direct threat to self-possession: "At the very first whiff of it my brain and my imagination were beyond all control. A thick, black cloud swirled before my eyes, and my mind told me that in this cloud, unseen as yet, but about to spring out upon my appalled senses, lurked all that was vaguely horrible, all that was monstrous and inconceivably wicked in the universe" (*OI*, 793). After solving the murder through this experiment in "immersive toxicology,"[12] Holmes sends the killer—along with his knowledge of the root—back to central Africa.

Classic detective fiction frequently deploys olfaction as a tool for detecting transgressive, racialized bodies and for controlling their atmospheric incursions on the spaces of white respectability.[13] Anticipating Holmes's encounters with Black atmospheres, the Bornean orangutan figuratively sniffed out by Poe's Dupin indexes a common stereotype associated with Black and brown bodies by practitioners of scientific racism. The racial implications of the deodorizing detective echo the role of bloodhounds used to discipline fugitive slaves. Given Poe's southern origins and the racially loaded orangutan at the heart of his formative detective story, we might consider whether the genre was influenced as much by the slaveholder's bloodhounds as it was by James Fenimore Cooper's narratives of wilderness tracking (as Walter Benjamin famously argued).[14] Mark Twain gestures toward this line of influence in "A Double-Barreled Detective Story" (1902)—a parody in which Sherlock Holmes's rational method is eclipsed by the tracking skills of a detective born with a preternatural sense of smell. In Twain's story, the detective's hyperosmic condition is referred to as "the gift of the bloodhound" because it was supposedly acquired when bloodhounds were set upon his mother shortly before his birth.[15] Smell's narrative function as a means of detecting, avoiding, or removing Blackness reflects its powerful role in historical arguments for segregation: as sensory historian Mark Smith has documented, advocates of segregation claimed not only that they could make racial distinctions based on the smell of Black bodies but also that desegregation would be repugnant because "Negroes have a smell extremely disagreeable to white people."[16] The racial underpinnings of olfactory detection persist in the use of drug sniffing dogs by contemporary police: in 2011, the *Chicago Tribune* reported a vast discrepancy between the success rate of drug sniffing dogs used at traffic stops for "Hispanic" and other drivers.[17] When influenced by the conscious or unconscious biases of their handlers, sniffer dogs may be just another mechanism for racial profiling.

In nineteenth- and early twentieth-century narratives of the deodorizing detective, Holmes and Watson's intimate encounter with the Devil's Root is the exception to the rule. Dupin and Holmes are seldom threatened by their recreational intoxicants, and, despite his regular and frequently deliberate exposures to London's panoply of smells, Holmes never experiences their cumulative effects. As Taylor notes, London's "abnatural" atmosphere *enables* Holmes's detection; with the exception of the Devil's Root, the atmosphere does not debilitate him. The nineteenth-century detective narrative's tendency to reduce criminality to the actions of individual perpetrators assumes a teleological, procedural model of deodorization: the detective traces the scent to its deviant source in order to contain or banish it. For many in the nineteenth century, however, unpleasant odors were recognized as environmental health threats—miasmas resulting not from individual crimes but from structural (and, often, infrastructural) inequities. Although miasma theory gave way to the germ theory of disease transmission in the later part of the century, the perception of smells as potentially debilitating substances persisted in popular health discourses. Whereas early detective fiction frequently frames the detective as an agent of olfactory surveillance and control, twentieth-century narratives of hyperosmic detection channel the genre's olfactory obsessions into critical accounts of differential deodorization in which the work of detection runs up against the uneven, inequitable distribution of smells across spaces and communities.

Environmental Detection

If hyperosmic sensitivity enables the work of detection, it also makes trans-corporeal material agency a source of anxiety in detective fiction—particularly as twentieth-century authors shifted the genre's focus to increasingly stratified and polluted settings. As detectives become intoxicated, they register a model of environmental entanglement that questions the viability of approaches to deodorization that prioritize the removal of deviant bodies. Conflating detection with exposure, smell unsettles the ideas of ratiocination, bodily immunity, and interpretive control inherent in classic detective fiction. Instead of interpretively reconstructing past events from the traces they leave behind, smell introduces plots of environmental detection in which the threat, or crime, is materially present in the atmosphere—and thus already present in the detective's body. As art historian Caroline Jones writes, olfaction calls forth new modes of thinking: "Tracing the path of smells requires thinking by sniffing, tracking the logic of stench in trajectories of the self."[18]

The concept of environmental detection indicates a tendency found (frequently in suppressed or marginalized moments) throughout detective fiction that anticipates the contemporary subgenre of eco-detective fiction represented by novels such as Percival Everett's *Watershed* (1996), Paolo Bacigalupi's *The Water Knife* (2015), and Donna Leon's *Earthly Remains* (2017)—as well as investigative documentaries that bring olfactory detection (alongside other senses) to bear on risk perception, such as Judith Helfand and Daniel Gold's *Blue Vinyl* (2002), Josh Fox's *Gasland* (2010), and Jon Whelan's *Stink!* (2015). Because of its trans-corporeal, chemical qualities, olfaction's connection with the environment opens onto an "interactionist" ontology wherein the detective's body is co-constituted by the environments she is investigating.[19] The object of the hyperosmic's environmental detection is not simply a transgression that has already occurred but harmful toxins circulating between atmospheres and bodies: not an absent event traced by clues left behind but the atmospherically dispersed agents of slow violence. The fantasy of environmental immunity that underpins the detective conceived as a "private eye" gives way to a model of the detective as "public nose"—an investigator whose sensory and cognitive capacities cannot be extricated from olfactory exchanges with differentially deodorized public spaces.

"John Archer's Nose" (1935), the last story published by the Harlem Renaissance author Rudolph Fisher, stages the tension between two interpretations of smell: on the one hand, as a sign of individual morality and behaviors; on the other hand, as a material constituent of risk-laden atmospheres. Fisher's text features a multilayered olfactory plot: if olfaction enables the story's detective figures to solve a murder, noxious air remains as a dispersed material agent of slow violence that exceeds the detective plot's denouement. In the story, detective Perry Dart is assisted by the hypersensitive nose of his friend Dr. Archer, who eventually connects a peculiar smell in the bedroom of a murdered boy with the "evil-smelling packet" of medicinal roots he saw around a dead baby's neck earlier that day.[20] Dr. Archer traces both deaths to the supposed ineffectiveness of root medicine: he believes that the baby died (of suffocation due to untreated status lymphaticus—"literally choking to death in a fit") because its parents relied on folk "superstition" rather than modern medicine and X-ray treatments; and he deduces that the baby's grieving father murdered the son of his root medicine provider as an act of retribution ("JA," 186).

As Dart and Dr. Archer discuss the smells encountered at the crime scene, their banter presents a remarkable metacommentary on the complex connections between odors, language, literary genres, and Black urban geographies:

"M-m. Peculiar—very. Curious thing, odors. Discernible in higher dilution than any other material stimulus. Ridiculous that we don't make greater use of them."

"I never noticed any particular restriction of 'em in Harlem."

. . . "Odors, *should* be restricted," [Dr. Archer] pursued. "They should be captured, classified, and numbered like the lines of the spectrum. We let them run wild—"

"Check."

"And sacrifice a wealth of information. In a language of a quarter of a million words, we haven't a single specific direct denotation of a smell."

"Oh, no?"

"No. Whatever you're thinking of, if [sic] it is an indirect and nonspecific denotation, linking the odor in mind to anything else. We are content with 'fragrant' and 'foul' or general terms of that character, or at

best 'alcoholic' or 'moldy,' which are obviously indirect. We haven't even
such general direct terms as apply to colors—red, green, and blue. We
name what we see but don't name what we smell."

"Which is just as well."

"On the contrary. If we could designate each smell by number—"

"We'd know right off who killed Sonny."

"Perhaps. I daresay every crime has its peculiar odor."

"Old stuff. They used bloodhounds in *Uncle Tom's Cabin*."

"We could use one here." ("JA," 193–94)

While Dr. Archer's desire for a comprehensive taxonomy of odors in the
service of surveillance takes center stage in this passage, Dart's incongruous responses shift our attention to the racial implications of olfactory
surveillance. Dart's comment about the lack of odor "restriction" in
Harlem invokes the neighborhood's disproportionate exposure to problems with sanitation, ventilation, crowding, and industrial pollution.
Rather than reducing Harlem's exposure to odors, Dr. Archer's wish to
"restrict" odors would involve only classifying them with words or numbers—a dream of total olfactory rationalization and control. This would
support the detection of individual crimes according to their "peculiar
odor"—a process that Dr. Archer concedes is comparable to the use of
bloodhounds to track fugitive slaves. The doctor's nose traces crime to
individual rather than social causes—to the "peculiar odor" rather than
the intractable background atmospheres to which most Harlem residents have become desensitized by prolonged low-level exposures.

Ironically, the "peculiar odor" that exposes the killer in this case is
the smell of African American folk medicine. Aligning what he perceives to be superstitious racial beliefs with smell, Dr. Archer's analysis
directly contrasts the deodorizing influence of modern medical technologies with the "evil-smelling" roots. Dr. Archer's eagerness to use "X-
ray treatments" to melt away the baby's inflamed thymus reflects Fisher's
own career as a successful radiologist; ironically, however, the diagnosis
and X-ray treatment of an "inflamed thymus" were controversial in the
1930s and eventually proven to be "as mythical as the therapeutic effects
of fried-hair charms."[21] Meanwhile, the rootwork that is so vehemently
rejected by Dr. Archer invokes the long tradition of conjure and hoodoo
in African American culture. In the 1920s and 1930s, mail-order curio

companies made these practices more readily available to growing Black urban communities. In her study of the African American spiritual products industry, Carolyn Morrow Long describes a range of scented products—from perfumes and powder sachets to the spicy scents of High John the Conqueror Root and Van-Van Oil (an oil scented with vervain or lemongrass)—that circulated through the mail-order catalogs and spiritual supply stores of the 1930s.[22] Although the magical properties attributed to these products are frequently dismissed as superstition (as in Crafton's comment about "fried-hair charms," above), hoodoo and rootwork promised recent Black migrants to the city the possibility of taking an active role in air conditioning. The powers attributed to these materials—which included enhancing charisma, warding off enemies, cleansing household spaces, and inspiring love—may not have been entirely unfounded: smell's capacities to evoke collective and individual memories, along with its influence on affects and behaviors, may exert considerable (though not easily measurable) effects on physical and mental health. Among the antebellum antecedents of these mail-order conjure materials were practical interventions such as "powders designed to aid runaways by throwing tracking dogs off their scent."[23]

If Fisher's hyperosmic detective stigmatizes rootwork as a harmful and retrograde superstition, the story also offers a critical counternarrative that complicates the figure of the deodorizing detective. Although Fisher never directly acknowledges it, the true agent of violence in "John Archer's Nose" may be the health effects of atmospheric stratification. It turns out that the murdered boy had a terminal case of tuberculosis—a contagious respiratory disease that disproportionately affected African Americans (the tuberculosis rate in Harlem was five times greater than the rest of Manhattan's),[24] and that strongly correlated with poor conditions of housing and ventilation. It is thus doubly significant that the killer in this "locked room" mystery entered the boy's room through the building's air shaft, a common ventilation feature in Harlem that Fisher elsewhere depicted in graphic detail reminiscent of naturalist description: "An airshaft: cabbage and chitterlings cooking[;] waste noises, waste odors of a score of families, seeking issue through a common channel; pollution from bottom to top—a sewer of sounds and smells."[25] In order to single out an individual perpetrator, Dr. Archer has to navigate and suppress Harlem's broader panoply of odors: in other stories, Fisher describes Harlem's atmosphere as "vile—hot, full of breath and choking perfume"; "Waste clutters over it, odors fume up from it, sewer-mouths gape like wounds in its back."[26] If "Lenox Avenue is for the most part the boulevard of the unperfumed 'rats,'"[27] it is because Harlem's atmosphere has already been compromised by urban planning, immiseration, and negligent landlords. Whereas Sherlock Holmes could deodorize his encounter with a Black man by resorting to his scent bottle, Fisher's Black detective figures are confronted with the systemic problem posed by infrastructures that permeate Harlem's air with risk. As Bruce Robbins writes, "Infrastructure smells . . . because attention is not paid, because it is neglected. And it is neglected because it belongs to the public domain, all other tokens of belonging effaced, owned in effect by no one. The smell of infrastructure is the smell of the public."[28] Fisher's story ironically dramatizes the tension between Harlem's panoply of olfactory burdens and the respiratory health of the hyperosmic detective: as Dr. Archer puts it, "I'm going to locate that odor if it asphyxiates me" ("JA," 213).

Fisher's attention to infrastructural racism resonates with the "air of fatality" that Sean McCann discerns in hard-boiled crime fiction—a genre that reinvigorated the detective story from the 1930s to the 1960s.[29] Whereas classic detective fiction purged deviant odors in order to restore a transparent social order, hard-boiled stories—influenced by literary naturalism's portrayals of humanity amid a swirl of environmental forces[30]—remained cynical about the prospect of "clear[ing] the atmosphere."[31] To be sure, hard-boiled authors sometimes indulge in moments of olfactory racialization, as when Dashiell Hammett notes the "unmistakable . . . smell of unwashed Chinese" or when Raymond Chandler writes, "He had a sort of dry musty smell, like a fairly clean Chinaman."[32] But they are distinguished by their interest in depicting an atmosphere of generalized corruption: as Chandler puts it, "It is not a fragrant world, but it is the world you live in."[33] In the amoral world of hard-boiled crime fiction, smell does not just provide the detective with clues—it manifests as a trans-corporeal index for social corruption and atmospheric stratification. In *The Big Sleep* (1939), for example, Chandler juxtaposes the cloying scent of General Sternwood's orchid hothouse with the pungent smell of the oil sump holes that made the Sternwoods rich. In addition to indicating divisions of space and class, odors have potential consequences for health and cognition: in an auto garage, "the smell of the pyroxilin paint was as sickening as ether"; down by the Sternwoods' oil wells, "the smell of that sump would poison a herd of goats."[34] Rather than enabling the detective to sniff out criminals, smell threatens Marlowe with physical and mental debilitation. Far from serving as a clue, the ether-like smell of paint, which "drugged the close air of the garage,"[35] dulls Marlowe's attention enough for him to be caught off guard and captured. Chandler's detective is not a dispassionate cartographer of the city's ambient smells but a porous subject co-constituted by the atmospheres he traverses.

In his hard-boiled Harlem detective series, Chester Himes dramatizes the contradictions between the policing of individual crimes and the subtler workings of structural violence. *The Heat's On* (1961) stages a temporary and collective climate of hyperosmia, as a heat wave amplifies Harlem's "atmospheric pressures"[36] and ambient odors:

> Heat was coming out of the pavement, bubbling from the asphalt; and the atmospheric pressure was pushing it back to earth like the lid on a pan.
>   ... An effluvium of hot stinks arose from the frying pan and hung in the hot motionless air, no higher than the rooftops—the smell of sizzling barbecue, fried hair, exhaust fumes, rotting garbage, cheap perfumes, unwashed bodies, decayed buildings, dog-rat-and-cat offal, whiskey and vomit, and all the old dried-up odors of poverty.[37]

Himes frames insomnia, gambling, knife fights, and "evil" itself as consequences of the neighborhood's lack of air conditioning: "It was too hot to sleep. Everyone was too evil to love" (*HO*, 30). Sustained by a convergence of structural inequities, these everyday "odors of poverty" are coterminous with the "smell of [inadequate] infrastructure."[38]

Himes later revisited this passage in his unfinished, final Harlem novel, *Plan B* (1993), expanding its olfactory prose into two pages of baroque excess. Early in that novel, a long paragraph catalogues Harlem's indoor stinks, culminating in "yearly accumulations of thousands of unlisted odors embedded in the crumbling walls, the rotting linoleum, the decayed wall paper, the sweaty garments, the incredible perfumes, the rancid face creams and cooking fats, the toe jam, the bad breath from rotting or dirty teeth, the pustules of pus."[39] The following paragraph explains that, despite people's beliefs in the "fresh air" of the outdoors, Harlem's outside air was no better: "Outside there were all the impurities generated by their worn-out automobiles, their brimming garbage cans, the dog shit and cat shit, the putrefying carcasses of rats and cats and dogs and sometimes of meat too rotten even for the residents to eat" (*PB*, 51–52). Himes's catalogues of stenches insistently connect atmospheric "impurities" with the economic and political issues embodied by poorly maintained homes, rotten food, inadequate dental care, substandard automobiles, and failures of municipal waste removal. Even cancer—a possible long-term consequence of all these stenches— becomes another source of stench: "It stank from . . . body tissue rotten from cancer" (*PB*, 51).

In *The Heat's On*, the Harlem detectives Grave Digger Jones and Coffin Ed have a conflicted relationship with the detective's deodorizing profession. Early on, Himes alludes to an earlier novel in the series in which Coffin Ed shot a kid who threw perfume at him, mistaking it for acid.[40] On two occasions, the detectives unsuccessfully try employing a dog to "sniff around" (*HO*, 99, 147). A later scene literally deconstructs the figure of the sniffer dog: believing that a key has been hidden in the dog, the drug dealer Sister Heavenly chloroforms it and systematically dissects it, releasing new odors into an already putrid hotel room: "The hot poisonous air inside of the room, stinking of blood, chloroform and dog-gut, was enough to suffer the average person. But Sister Heavenly stood it" (*HO*, 171). Like the sniffer dog, Himes's detectives fail to locate the missing shipment of heroin that drives the novel's plot: they identify and stop (often by killing) individual culprits, but eventually discover that the five kilograms of heroin were unwittingly thrown into an incinerator. As the novel concludes, this incinerated heroin disperses into Harlem's atmosphere, blending with both the catalogue of stenches and the intoxicating atmospheres of opium, incense, and marijuana described earlier in the novel. Not only do the detectives (who frequently rely on extralegal violence) become morally associated with the criminals in Harlem's generalized atmosphere of corruption, but their interventions actually increase the atmosphere's toxicity by contributing the suffocating smells of cordite (from gunshots), the pheromonal "smell of terror . . . like a sickening miasma" evoked by Coffin Ed's menacing presence, and the fumes of burning heroin (*HO*, 174).

Blood Shot (1988), Sara Paretsky's fifth hard-boiled novel featuring the female detective V. I. Warshawski, leverages the genre's dual modes of olfactory representation—smell as both clue and airborne risk factor—to stage the economic and political machinery of environmental "slow violence." Although the novel's central characters are white working-class women, its account of environmental violence is set in South Chicago—an area whose population is 93 percent Black. As environmental sociologist David Pellow notes, South Chicago has been described as "one of the greatest ecological disasters in the history of North America," where residents "breathe in an estimated 126,000 pounds of toxic pollutants emitted into the air each day and are surrounded by the most landfills per square mile in the United States."[41] Environmental justice activist Hazel Johnson "has often charged that environmental racism in [South Chicago] is 'another form of genocide.'"[42] Although Paretsky disingenuously downplays these racial disparities in order to underscore the class dynamics of environmental injustice, her novel offers a vivid sensory account of everyday atmospheric violence in South Chicago. *Blood Shot* begins with detective Warshawski reencountering the long forgotten smell of the neighborhood in which she was raised: "I had forgotten the smell. Even with the South Works on strike and Wisconsin Steel padlocked and rusting away, a pungent mix of chemicals streamed in through the engine vents. I turned off the car heater, but the stench—you couldn't call it air—slid through minute cracks in the Chevy's windows, burning my eyes and sinuses."[43] Whereas writers frequently deploy smell to evoke powerful place-based memories, the smell described here draws attention only to itself. The detective is no sooner introduced than her perceptual faculties are debilitated by an indecipherable and inescapable "pungent mix of chemicals."

Some of these airborne chemicals are at the center of the novel's plot, as Warshawski investigates a series of cover-ups and a murder aimed to suppress the occupational and environmental health effects of Xerxine, an industrial cleaning solvent manufactured in the South Side. As a retired company doctor explains, "The way they used to make it, it left these toxic residues in the air. . . . If you breathe the vapors while they're manufacturing it, it doesn't do you a whole lot of good. Affects the liver and kidneys and central nervous system and all those good things. . . . You know, they didn't run the plants to kill the employees, but they weren't very careful about controlling how much of the chlorinated vapors got into the air" (*BS*, 132). After being left for dead in a pungent, chemical-filled marsh, navigating a "thick mist carrying the river's miasmas" (*BS*, 318), and taking down a gangster and a corrupt politician in a chemical plant, Warshawski worries about the effects of her many exposures to airborne toxins over the course of the narrative: "I shut my eyes, but I couldn't keep out the clamor, or the murky Xerxine smell. What would my creatine level be after tonight? I pictured my kidneys filled with lesions—blood-red with black holes in them, oozing Xerxine" (*BS*, 333). The novel's title, *Blood Shot*, turns out to refer not to bloodshot eyes or to gunshots but to the slow violence that toxic chemicals introduce into the bloodstreams of workers, local communities, and the detective herself.

The most recent incarnation of the deodorizing detective is the eponymous protagonist of *The Sniffer* (2013–)—a popular Ukrainian television series directed by Artyom Litvinenko and internationally distributed by Amazon Prime and Netflix. Although its provenance is located at some distance from the US detective fiction (and the unavoidable influence of Doyle) that I have discussed so far, the show's many references to Sherlock Holmes and the conventions of Hollywood police procedurals position it as one of the latest, international installments in the hyperosmic detective tradition. Working with the Special Bureau of Investigations, the show's reclusive police consultant, Käro, relies on his hyperosmic talents to reconstruct crime scenes. Blending olfactory data with his extensive knowledge of chemistry and related fields, he is able to deduce the age, gender, recent contacts, smoking habits, food preferences, weapons, and countless other characteristics of those present at the crime scene. When he cannot solve cases in situ, the Sniffer continues his investigations in his home—a hermetically sealed apartment where he conducts olfactory experiments in a fully equipped laboratory. At the center of the show are the Sniffer's virtuosic olfactory capacities, which are often dramatized through the formal innovation of staging his analysis of crime scenes with CGI-animated gaseous bodies and props. These aspects of *The Sniffer* underscore how hyperosmia empowers its protagonist to perceive invisible material traces and to leverage these traces in the service of surveilling and containing a motley collection of terrorists, kidnappers, murderers, thieves, art forgers, sex criminals, and traffickers.

The Sniffer's hyperbolic rendering of the olfactory detective stages the immense architectural and social efforts necessary to prop up the hyperosmic detective as a figure of pure rationality. For, as the series slowly reveals, Käro suffers from acute environmental hypersensitivity: his surly personality is not (or not only) the product of machismo, but the result of the strain and unease with which he tolerates the barrage of city smells outside his home. In a rare moment of self-reflection, he offers this description of his condition: "Imagine a person who lives without a skin, like a snail without its shell."[44] When the show is not concerned with solving crimes, *The Sniffer* reflects on how its protagonist compensates for his condition of radical olfactory exposure. His hypersensitivity—reflected in his irritability, solitude, and inability to eat impure foods or to tolerate the presence of others without commenting on their odors—compromises his relationships with his ex-wife, son, and new love interest. His home—a pristine apartment that appears to be the only inhabited unit in a high-rise building—is accessible only by a private elevator in which visitors must undergo an ultraviolet decontamination protocol. In order to employ hyperosmia without succumbing to its intoxicating effects, the Sniffer must occupy the difficult position of a misanthrope socially distanced from the world in a deodorized bubble—ironically, a bubble with a laboratory chock full of synthetic chemicals that somehow do not affect him. As in most serial detective fiction, the Sniffer's body bears no cumulative traces of its past exposures or chemical body burden: despite being "a snail without a shell" when it comes to atmospheric exposure, his body seems repositioned as a blank slate at the beginning of each new episode. The serial form's tendency toward bodily renewal at the beginning of each new installment resolves the tension between hyperosmia's everyday debilitations and its status as an extraordinary crime-solving ability. This enables *The Sniffer* to reframe masculinity itself—not as an invulnerable body distanced from its surroundings, but as a body that can both leverage and manage its environmental entanglements. While *The Sniffer* takes the hyperosmic detective's environmental detection to its logical endpoint by dramatizing Käro's sometimes debilitating environmental sensitivity, it simultaneously glosses over the chronic symptoms and pervasive exposures that distinguish illness narratives by people with MCS. The following section considers how these narratives of chemical injury mobilize environmental detection and the figure of the hyperosmic detective in their efforts to document and communicate embodied interactions with atmospheric risks.

Hyperosmia and Risk in MCS Narratives

Although it has been the subject of groundbreaking memoirs, ethnographies, clinical studies, and academic research, MCS—a frequently debilitating condition characterized by hypersensitivity to a range of toxic chemicals—continues to be both culturally and medically derecognized and often dismissed as a psychosomatic condition.[45] Because it is a "relational illness" whose symptoms are connected with the behaviors of others, Steve Kroll-Smith and H. Hugh Floyd argue that "important, perhaps critical, to a person's management of MCS is her ability to persuade other people that they are partly responsible for her misery and must change if she is to successfully manage her symptoms. People with MCS must narrate their illness stories in order to survive."[46] Denied the recognition of medical experts, people with MCS produce narratives to validate their experience and to enlist others to assume responsibility for maintaining a safe environment. As Alaimo writes in her definitive study of MCS memoirs, "The peculiar (auto)biographies of those with MCS have become a recognizable genre, featuring descriptions of toxins followed by descriptions of their effects."[47] Alaimo goes on to reflect on these authors' tendency to focus on trans-corporeal materialities: "Social relations fade in these eerie accounts, as the most influential forces in the authors' medical environmental/life histories are objects and substances, commonplace matters that would escape notice were it not for a conception of MCS."[48]

Among the most ubiquitous of these "commonplace matters," ambient odors evoke considerable attention and anxiety in MCS narratives. This is in part because—unlike other potentially intoxicating senses such as touch and taste—smells are invisible, mobile, spatially dispersed, and often difficult to avoid. The risks posed by unanticipated smells demand constant atmospheric vigilance and respiratory choreography for those with environmental sensitivity: for example, Mel Chen notes that walking in the city requires constantly scanning for the possibility of passing cars, cigarettes, perfume, and sunscreen and adjusting their breath accordingly: "Before [other pedestrians] near, I quickly assess whether they are likely (or might be the 'kind of people') to wear perfumes or colognes or to be wearing sunscreen. I scan their heads for smoke puffs or pursed lips pre-release; I scan their hands for long white objects, even a stub."[49] Even apparently stable objects present potential threats: "Substances made of volatile organic compounds such as foam, adhesives and plastics off-gas when the instability of the molecules cause them to escape the form of the object they were fused to, often releasing an odor."[50] Because such airborne chemical risks have been neglected, obfuscated, misrepresented, and medically derecognized, narratives of chemical sensitivity frequently take on the conventions of detective fiction, mobilizing smell to sense—and make sense of—airborne toxins and their embodied effects. The vulnerability of olfaction in these accounts stages the broader, universal human condition of the "defencelessness of breathing."[51]

MCS narratives also dwell on olfaction because hyperosmia is one of the condition's characteristic symptoms. Whether through physiological changes or the constant practice of olfactory vigilance, many people with MCS report a dramatically heightened sense of smell. Bonnye Matthews notes that hyperosmia is a common experience for those with MCS: "For example, a chemical sensitive who is experiencing acute sense of smell will be able to identify the level of personal hygiene of each person with whom he shares an elevator; recognize that a person waiting for a light to cross a street is sick (when it is not visually apparent); trail the path taken through a building by someone wearing perfume; and correctly list the contents of a metal lunch pail."[52] For the chemically sensitive, such enhanced powers of olfactory detection are accompanied by an acute vulnerability to the debilitating force of ambient smells. As "Jennifer" observes in her MCS narrative, "Now I can't go near a store without feeling sick from the smells—which I couldn't even smell when I was feeling well."[53] Underscoring the social and relational repercussions of olfactory hypersensitivity, Gail McCormick writes, "Work performance, relationships and community ties collapse when your olfactory system is so heightened that you become ill from the smell of laundry products on the clothes of someone sitting all the way across the room."[54] For Hermitra Elan*tra Vedenetra, the onset of MCS not only makes everyday smells more noticeable but transforms them into agents that disgust and sicken her, displace her from a series of familiar spaces (she ends up relocating to the high mountain desert of Arizona), and constantly threaten physical assault: "I was constantly fighting against a barrage of smells and odors coming at me from all sides, overpowering me, knocking me down again and again."[55] Like MCS, hyperosmia is stigmatized by the medical profession as a psychosomatic condition: "The *Merck Manual* used by physicians has only one thing to say about the acute sense of smell: 'Hyperosmia' (increased sensitivity to odors) usually reflects a neurotic or histrionic personality' (15th edition, page 1357)."[56] Whereas those with MCS experience their hyperosmic sensitivity as corroborating evidence that their symptoms are triggered by odors, the *Merck Manual* encourages physicians to view hyperosmia as further evidence of the MCS patient's psychological deviance.

Researchers who have studied MCS as a neurological (rather than merely psychosomatic) condition have noted the importance of olfaction as a potentially debilitating interface between sensitive subjects and environmental substances. In "MCS: Trial by Science," neurological researcher Donald L. Dudley suggests that the medical community's failure to identify "possible initiators of [MCS]" may stem from its "general lack of interest in the olfactory system, which has never represented a popular or fashionable area of research."[57] According to Dudley, this avoidance of olfactory research can be attributed to "authoritative medical textbooks since at least 1875; the use of technology better suited to other systems (e.g., the immune system) to study the olfactory system; the lack of adverse effect occurring from ablation of olfactory tracts in the brain (which has been misinterpreted as evidence that the system must have little value); the supposed failure to identify neurotransmitters in the olfactory system; and the supposed failure to identify any essential role this system could have in disease production."[58] Drawing on experimental data gleaned from twenty subjects with MCS (each exposed to substances to which they claimed sensitivity), Dudley hypothesizes that "olfactory signals release excitatory amino acids, which lead to cell injury," "diffuse, similar, and disturbingly severe changes" in responses to sensory stimuli, and increases in "the psychophysical measurements of disability."[59] Another influential study led by alternative medicine expert Iris Bell adapts the concept of "kindling" to explain how low-level chemical exposures in the olfactory system can trigger reactions in individuals with MCS.[60] The olfactory system—which "permits direct access . . . to the olfactory bulb for a wide range of environmental chemicals"—enables substances to directly affect the limbic system, a key part of the brain involved in mediating emotions, memories, and learning.[61] Kindling, the authors explain, "is a special type of time-dependent sensitization of olfactory-limbic neurons [that] involves the ability of a repeated, intermittent stimulus . . . that is initially incapable of eliciting a response eventually to induce a motor seizure from later applications of the same stimulus."[62] According to their research, the chemical kindling of olfactory-limbic neurons could be "the neurobiological mechanism" that amplifies responses to low-level exposures in people with MCS.[63]

One common scenario of environmental detection in MCS memoirs is their tendency to reconstruct the initial onset of symptoms by detailing suspicious odors followed by physiological changes. For example, Jacob Berkson's *A Canary's Tale* (1996)—an experimental epistemological memoir that Alaimo characterizes as "the *Moby-Dick* of MCS"[64]—opens with a "foul odor" emanating from the author's recently fumigated home. After noticing the odor (which turns out to be Dursban, a toxic Dow Chemical product), Berkson reports, "I began to feel bad. My eyes were tearing. My nose was irritated. My head hurt. I became nauseated."[65] The following ten pages trace the extermination company's various efforts to mitigate the odor through vents, plugs, and fans as Berkson's health declines. Framing the kindling of MCS as the emergence of a new epoch, Berkson titles his memoir's chapters after the number of years that have passed since his initial exposure: for example, "Year One: 1988 A.D."[66] In "My Experience with Chemical Sensitivity" (1998), Bonnye Matthews notes that her capacity to smell became both acute and unbearable at the onset of MCS: "I recall that out in the halls I could identify where every person had been. They left trails of scent— perfume, hairspray, lack of personal hygiene, and other odors. Each was distinct, and all were equally discernible simultaneously. I could have followed any one of them blindfolded."[67] However, she notes that "I did not want that knowledge" because each of these airborne odorants triggered debilitating reactions.[68] In another account recorded by

Kroll-Smith and Floyd, an environmental resources inspector first falls ill when responding to neighbors' complaints about "caustic odors" in an abandoned used car lot:

> We started smelling strange things coming from the ground. At that point, the state police should have pulled us back. No one was wearing a respirator. But everyone was so excited that we finally found something out there, that we proceeded on our merry way. The bigger the smells were, you know, that was pay dirt. We had this guy digging. I was just following my nose, smelling, stopping, pointing, and someone would dig. I was like a hunting dog.
>
> Once we collected the samples, and the excitement of the big discovery was not so exciting, I noticed the smells burning my nose, eyes, my throat, my skin, and such. And it was a strange feeling. The guy with the shovel had to call me a couple of times, because apparently I was in a rapture of the deep, kind of like I had crawled into a big shell and couldn't hear the world.[69]

At first acting like a "hunting dog" or olfactory detective, the environmental inspector falls ill from the very smells he is attempting to expunge. Doing the work of deodorization that supports fantasies of the hermetically sealed individual body, he is drawn into an entirely different way of inhabiting the world. When the newly reactive subject emerges from his cocoon-like "shell," he finds himself enmeshed in previously unnoticed environmental intimacies.

These scenes of MCS inception are characterized not only by noxious odors but by a pervasive atmosphere of uncertainty about what is happening to the subject's body, mind, and moods. As Kroll-Smith and Floyd explain, chemically reactive people must rely on their own senses and embodied experiences to understand and articulate the "new body" they inhabit—not biomedicine's conception of the immune individual as a "body worth defending," but a body trans-corporeally co-constituted by its environment (including the bodies of others).[70] People with MCS improvise a "practical epistemology" that affirms the importance of embodied experiences derecognized by the medical community.[71] As Alaimo observes, everyday uncertainties about possible chemical exposures give rise to experimental practices of citizen science: "The person with MCS may be understood as a sort of scientist, actively seeking knowledge about material agencies, and, simultaneously, as the instrument that registers those agencies. In MCS (auto)biographies, the body often appears as something akin to a scientific instrument, in that daily life becomes a sort of experiment: what happens when I go there, breathe that, touch this?"[72] In her "Notes from a Human Canary," Lynn Lawson characterizes this process of self-experimentation as "detective work":

> One night about a month after I was diagnosed, I smelled formaldehyde on my pillowcase. Formaldehyde, a suspected carcinogen, is in many, many products, including synthetic fabrics such as cotton/polyester sheets. I immediately put some old cotton sheets and pillowcases on my bed. A few days later, I detected the same smell in soap from a filling-station dispenser. Now I avoid using public soap dispensers and try to carry my own soap. And once again I hang my all-cotton sheets on lines in our basement after they have been washed in our washing machine with a plant-based liquid soap without fabric softeners. Fabric softeners from neighbors' dryers and others' clothes now smell nauseating to me.
>
> One's sense of smell is invaluable in detecting possible chemical injury from modern synthetic products.[73]

Lawson uses her sense of smell to identify and evade potential toxins, while her olfactory vigilance in turn sharpens her olfactory capacities: once she has noticed the smell of formaldehyde, she becomes capable of "detect[ing]" its presence elsewhere.[74] Like many other writers with MCS, Lawson comes to understand her sense of smell not only as a source of vulnerability but as an improvable tool of risk detection— perhaps the most widely accessible (though commonly disparaged and dangerously underutilized) resource of citizen science.

In *Poisoned: How a Crime-Busting Prosecutor Turned His Medical Mystery into a Crusade for Environmental Victims* (2017), Alan Bell expands this trope of detective work into a fully fledged "medical mystery." Bell approaches familiar elements of MCS memoir—the onset of symptoms in a "sick" office building, his frustrated search for an accurate medical diagnosis, his search for a safer living space, his epistemological quest to learn about the disease—with the legal training of a former criminal prosecutor. *Poisoned* charts a trajectory from Bell's early legal career prosecuting individual defendants (allegedly involved with organized crime and drug trafficking) in Florida to his legal advocacy for victims of environmental injury resulting from sick buildings, occupational illnesses, pesticide exposure, and incinerators sited in African American communities. After provisionally resolving his own "medical mystery" by consulting (and convening, as founder of the Environmental Health Foundation) an emerging network of researchers focusing on MCS and environmental health, Bell learns that the drug Neurontin (gabapentin) can help manage his reactions. At this point, he begins offering other chemically injured people support as a sort of ad hoc environmental investigator. He reports, "I could now determine with some accuracy when toxic chemicals were around me. I was like a drug-sniffing dog able to detect low levels of toxins that other people couldn't sense."[75] Because taking Neurontin enables Bell to minimize his chemical reactivity, he can use his olfactory sensitivity to locate toxins: "Unorthodox or not, my ability to sniff out or 'feel' the presence of toxins was actually pretty straightforward and simple. Some victims would call me to say they thought their workplace or home was making them sick, but they weren't sure why. I'd go on site to help them figure out the likely source of their illness. If there was black mold or another toxic chemical in their environment, I could sense it. My lungs would immediately seize up, or I'd feel an intense sinus pain" (P, 170–71). Detecting toxins like a "drug-sniffing dog," Bell puts his body on the line to produce evidence of environmental toxicity. Although he puts himself at risk of tightened lungs and sinus pain, Bell's hyperosmic detective work also serves to shore up his masculinity and, to some extent, his sense of bodily integrity: Neurontin enables him to use his vulnerable, porous body to rescue others. The arc of Bell's career is oriented by a focus on "organized crime" and the traffic in intoxicants—only the intoxicants are no longer criminalized narcotics, but everyday chemicals propagated by corporations benefiting from weak legal regulations and putatively strict medical standards of "evidence." Bell comes to conceive of his role as helping to "expose this ultimate crime—a crime so vicious that it leaves millions of victims in its wake; a crime so insidious that the villain is often invisible" (P, 238). As an embodied tool that helps give direction to technologically supported "expert" methods of measuring toxicity, Bell's sense of smell plays a crucial role in this project of detecting insidious, corporate "crimes" of slow violence.

As Kroll-Smith and Floyd argue, the burden of MCS narratives is to persuade others to join in the recognition of this "new somatic text": "From changing something as personal as avoiding the use of a scented hair spray to rewriting a federal public housing code to accommodate the habitat needs of the environmentally ill, society is representing the existence of a new body" (P, 145). Hyperosmia communicates this mode of porous and interactive embodiment by reordering the modern hierarchy of the senses, at once appealing to the commonly available but undervalued sense of smell and dramatizing the potential toxicity of synthetic scents. Through this vigilant attention to odors—often juxtaposed with their presumed embodied effects—MCS narratives also recode smells in material terms. This olfactory rhetoric validates both smell and suffering as embodied experiences that challenge the privileging of the visual inherent in the etymology of "evidence." Instead of functioning as free-floating signifiers of freshness, sex, and a range of "natural" associations, synthetic scents come to signify what they materially entail for chemically reactive authors: nausea, migraines, fatigue, gastrointestinal discomfort, respiratory problems, muscle pain seizures, and cognitive difficulties. This recoding brings the semiotics of scents back to their material basis in highly reactive volatile organic compounds—substances, commonly found in scents, that have been associated with a range of short- and long-term health conditions.[76] Because, in many cases, MCS is first kindled through an olfactory pathway and subsequently triggered by a vast range of everyday smells, these narratives attune both reactive and nonreactive readers to the potential toxicity of the everyday atmospheres they inhabit and inhale.

If hyperosmia enables MCS narratives to communicate sensory experience and associated perceptions of risk in embodied, everyday terms, it may also have the effect of circumscribing the scope of readers' engagement with environmental health issues. As Matthews notes, "Our tendency is to ignore the existence of substances we cannot smell or delight in those with a pleasant scent. That tendency can prove harmful, if not deadly."[77] While the pleasant scent of perfumes and fabric softeners can be recoded through association with debilitating health effects, hyperosmia cannot directly engage with the considerable risks posed by odorless toxins. It also risks reinscribing—even exacerbating—cultural influences on olfactory perception: which cooking smells and personal care products are perceived to be noxious may not be entirely extricable from issues of ethnicity, class, and culture. Hyperosmic MCS narratives are further limited by a tendency to feature the struggles of individual breathers endangered by the presence of atmospheric substances. What this communicates to readers is the visceral urgency of moving to a place with more breathable air: Bell, for example, draws on his enormous family wealth to move from Florida to the Arizona desert, an MCS community in Texas, a stone castle in Cabo San Lucas, and finally to the California coast in search of less toxic atmospheres. Many MCS authors and/or chronic respiratory conditions resettle in the Southwest, compelled to reenact settler colonial patterns whereby health-seeking migrants with tuberculosis and asthma helped fuel settler population growth throughout the region.[78] Finally, MCS narratives' intense vigilance concerning the harmful effects of everyday consumer decisions regarding personal care products, perfumes, colognes, cigarette smoking, and pesticides may draw attention away from broad and geographically uneven patterns of atmospheric violence, even as it promotes social recognition of MCS and support for fragrance-free spaces. How can the direct sensory appeals (and aversions) of hyperosmia be redirected from individual breathers to the broader dynamics of slow violence?

Alison Johnson, a chemically sensitive author who has edited two collections of MCS narratives, identifies military veterans with Gulf War Syndrome, office workers in "sick buildings" (including the EPA headquarters), 9/11 responders and cleanup workers, oil spill cleanup workers, and residents of post-Katrina New Orleans as populations especially vulnerable to chemical poisoning; her books also include clusters of narratives by painters, beauticians, and domestic caretakers.[79] The numerous MCS cases clustering around war, industrial accidents, catastrophic events, and chemically intensive occupations convey the extent to which chemical sensitivity disproportionately affects working-class populations. Whereas MCS networks and the condition's most prominent spokespeople have been white and relatively privileged, Johnson presents several testimonies by chemically injured people of color. For example, the siblings Tomasita and Moises recount how they both fell sick after being exposed to an unknown scent while cleaning up a guest house: "Suddenly I had the feeling of being gassed, and I felt like something was encompassing me. . . . I felt like I had just taken a chug of perfume or something like that because my mouth tasted like perfume."[80] While they graphically recount the gruesome experience of being enveloped and violated by an unknown smell, the narratives of Tomasita and Moises also provoke questions about the many laborers in fields such as intensive agriculture, domestic work, construction, and cosmetology—frequently immigrants with limited access to health care, literacy, and MCS networks who lack opportunities to bear witness to their experiences of chemical sensitivity.

Although MCS often has the effect of (at least temporarily) isolating people from their communities and social relationships, Terri Crawford Hansen (Winnebago) writes that "in many ways my life has changed for the better" after formaldehyde exposure in her newspaper office triggered her symptoms.[81] Hansen's social losses (divorce, losing custody of her daughter, and leaving her job) were counterbalanced by stronger connections with her mother's Winnebago ancestry: "It wasn't until after I quit my job that I became Indian. After I had to quit my job, I started volunteering in the Indian community. That was good for me, to go back to my roots. My mother was all Indian. She was removed from the reservation at the age of three because her mother died. She was adopted by a family in Portland and never developed an interest in her Indian heritage" (TCH, 203). Volunteering in a local (unspecified) Native American community, Hansen puts herself at risk of further exposures. As she notes, "The prevalence of MCS is higher in the Indian community that in the general population . . . 31 percent of the Native Americans surveyed [by New Mexico's Department of Health] identified themselves as chemically sensitive, compared to 17 percent in the general population" (TCH, 203). Hansen explains that Native Americans' vulnerability is likely connected to the fact that "more toxic wastes are dumped on reservations than anywhere else in the United States" (TCH, 204). Instead of escaping to a safer, "purer" atmosphere, Hansen exposes herself to disproportionately polluted spaces in order to assist and advocate for her community: Hansen has authored numerous articles documenting chemical poisoning among Native Americans, and she founded the National American Indian Environmental Illness Foundation. She employs

Indigenous therapies to manage her condition, reminding us that ideas about "purity" are culturally variable: "Every morning and every evening I burn and smudge sage or sweetgrass to purify myself and my home" (TCH, 201).[82] MCS sensitizes Hansen to her Native American descent, as well as the chemical consequences of settler colonialism for Indigenous lands throughout the United States. Yet despite its role in triggering her chemical sensitivity, Hansen does not rely on olfaction to make these connections: instead, she turns to the data provided by health surveys. Like the clusters of short narratives collected by Johnson, Hansen's narrative shifts the scope of environmental detection from individual olfactory experience to broader patterns of damage resulting from differential deodorization.

Simultaneously an organ of olfactory knowledge and olfactory invasion, the detective's nose catalyzes diverse responses to modernity's atmospheric risks: nineteenth-century efforts at deodorization and olfactory control, the systemically poisoned atmospheres of hard-boiled crime fiction and Fisher and Himes's Black detective narratives, and the chemically sensitive "detective" figures who employ their noses to sniff out systemic environmental risks rather than criminalized individuals. The hyperosmic detective indicates how trans-corporeal modes of embodied knowledge and ecological relation have always haunted the genre of detective fiction. In addition to situating detective fiction as a genre with important environmental implications, the literary history of the hyperosmic detective illuminates the tension between individualized criminality and environmental violence. In many twentieth-century and contemporary narratives, the activity of sniffing out criminals draws detectives into new, intimate understandings of environmental toxicity. Through olfaction, intoxication—frequently stigmatized as a sign of irrationality and criminality—becomes an invaluable yet potentially debilitating epistemological tool for detectives navigating modernity's stratified atmospheres.

While their direct and detailed accounts of smell are effective in communicating emergent, trans-corporeal ways of knowing the effects of anthropogenic atmospheres upon individual bodies, hyperosmic narratives have not been so effective when it comes to communicating the spatial and demographic patterns of atmospheric violence. As I argue in the following chapter, literary naturalism—along with twentieth- and twenty-first-century environmental justice narratives that draw on naturalist techniques—leverages olfactory description to address atmospheric disparities at the level of aggregate populations. In these works, atmospheric risks taken in through olfactory pathways are most devastating when characters notice them least. Whereas the relative mobility of detectives and some authors with MCS (who are frequently forced to move in search of safer spaces) frequently exposes them to new and unfamiliar smells, characters in naturalist novels tend to be immersed in (and thus become habituated to) a circumscribed smellscape. Without the detectives' hyperosmic sensitivity and deodorizing sensibility, naturalist characters could be said to be *hypo-osmic*: whether through desensitization, habituation, or denial, they hardly notice or think about the smells to which they're chronically exposed.

2

Naturalist Smellscapes and Environmental Justice

In an effort to counteract an affliction that gradually transforms him into a "brute," the protagonist of Frank Norris's *Vandover and the Brute* (1914) turns to the uplifting influence of art. But despite his "natural" talents as an artist, Vandover has trouble concentrating in his life-drawing class: "Vandover was annoyed at his ill success—such close attention and continued effort wearied him a little—the room was overheated and close, and the gas stove, which was placed near the throne to warm the model, leaked and filled the room with a nasty brassy smell."[1] Although Norris mentions this art studio's gas leak only in passing, its smell evokes a range of tensions that I argue are central to his novel and to the broader tradition of literary naturalism: the tension between vision and the so-called lower senses, the tension between modern improvements (such as indoor heating) and unintended environmental externalities (such as a gas leak), and the tension between aesthetic objects and the material atmospheres they inhabit and describe. Underlying all these tensions is the problem of uncertainty: does Vandover notice the "nasty brassy smell" of leaked gas because he loses his concentration, or does he lose his concentration and succumb to "weariness" because he has been breathing leaked gas—along with paint fumes[2]—in a poorly ventilated, overheated room? Instead of counteracting his physical and mental decline, the atmosphere of Vandover's drawing class seems to exacerbate his malaise. This passage dramatizes what Ulrich Beck calls "reflexive modernization"—or modernization's tendency to produce concerns about modernization's risks[3]—on the level of aesthetic practice: the heating apparatus designed to ensure the comfort of the nude art model is emitting gas that possibly hinders Vandover from drawing the model.

The gas leak in Vandover's art studio exemplifies an underexamined motif that I argue is crucial to understanding naturalism's complex engagements with processes of environmental determinism or constraint:

the uneven composition and distribution of air. As Lawrence Buell has suggested, environmental "discourses of determinism"—which often feature cities, factories, and other "impure" environments—offer an important counterbalance to an American tradition of environmental thinking that largely derives from Romantic ideals about "Nature" and purity.[4] Whereas the animal and the machine have furnished literary naturalism's most familiar metaphors for a world of inhuman forces, air represents a vehicle for thinking about environment that refuses easy oppositions between wild "Nature" and artificial "machines."[5] As Jennifer Fleissner has noted in a different context, our tendency to emphasize naturalism's hyperbolic narratives—in which nature is seen in either nostalgic or revitalizing terms—tends to obscure how naturalist authors enacted "a far more nuanced and serious confrontation with the meanings of 'nature's changing status in the modern world."[6] Air—which consists of shifting combinations of anthropogenic emissions, animal and plant exhalations, and dust particles of nearly everything—offers a complex yet often overlooked index of "nature's changing status in the modern world." As Choy puts it in his groundbreaking work on air pollution in Hong Kong, "Air functions . . . as a heuristic with which to encompass many atmospheric experiences. The abstraction of air does not derive from asserting a unit for comparison or a common field within which to arrange specificities, but through an aggregation of materialities irreducible to one another (including breath, humidity, SARS, particulate, and so on). Thinking about the materiality of air and the densities of our many human entanglements in airy matters also means attending to the solidifying and melting edges between people, regions, and events."[7] In addition to calling attention to our material interactions with multiple atmospheric substances, air embodies the frequently overlooked flow of lively materials between differentiated spaces and across geographic scales. Air is thus an important element for theorizing social relations and affect in material terms: "Thinking more about air, that is, not taking it simply as solidity's opposite, might offer some means of thinking about relations and movements—between places, people, things, scales—means that obviate the usual traps of particularity and universality."[8]

In naturalist fiction, air functions as a diffuse yet significant vehicle (both metaphor and metonymy) for environmental influence. At the same time, naturalist writers' tendency to vacillate between metaphoric, affective, and material treatments of air—air as a social "atmosphere," as an evocative smell, or as a toxic cloud—dramatizes both the stratification of air (which enables health and sociability in some places, while inducing exhaustion and illness in others) and the uncertainty that characterizes many experiences of environmental risk, particularly among vulnerable populations. Unlike the hyperosmic narratives discussed in chapter 1, naturalist fiction depicts characters and populations who are relatively insensitive to the atmosphere and its embodied consequences. By contrast with the characters they depict, however, naturalist narrators are acutely aware of how the chemical composition of air varies across spaces and class boundaries as well as how airborne toxins can affect bodies, minds, and moods on both individual and collective scales.[9] At once animated and animating (or deadening) in its effects, air calls for a reassessment of Georg Lukács's influential dismissal of naturalism as a genre whose overemphasis on describing physical details reifies humans as passive, mechanistic beings. Whereas Lukács claims that "the descriptive method lacks humanity [and transforms] men into still lives," describing the liveliness of nonhuman materials such as air illuminates the trans-corporeal becomings that condition human mood, embodiment, and action.[10] In "The Language of the Stones: Literary Naturalism and the New Materialism," Kevin Trumpeter argues that naturalism shares important conceptual ground with new materialism, noting that Bruno Latour's methodological privileging of description "is consonant with the emphasis on description in the 'experimental' novels of naturalism."[11] In underscoring the ways in which we are conditioned by differentially deodorized atmospheres, naturalist smellscapes offer a productive site for putting new materialist insights in dialogue with environmental justice concerns.

Like much urban and industrial writing, naturalism devotes considerable attention to air's appearance: the writings of Frank Norris, Stephen Crane, Theodore Dreiser, and Jack London are shot through with smoke, steam, fog, dust, and soot. Rather than focusing on these visual markers of air pollution, however, I explore a mode of representing air that violated both Enlightenment aesthetics and Victorian decorum: naturalist descriptions of smells (particularly unpleasant ones). Associated with passive reception, physical permeability, corporeal excess, involuntary responses, and disease transmission, the sense of smell unsettles liberalism's fiction of the rational, individual subject of free choice. Air is simultaneously an aesthetic medium of scent and a biopolitical medium that conditions life and death: airborne chemicals may convey not only disgust or enjoyment but also environmental slow violence that insidiously disperses environmental harm across space and time. Distributed unevenly across space, smells also condition subtle gradations of capacity and debility: in addition to killing, they can temporarily or chronically affect one's embodiment, cognition, and mood.[12] Yet smell is also something to which we become habituated: the more we're entangled with it—the more a smell enters our bodies and sticks to our clothing—the less we notice it. Smell thus offers naturalist writers an especially effective means for dramatizing both the uneven distribution of bad air and people's involuntary—frequently debilitating—corporealization of airborne particulates. To the extent that it serves as a visceral yet indefinite index of airborne toxins, smell can sensitize us to everyday pathways of trans-corporeal material agency.

Beginning with an analysis of olfactory environments in *Vandover*, this chapter shows how naturalist narratives of mental and physical decline intersect with the genre's obsessive mapping of place-based smells. Next, I consider how the twentieth-century authors Ann Petry and Helena María Viramontes—whose works have significant affinities with earlier naturalist novels—extend Norris's thematic treatment of air as a debilitating medium by dramatizing the connections between airborne toxicity and race- and class-based inequalities. While critics have traced the influence of naturalism on twentieth-century genres such as protest novels, film noir, hard-boiled crime fiction, and science fiction,[13] my focus on environmental justice fiction illuminates a strain of "neo-naturalism" that runs through all these other genres, infusing their plots with diffuse manifestations of environmental slow violence. The threads that run from turn-of-the-century naturalism to environmental justice fiction illustrate how the formal innovations of Norris and his contemporaries have been reappropriated from their imperialist, Anglo-Saxonist origins and rechanneled toward antiracist projects.

Vandover's Smellscapes

While modernization is often associated with a drive to eradicate undesirable smells, it would be more accurate to say that the dramatic growth of US cities and industrial production beginning in the 1880s introduced disorienting and rapidly shifting "smellscapes"—to invoke geographer J. Douglas Porteous's term for the way in which places can be characterized by particular smell combinations.[14] The rapid and chaotic growth of urban spaces and populations proliferated technologies of differential deodorization that unevenly distributed smells emitted by smokestacks, steam laundries, construction materials, paint, cleaning products, gas lamps, unfamiliar foods, and diverse bodies, human and nonhuman. The cultural, ethnic, and class diversity of cities—as well as the vast populations served by urban infrastructure—gave rise to new anxieties about identity, hygiene, and contagion: smells perceived to be "repulsive" could index class and ethnic disparities, failures of urban planning and infrastructure, or the potential for disease transmission. Differentiated smellscapes thus offer an important perspective on the "microclimatic 'splintering of the atmosphere'" into compartmentalized and stratified breathing spaces—a process that Sloterdijk frames as the material basis of modern alienation, or people's increasing "inaccessibility to the differently minded, differently enclosed, and differently air-conditioned."[15] These complex and shifting smellscapes gave rise to aesthetic experiments with *toposmia*—Drobnick's neologism (combining the Greek words for "place" and "smell") for a field of aesthetic inquiry concerned with "the spatial location of odours and their relation to particular notions of place."[16] Drobnick provides a typology of artistic practices of toposmia, arguing that they may reinforce visual topographies with supporting smells, trace the affective means by which smells induce place-based identifications, or explore "dialectical odours" that strategically "use smell as an intervention into and means to critique . . . abstract or essentialist political conceptions of space."[17] Smell is thus an important medium for understanding the affective capacities of air—what atmospheric geographer Peter Adey calls the "material-affective ecology of a place[,] the qualities of the city that . . . imbue its material and biological fabric with affect."[18]

The widespread association of unpleasant smells with poor hygiene and risk derived from the nineteenth-century miasma theory of disease. As British public health expert Edwin Chadwick put it in 1846, "All smell is, if it be intense, immediate acute disease; and eventually we may say that, by depressing the system and rendering it susceptible to the action of other causes, all smell is disease."[19] As Corbin writes in his study of odor in nineteenth-century France, "The increased importance attributed to the phenomenon of air by chemistry and medical theories of infection put a brake on the declining attention to the sense of smell. The nose anticipates dangers; it recognizes from a distance both harmful mold and the presence of miasmas."[20] In the Progressive Era United States, smell was perceived to be both a nuisance and a public health threat: in 1891, for example, the Fifteenth Ward Smelling Committee embarked on a voyage up Newtown Creek to determine the sources of pungent and reportedly debilitating odors in Brooklyn, Queens, and parts of the Lower East Side.[21] Although germ theory (already widely accepted in Europe) was gaining influence in the United States at the end of the nineteenth century, historian JoAnne Brown notes that "older etiological concepts of putrefaction, miasmas, and filth [as disease agents] persisted in the popular culture well into the twentieth century."[22] Miasma theory—or the notion that disease transmission is facilitated by poor air quality—underscores the connections between olfactory aesthetics and public health. In addition to mapping place-based smells, toposmia can produce olfactory maps of environmental inequality, tracing not only how odor contributes to affect and memory but also how unevenly distributed smells can debilitate or kill through trans-corporeal means.

Naturalism was the first American aesthetic movement to explore these links between air quality, health, and disease.[23] Examples include the fetid odors and lung disease (as well as the "woody fragrance" of the Quakers) that suffuse Rebecca Harding Davis's proto-naturalist "Life in the Iron Mills" (1861);[24] Buck sniffing the "fresh morning air" in *The Call of the Wild* (1903); the "subtlest, most enduring odor" of Gilman's yellow wallpaper (possibly arsenic dust from the pigment);[25] the "strange and unspeakable odors" and "unholy atmospheres" that assail Crane's protagonist "like malignant diseases with wings" in "An Experiment in Misery" (1894);[26] the "subtly strong odor of powder-smoke, oil, wet earth" that causes "alarmed lungs . . . to lengthen their respirations" in Crane's

"In the Depths of a Coal Mine" (1894);[27] the opposition between rancid forecastles and healthy salt air in Norris and London's seafaring novels; the theme of "bad air" that Rose Ellen Lessy has traced in the works of Edith Wharton;[28] *Sister Carrie*'s (1900) juxtaposition of dazzling social "atmospheres" with suicide by gas inhalation;[29] and *The Jungle*'s (1906) suggestion that the suffocating stenches of industrial meat rendering contribute to the diseases that debilitate and kill several key characters.[30] Anticipating the olfactory reading of Norris that I provide below, Ernest Marchand observed in 1942 that "an interminable catalogue of odors might be compiled from the work of [Frank] Norris."[31] In their diffuse references to air—an element that frequently hovers in the barely perceived background—naturalist writers practice a mode of "ambient poetics"[32] attuned to the intoxicating qualities of airborne materials. In virtuosic passages such as Zola's famous catalogue of cheeses and Upton Sinclair's account of the "strange, pungent odor" that takes hold as his characters approach the slaughterhouses, naturalist fiction suspends plot development in favor of olfactory description. This technique of olfactory description subverts the classical visual trope of *ekphrasis*: rather than verbally render a visual artwork, olfactory ekphrasis makes an extensive and necessarily imprecise effort to describe an odor. Their fascination with the supposedly atavistic sense of smell led critic Max Nordau to deride the fiction of "Zola . . . and his disciples" as an olfactory offense:[33] "The books in which the public here depicted finds its delight or edification diffuse a curious perfume yielding distinguishable odours of incense, eau de Lubin and refuse, one or the other preponderating alternately. Mere sewage exhalations are played out. The vanguard of civilization holds its nose at the pit of undiluted naturalism, and can only be brought to bend over it with sympathy and curiosity when, by cunning engineering, a drain from the boudoir and the sacristy has been turned into it."[34] Corbin, however, explains Zola's olfactory predisposition as a capacity for engaging with public health concerns: "Zola transposed into novels—very belatedly—the obsession with smells that had haunted medicine before Pasteur. His descriptions of the odors of public and private places, of the dwellings of both rich and poor, reflected the sort of obsessions found in the writings on sanitary reform around 1835 after the great cholera morbus epidemic."[35]

While critics such as Bill Brown and Kevin Trumpeter have illuminated the social liveliness of *things* in realist and naturalist novels,[36] scholars of these genres tend to overlook the "animacy" of air—to adapt Mel Chen's term for the capacity of language to attribute degrees of liveliness to bodies, things, and environmental materials such as toxins.[37] In these writings, air functions as both a metaphor for stratified social milieus (it tends to be more hazardous in spaces occupied by the poor) and an uneven medium of physical and mental health. For example, in *The People of the Abyss*—his 1903 account of "precarious" living conditions in East London—Jack London offers a toposmic account of how "the manifold smells of the day" mix and persist in the small, overcrowded room that serves as kitchen, laundry room, living room, and bedroom for a large family. Elsewhere, describing the slow deaths caused by occupational dust inhalation, London writes, "Steel dust, stone dust, clay dust, alkali dust, fluff dust, fibre dust—all these things kill, and they are more deadly than machine-guns and pom-poms."[38] London's metaphor of the "abyss" names a vicious downward spiral whereby environmental factors slowly debilitate the minds and bodies of the poor, leaving them more vulnerable to new environmental risks connected with ever poorer living and working conditions.

Vandover and the Brute charts just such a vicious cycle of decline by following its protagonist's trajectory across a range of intoxicating smellscapes. The novel traces the moral and physical degeneration of Vandover, a young aspiring painter who graduates from Harvard, rapes a young woman, causes her suicide, indulges increasingly in alcohol and long baths, inherits his father's real estate holdings, fritters away his inheritance on fancy dinners and gambling debts, and ends up working as a janitor in a row of cheap working-class cottages. Along the way, he slowly succumbs to *lycanthropy-mathesis*, a nervous disease supposedly linked to syphilis,[39] which impairs Vandover's vision and coordination and eventually causes him to act like a wolf, running around naked on all fours while compulsively barking the word "Wolf!" *Vandover* was the first novel Norris completed (in 1895), but it was published posthumously in 1914, twelve years after the author's death. Russ Castronovo attributes the delay in publication to publishers' concerns about the book's lewd and "immoral" content: "There was no saving a novel where portraits of harem girls bathing and other racy paintings hang from the walls[,] wine flows freely[,] women talk coarsely[,]" and the protagonist nearly vomits in a church from a hangover.[40] Although *Vandover* received mixed reviews when it was first published,[41] it has since re-emerged as an important text for new historicist critics such as Walter Benn Michaels, June Howard, Katherine Fusco, and Gina Marchetti, who frame Vandover's degeneration as an expression of the era's anxieties about the capitalist economy, urban environments, mass entertainments, class mixing, and the atavistic "brute" within. While my analysis builds on these contextual readings, I focus on the centrality of smell as a formal influence and environmental motif that links *Vandover* with twentieth-century fiction concerned with intersections between social inequality and toxic atmospheres. While *Vandover* is representative of an interest in the materiality of smell found across many naturalist texts, it is nevertheless distinguished by Norris's persistent formal engagement with questions of habituation, uncertainty, and diffusion arising from everyday, low-level exposures to environmental toxins.

Vandover stages a tension between visual and olfactory aesthetics, pitting the aspiring painter's control of lines and color against his susceptibility to San Francisco's varied and frequently toxic smellscapes. In a degenerative process that allegorizes Kant's hierarchy of the senses, Vandover's ambitions and independent will are gradually eroded by the lower senses as he overindulges in chocolates in the bathtub, reads sensationalistic novels, and inhales the scents of alcohol and food and the perfumed "odour of abandoned women" (*V*, 73). According to Kant, vision, hearing, and touch perceive the surface of objects, while taste and smell involve "the most intimate taking into ourselves"—an intimacy that, he adds, "can be dangerous to the animal."[42] For Kant, smell is both "contrary to freedom" and "even more intimate" than taste.[43] As Drobnick explains, smell threatens Kant's "central aesthetic tenets" of disinterestedness (insofar as "smells are highly subjective and directly implicate the beholder's body") and autonomy (insofar as smells are perceived passively, appeal to the limbic system, and call forth visceral physiological responses).[44] Just as smell's excessive intimacy threatens to undermine the liberal subject's capacities of reason and will, Vandover finds himself increasingly unable to act on his moral judgments over the course of the novel. At the same time, his foul inhalations contribute to Vandover's physical decline and his increasing susceptibility to a nervous condition that Norris frames in both emasculating and atavistic terms.[45] Smell thus plays a pivotal role in Vandover's vicious cycle of decline: bad air renders him increasingly susceptible to lycanthropy, and his psychological transformation into a wolf may in turn sharpen his sense of smell. The novel's plot approximates the trajectory of sensory decline mapped out by Nordau in his caustic account of Zola's naturalism: "To make [a man] conceive the phenomenon of the world, its changes and causes of motion, by a succession of perfumes, his frontal lobe must be depressed and the olfactory lobe of a dog substituted for it."[46]

Norris tracks Vandover's decline across a range of unpleasant—and possibly noxious—smellscapes. The novel begins with a sort of primal scene that juxtaposes the death of Vandover's "invalid" mother with "the smell of steam and of hot oil" at a train station: this juxtaposition immediately positions Vandover as a product of both his mother's body and the smell of train exhaust (V, 41, 42). At the Imperial barroom, where Vandover frequently drinks with college chums and prostitutes, "a heavy odorous warmth in which were mingled the smells of sweetened whisky, tobacco, the fumes of cooking, and the scent of perfume, exhaled into the air" (V, 71). The previously healthy Vandover becomes sick for the first time amid the foul air of a ship: "The cabin was two decks below the open air and every berth was occupied, the only ventilation being through the door. The air was foul with the stench of bilge, the reek of the untrimmed lamps, the exhalation of so many breaths, and the close, stale smell of warm bedding" (V, 120). In this scene, Norris explicitly attributes Vandover's illness to the air: "The continued pitching, the foul air, and the bitter smoke from the saloonkeepers' cigars became more than Vandover could stand. His stomach turned, at every instant he gagged and choked" (V, 121). At one of Vandover's art studios, the casts of celebrated classical statues are surrounded by an atmosphere that is filled with artistic materials, yet (for that very reason) unsupportive of the artistic process: "A strong odour of turpentine and fixative was in the air, mingled with the stronger odours of linseed oil and sour, stale French bread" (V, 79). When Vandover attends the opera, aesthetic experience is again accompanied by bad air: "The atmosphere was heavy with the smell of gas, of plush upholstery, of wilting bouquets and of sachet. A fine vapour as of the visible exhalation of many breaths pervaded the house. . . . The air itself was stale and close as though fouled by being breathed over and over again" (*V*, 174). Vandover's living quarters become progressively stuffier as well: at one hotel "the air of the room was thick and foul, heavy with the odour of cooking, onions, and stale bedding. It was very warm; there was no ventilation. . . . He was glad to be warm, to be stupefied by the heat of the bedding and the bad air of the room" (*V*, 243). Rendered passive and sensuous by so many smells, Vandover is not only "stupefied" by his home's bad air—he's "glad" to be stupefied. The novel concludes with Vandover working as a house cleaner, immersed in both the stench of rotting filth and the smell of cleaning products: "Now he was cleaning out the sink and the laundry tubs. They smelt very badly and were all foul with a greasy mixture of old lard, soap, soot, and dust; a little mould was even beginning to form about the faucets of the tubs" (*V*, 259). The novel maps Vandover's regression by moving from sensual and cloying scents in spaces of luxury to the cheap boarding houses and cottages in which Vandover must live and work after gambling his inheritance away.

Norris's deployment of toposmia throughout *Vandover* formally underscores three facets of low-level exposure: habituation, uncertainty, and diffusion. Norris enacts our tendency to become habituated to smells by describing them in passing early on in each of the novel's scenes: soon after being perceived, even the foulest smells fade into the background. This phenomenon of olfactory habituation—or what Drobnick terms "olfactory fatigue"[47]—dramatizes how low-level exposures to "bad air" can function through the gradual, accretive temporality of slow violence: for even intolerable smells become tolerable with time. Moreover, as Nixon explains, the spatial and temporal dispersal of widespread low-level exposures has a camouflaging effect: they're present everywhere, but in barely noticeable quantities. Olfactory habituation in Norris's narration parallels the process of sensory habituation that propels Vandover's decline: always on the lookout for "fresh excitement that . . . could rouse his jaded nerves," Vandover indulges in increasingly extreme forms of gambling and consumption until the thrill of losing fantastic sums of money becomes the only novelty left to him.

Vandover's juxtaposition of physical and mental degeneration with foul smells also stages what environmental historian Michelle Murphy calls "the problem of uncertainty." In her study of the emergence of "sick building syndrome" in the 1990s, Murphy explains that office workers voicing health concerns about harmful chemicals in office buildings negotiated "domains of imperceptibility" generated by scientific standards of proof. In the face of so much uncertainty, Murphy argues, it is necessary to "historiciz[e] the techniques through which 'exposure,' as an effect between buildings and bodies, became a phenomenon people could say, feel, and do something about."[48] While Murphy traces the techniques enacted by scientists, corporate experts, and labor activists, I argue that the naturalist novel was also an important cultural tool for reconfiguring domains of imperceptibility. Although it seldom specifies direct causal relations between airborne particles and physiological reactions, Norris's novel insinuates correlations between the foul air that pervades *Vandover*'s environments and the protagonist's debilitation. Relegated to the edges of perceptibility, airborne particles are usually invisible and sometimes scentless; their biological effects are difficult to prove. When the foul air on the ship is juxtaposed first with a Salvation Army worker's violent, choking cough and then with Vandover's nausea, the novel only implies direct causation. Similarly, Norris's repeated descriptions of Vandover's mind as "clouded" and "enwrapped [in] fog" suggest the trans-corporeal influx of bad air, but only through metaphorical association.[49] The near imperceptibility of airborne toxins—along with the impossibility of ascertaining definite etiologies of harm—makes environmental miasmas a frequent subject of the "compulsion to describe" that Fleissner identifies as a definitive formal feature of naturalist writing. Grounded in a "feeling of incompleteness" and a compulsive sense of doubt, this compulsion to describe takes the form of "an endless, excessive attempt to gain control over one's surroundings that reveals one's actual lack of control and concomitant frozenness in place."[50] In spite of the novel's pervasive uncertainty concerning smells, Norris consistently correlates health with air quality, as when Vandover's episode of incessant barking in a stuffy barroom is temporarily relieved "after a few minutes in the open air" (*V*, 233), or when working-class tenants complain to their landlord of "a certain bad smell that was supposed to have some connection with a rash upon the children's faces" (*V*, 259). The incapacity to shift from consecutive correlations to positive proof—frequently resulting from constrained access to scientific expertise on the part of vulnerable populations—persists in many twentieth-century accounts of environmental injustice.

The tenants' complaint about "bad smell" possibly correlated with "a rash upon the children's faces" points to the extensive diffusion of airborne pollutants. While Norris focuses on Vandover's predicament, he frequently hints at the ubiquity of environmental risks among the urban poor. Vandover's entanglement with filth and chemical soap smells in the novel's concluding scene is doubled not only by the correlation of "bad smell" with the children's rash but also by the fact that he is cleaning the cottage of a burnisher's family. The burnisher—who polishes floors or machinery at the factory across the street—is also a subject of occupational chemical exposure: "an odour as of a harness shop hung about him" (*V*, 263). Norris's description of one of Vandover's boarding house rooms registers the larger scope of toxic exposure: "close by, from over the roofs, the tall slender stack upon the steam laundry puffed incessantly, three puffs at a time, like some kind of halting clock. The room became more and more close, none of them would take the time to open the window, from ceiling to floor the air was fouled by their breathing, by the tobacco smoke and by the four flaring gas-jets" (*V*, 222). What good would opening the window do here, with the laundry steam stack puffing like clockwork just outside? In a later scene, the steady puffs of this smokestack—"each sounding like a note of discreet laughter interrupted by a cough" (*V*, 239)—ominously blend into the city's general atmosphere:

> The clouds had begun to break, the rain was gradually ceasing, leaving in the air a damp, fresh smell, the smell of wet asphalt and the odour of dripping woodwork. It was warm; the atmosphere was dank, heavy, tepid. . . . Not far off the slender, graceful smokestack puffed steadily, throwing off continually the little flock of white jets that rose into the air very brave and gay, but in the end dwindled irresolutely, discouraged, disheartened, fading sadly away, vanishing under the night, like illusions disappearing at the first touch of the outside world. As Vandover leaned from his window, looking out into the night with eyes that saw nothing, the college slogan rose again from the great crowd of students who still continued to hold the streets.
>
> "Rah!, rah, rah! Rah, rah, rah!" (*V*, 237)

Here, the gradual, meticulously described "vanishing" of white jets of smoke is tinged with psychologically debilitating affects: irresolute, discouraged, disheartening, sad. If smoke becomes invisible, it remains materially dispersed throughout the city air, possibly contributing not only to "the queer numbness that came upon [Vandover's] mind [and] enwrapped his brain like a fog" (V, 238) but also to the animalistic behavior of the crowd of drunken students puffing mechanical, inarticulate monosyllables after a football victory: "Rah!, rah, rah!" Hinting at indefinite connections between the vanishing smokestack puffs and variegated symptoms of intoxication, Norris communicates both the uncertainty inherent to representations of environmental risk and the generalized sense of anxiety that Beck argues is characteristic of risk society.[51]

Vandover's olfactory anxieties support discourses of racial degeneration even as they develop the groundwork for critically considering the environmental determinants of race. On the one hand, mapping urban smells serves to enhance Norris's allegory of industrial modernity's emasculating effects on white masculinity. The passive, atavistic, and emasculating implications of smell in the novel support critical accounts of the anxious opposition between white male degeneration and imperial remasculinization that structured many naturalist narratives of adventure and decline: as Molly Ball argues, naturalist texts such as *Vandover* mobilized the figure of the male neurasthenic to claim vulnerability as a property of privileged white men.[52] On the other hand, environmental determinism was fundamentally at odds with race thinking: as Julie Sze notes, "[Miasma theory] suggested that economic class and living conditions, rather than character or morality, were the sources of disease."[53] As I show in the next section, Norris's aesthetic engagements with smell as a medium for perceiving threats to environmental health have been taken up by twentieth-century writers explicitly concerned with racialized health disparities. If naturalist narratives frequently naturalized racial and class inequality, their formal experiments with air also developed a mode of environmental representation oriented not toward the crypto-racist wilderness ideal but toward modernity's proliferating "nature-cultures."[54]

Atmo-terrorism in Environmental Justice Literature

As Lawrence Buell has noted, ecocriticism's origins in Romantic "nature writing" led the field to neglect how naturalism's "discourses of determinism" might illuminate the social consequences of "impure" environments, such as the city.[55] As an influential yet frequently over-looked point of reference for American environmental thinking, literary naturalism interrogates ecological entanglements suppressed by the idealization of pure "Nature." This section explores the contributions that naturalism has made to environmental narrative by tracing a tradition of environmental novels devoted to mapping the uneven distribution of risks—a tradition that preceded and may have helped orient the emergence of the environmental justice movement in the 1980s. Environmental fiction in a neo-naturalist mode extends naturalism's stagings of "bad air" as a medium contributing to environmental health disparities, treating airborne toxins and the smell of risk as central political themes and formal concerns. At the same time, these authors delink environmental injustice from naturalism's investments in antimodern discourses of wilderness, imperialism, and "race suicide," attending instead to poor and racialized populations that bear the greatest burdens of environmental risk. Petry and Viramontes's olfactory engagements with atmospheric disparities bring Progressive Era naturalists' concern with modernity's differentiated smellscapes to bear on specific scenes of residential, infrastructural, and occupational slow violence: poorly maintained Harlem apartments, Central California's poisoned agricultural fields, and East Los Angeles neighborhoods cut up for freeway construction.

The toxic entanglements explored by these novelists illustrate how—particularly in the United States—race inflects the twentieth century's processes of atmospheric "splintering."[56] Sloterdijk coins the concept of "atmoterrorism" to describe the design and production of unbreathable atmospheres—a practice that he traces back to the origins of gas warfare.[57] Opposed to these unbreathable atmospheres are enclosed spaces that have been disconnected from the immediate atmosphere: according to Sloterdijk, this "principle of air conditioning" is based on the use of gas masks on the battlefield to produce a personal envelope of filtered, breathable air.[58] Sloterdijk traces how poison gas technology originated by military scientists and pesticide developers moved to the architecture of gas chambers, a supposedly "humane" and "peaceful" apparatus of execution that depends upon the efficient atmospheric separation of the chamber from the surrounding air.[59] The disproportionate exposure of Black and brown Americans to pesticides, smog, poorly ventilated spaces, gas leaks, and military experiments with mustard gas illustrates how differential deodorization distributes toxicity along racial lines.[60] These racial disparities in gas exposure are also evident in the history of the gas chamber in the United States: first used in Nevada's 1924 execution of the convicted murderer Gee Jon,[61] the gas chamber's supposedly "humane" executions (which witnesses described in gruesome terms as a slow process of death by choking) continued to be disproportionately imposed on racialized subjects. As historian Scott Christianson reports, "By the end of 1941 the gas chamber had claimed eighty-two lives, at least sixty-eight of them African American—many of them for crimes other than murder."[62] Whereas *Vandover* frames air pollution primarily by depicting mixed urban crowds in close quarters, Petry and Viramontes write in contexts in which legal, economic, and social forces superimposed uneven atmospheres onto historically sedimented racial disparities—contexts wherein "atmo-terrorism" has been both racialized in its imposition and racializing in its results (which frequently exacerbate existing conditions of immiseration, debilitation, and premature death).

The two authors I consider borrow a range of formal techniques from turn-of-the-century naturalists. In their narratives of disempowered, working-class characters confronted with everyday environmental constraints, Petry and Viramontes deploy distanced third-person narration, extensive passages of environmental description, characters who are relatively unaware of the forces that act upon them, and plot trajectories that emphasize immobilization and decline. Both these authors indirectly acknowledge naturalist precursors by echoing and repurposing formal and thematic elements of *Maggie* (1893), *Native Son* (1940), and *The Grapes of Wrath* (1939).[63] Instead of detailing all the formal and intertextual elements that link these works to earlier naturalists, I focus on how they build on naturalism's staging of air as a medium of life and health. In key passages devoted to the animacy of air, these authors detail how atmospheres transfer material supports of health between places and populations: in their novels, building maintenance, real estate investments, and corporate agriculture transfer resources and health to wealthier locations while abandoning inhabitants of Harlem and Central California to heightened health risks. In addition to demonstrating the influence of naturalism on environmental justice literature, Petry and Viramontes experiment with a range of formal techniques for representing airborne risks situated at the threshold of perceptibility. Their novels deploy smell to aid in characterization, to represent the insidious effects of everyday low-level exposures, and to convey the anxiety induced by the nearly imperceptible nature of some airborne toxins.

In *The Street* (1946), Ann Petry deploys smell to situate and develop characters in relation to environmental factors—a technique I term olfactory characterization. Narrated from multiple characters' perspectives, the novel focuses on Lutie Johnson's experience as a young Black woman struggling to raise her child amid Harlem's spatialized constraints on social reproduction.[64] *The Street* begins with a prolonged account of the cold November wind, which "found all the dirt and dust and grime on the sidewalk and lifted it up so the dirt got into their noses, making it difficult to breathe; the dust got into their eyes and blinded them; and the grit stung their skins."[65] Animating the dust, grime, and litter on the street, the wind obstructs the life chances of Harlem's humans. If, as Petry writes, streets "were the North's lynch mobs," then air serves as one of the street's most oppressive features, helping to "keep Negroes in their place" (S, 323). Elsewhere described as an "invisible hand" distributing grime and rubbish along the sidewalks, the Harlem wind emerges as an invisible antagonist—an atmospheric manifestation of the pervasive social and material antiblack climate that Sharpe theorizes as "the weather." In addition to confronting a series of racist employers and predatory men, Lutie Johnson struggles to survive the city's burdened atmosphere itself.

Throughout the novel, Petry invokes choking and suffocation as both physiological reactions and metaphors describing affective responses to life's constraints. With no window in the bedroom—"just an air shaft and a narrow one at that"—Lutie carefully considers how to ensure that her son Bub will have access to "air" in their new apartment (S, 14). As she scrutinizes the apartment, the importance of fresh air becomes more apparent: "She was conscious that all the little rooms smelt exactly alike.

It was a mixture that contained the faint persistent odor of gas, of old walls, dusty plaster, and over it all the heavy, sour smell of garbage—a smell that seeped through the dumb-waiter shaft" (S, 16). Lutie's determination to improve her son's situation prevents her from passively suffocating in this atmosphere. By contrast, Petry's descriptions of the mingled smells that pervade the building's apartments, hallways, and basement hint at an environmental explanation for the awkwardness and violence of the building's superintendent, who ogles women, sneaks into Lutie's bedroom, and eventually assaults her. When Petry writes that Jones's "voice had a choked, unnatural sound as though something had gone wrong with his breathing," it's unclear whether his choked voice results from his sexual arousal and mental agitation or from his prolonged exposure to the building's bad air (it could be asthma triggered by excitement, for example). Indeed, Jones's occupational exposure to chemicals is more intimate than Lutie's: when he spends an afternoon painting the building and firing the furnace, for example, he briefly steps out for "a breath of air . . . because the smell of the paint was in his nose, looked like it had even got in his skin" (S, 373). Mrs. Hedges, who rescues Lutie from Jones's assault, provides an environmental, trans-corporeal explanation for his behavior: she tells him, "You done lived in basements so long you ain't human no more. You got mould growin' on you" (S, 237). Mrs. Hedges, who is herself the victim of occupational debilitation (her face was disfigured in a furnace fire when she worked as a janitor), even considers environmental explanations for the physical appearance and comportment of minor characters: when one young man stops by the brothel she runs, she "wonder[ed] if a creature like this was . . . the result of breathing soot-filled air instead of air filled with the smell of warm earth and green growing plants" (S, 249).[66]

Petry's most extensive deployment of olfaction to convey characterization appears in chapter 14, which uncharacteristically assumes the point of view of Bub's schoolteacher, a white woman who hates teaching Black children in Harlem. Miss Rinner's reflections about her job are described through eight paragraphs devoted to describing a suffocating blend of odors: "the dusty smell of chalk, the heavy, suffocating smell of the pine oil used to lay the grime and disinfect the worn old floors, and the smell of the children themselves" (S, 327). While Petry's narrator notes that this peculiar mixture of smells is characteristic of all poorly maintained, forty-year-old buildings—not just classrooms located in Harlem—Miss Rinner feels disgusted by the smell of "rancid grease" on the children's clothing, which she eventually comes to think of as "'the colored people's smell,' and then finally as the smell of Harlem itself" (S, 328). By this point in the novel, Petry has already provided numerous economic and architectural explanations for the poor ventilation and musty smells of Harlem's low-income apartment buildings; Miss Rinner's reactions to these smells thus represent the process of stigmatization whereby the effects of the racially uneven distribution of air are misperceived as a racial characteristic: not the smell of poorly maintained, segregated schools and housing units, but "the colored people's smell"—"the smell of Harlem itself." As Smith has shown, this pattern of olfactory racialization became especially pronounced during the Jim Crow era, when white Americans relied on the "olfactory fiction" of racially distinct smells to shore up and police the color line.[67] Miss Rinner's horrified fantasy about a racialized smell that follows her into her own home is an allegory for racial thinking that misperceives effects as causes: because poor Black residents of Harlem inhabit unhealthy apartments and poorly maintained streets, white middle-class outsiders like Miss Rinner tend to perceive them as "ecological others"[68]— irresponsible environmental stewards who, according to Miss Rinner, are "probably diseased" and have "no moral code" (S, 332). Petry's deployment of olfactory characterization thus highlights the different ways in which characters interpret and respond to Harlem's suffocating smellscapes: Miss Rinner's stigmatizing essentialization of smells, Jones's resignation to their trans-corporeal influence, and Lutie's determined refusal to "get used to it" (S, 194).

Like Petry, Helena María Viramontes employs sensory detail and multiperspective narrative to underscore both the commonalities and differences among her character ensembles—as well as those between her characters and readers. In a 2010 interview, she says that the five senses are "the only things that are 'universal,' if you can call anything 'universal,' a word I hate. The thing of it is we all share senses."[69] For Viramontes, smell is (along with vision and hearing) among the three "easiest" senses for writers to use, particularly compelling because they extend across distances.[70] In her novels, smell mediates a critical approach to the concept of universality: it is a nearly universal sense with visceral appeal to readers, but it attests to the manifold ways in which bodies and sensoria are shaped by differentiated atmospheres. This blend of familiarity and viscerality makes olfaction particularly effective for achieving Viramontes's political and aesthetic aim of "exposing . . . injustices—not just for discussion, but to make people who have never even thought or experienced such things actually experience them."[71]

Whereas *The Street* underscores how Harlem's air physically obstructs (as wind) or affectively agitates (as gas, mold, and smell) characters like Lutie, Jones, and Miss Rinner, Viramontes's *Under the Feet of Jesus* (1995) stages the conditions of chronic pesticide exposure among Central California's migrant Chicanx farmworkers. Like *The Street*, the early pages of Viramontes's novel are filled with references to the agency of wind: it whistles, lifts a hat, clears the air, fans a dress, and "mentholate[s]" the air with the scent of eucalyptus.[72] But if wind appears to function as a metaphor for the "Holy Spirit" (*UF*, 31), it is also a carrier of chemical toxins. As Linda Nash has shown, the "inescapable ecologies" of industrial agriculture have prompted migrant farmworkers in Central California to develop a range of epistemological and political responses to pesticide exposure—including a reliance on smell as a readily available tool for detecting risks that are denied by both growers and health experts' overreliance on germ theory.[73] In one of the novel's climactic scenes, a teenage farmworker named Alejo is directly exposed to pesticides dropped by an unscheduled crop duster. Although this scene may seem improbable, it references numerous preventable "pesticide drift" incidents in which the "wayward movement of pesticides, often far from where they were applied," has directly exposed farmworker communities to potentially lethal chemical clouds.[74] As Jill Harrison writes in her study of environmental justice activism concerning this issue, "Pesticide drift incidents simply cannot be understood apart from the relations of oppression that characterize immigrant farmworking communities."[75] Alejo's direct exposure—along with its nearly instantaneous effects—is a condensed representation of the farmworker population's everyday exposures to agricultural pesticides. According to Curtis Marez, "In the 1990s . . . it was estimated that a thousand farm workers died every year from pesticide poisoning while over three hundred thousand got sick."[76] In order to counteract the "temporal camouflage" that renders low-level exposures imperceptible by dispersing their health effects across long time spans,[77] Viramontes incorporates a spectacular scene of direct exposure into her otherwise naturalistic novel.

Viramontes's olfactory description of Alejo's pesticide inhalation underscores the difficulty of perceiving environmental risks by noting the deceptive disjunction between smell and substance: "The lingering smell was a scent of ocean salt and beached kelp until he inhaled again and could detect under the innocence the heavy chemical *choke* of poison. Air clogged in his lungs and he thought he was just holding his breath, until he tried exhaling but couldn't, which meant he couldn't breathe. He panicked when he realized he was *choking*" (*UF*, 77, emphasis added). Initially, the smell of pesticide is nearly undetectable, camouflaged by the scent of the sea. When Alejo notices the presence of poison, what he detects is not an odor but a "heavy chemical choke"—not the smell of chemicals but his physiological *response* to the pesticide. At about the same time, a character named Perfecto, located at some distance from the spray, also inhales a trace of these chemicals: "The winds shifted and he breathed in a faint trace of saltwater and coughed" (*UF*, 78). Perfecto seems barely aware of the faint saltwater scent in the air, and the narrator does not directly attribute his cough to the scent. Juxtaposed with Alejo's dramatic poisoning, this indirect correlation between smell and physiological response dramatizes the insidious and everyday nature of low-level exposures.

The initially misleading nature of the pesticide's "scent of ocean salt and beached kelp" draws on Viramontes's own belated epiphany about the deadly significance of this scent. Although she worked in the fields with her family when she was young, it was not until much later—on a drive through California's Central Valley with her husband (chemical ecologist Eloy Rodriguez)—that Viramontes connected the smell of the sea with its chemical hazards: "My husband and I were driving to Vancouver when we passed through Fresno and I smelled that agricultural smell and said, 'Oh man I miss that smell, it smells like ocean.' And he turned to me and said, 'Helena, that's the pesticides.' That's what killed me! The scent of pesticides permeated our lives! It was a constant. Then I realized, 'Wow man, how much we have all been dosed by that?' But as workers we didn't think about it. It was pretty devastating to me to realize our lack of knowledge about the pesticides that had been poisoning us."[78] Only decades later, in the company of an expert in environmental toxicology, is Viramontes able to perceive this nostalgic scent as a poison that has "permeated" the lives of farmworkers. In the Central Valley, this smell may signify the ocean, but it is materially composed of chemicals with debilitating and potentially fatal effects: "That's what killed me!"

Characters in *Under the Feet of Jesus* suffer a range of ailments including a cleft lip, irritated eyes, muscle soreness, fatigue, chronic coughing, and other respiratory conditions. Although none of these conditions is directly attributed to pesticide exposure, the fact that they are endemic among the novel's migrant workers suggests the presence of a causal connection. Aside from industrial pesticides, Viramontes also details a range of everyday toxins that pervade the air her characters breathe. In an early scene, for example, Estrella opens a kitchen cabinet to discover there is no food—"Nothing . . . except the thick smell of raid and dead roaches and sprinkled salt on withered sunflower contact paper and the [empty] box of Quaker Oats oatmeal" (*UF*, 18). Given that both domestic pesticides like Raid and particulates from decomposing cockroaches have been linked to respiratory health conditions, this early scene both foreshadows and provides a wider, everyday context for the concentrated dose of pesticide that Alejo receives in the fields. Likewise, for Perfecto, the saltwater smell of pesticides induces involuntary memories of the smell of his stillborn child from decades earlier and a lover who died of cancer. The juxtaposition of cancer and stillbirth with the chemical smell of pesticide indicates an oblique yet ominous connection between chemical exposure and premature deaths, as does the pairing of human and insect responses to poisoned air: "Perfecto coughed into his fist, and his nose began to run and he blew his nose and sneezed again. Flies tumbled like leaves from the bushy trees, dropping onto his shoulders and then onto the ground" (*UF*, 80). The catastrophic scene in which Alejo is sprayed by a crop duster thus condenses years of low-level exposures spread across an entire population into a single instant, presenting a scene of direct poisoning with clear causal relationships that can be difficult to prove in more mundane cases of chronic illness. Yet even in Alejo's case, the aftermath is riddled with uncertainty: his debilitated condition—which other laborers refer to as "*daño* of the fields" (*UF*, 93)—has no definite medical diagnosis, and the novel tells us nothing more about him after Alejo's friends leave him at a hospital. The ambiguity of Viramontes's smells and the uncertainty of their effects call attention not only to the uneven distribution of risk factors but also (echoing Viramontes's anecdote about driving through the fields with her chemical ecologist husband) to the uneven distribution of scientific expertise and research on toxins that disproportionately affect racialized populations. In a world so riddled with unknowable toxins,[79] even the novel's scattered moments of lyrical resilience—as when Estrella finds music in an oatmeal box "full of empty" or when she enjoys the sensation of a breeze in her hair while standing on the roof of a barn—are overshadowed by airborne risk (*UF*, 20). For as the novel's flitting olfactory references make clear, neither the fluttering breeze nor the air inside the oatmeal box is truly "empty."

In *Their Dogs Came with Them* (2007), Viramontes turns to another instance of debilitating atmospheric exposure: the smells of dust, asphalt, tar, and automobile exhaust associated with freeway construction in East Los Angeles.[80] Despite decades of complaints, lawsuits, and protests by local residents, the construction of unsustainable transportation infrastructure to service predominantly white suburban commuters and consumers made East LA the unwitting "home to more freeways than any place in the country" in the decades following the 1956 Interstate and Defense Highways Act.[81] *Their Dogs* traces the everyday lives and interactions of young Chicanx characters during the peak decades of freeway construction, when entire blocks of homes were demolished to make room for "seven freeways and one massive interchange."[82] The plot tracks an ensemble of characters coping with conditions of vulnerability such as orphanhood, undocumented status, abandonment, sexual assault, depression, gender nonconformity, and gang violence; the characters' lives diverge and intersect "like freeway interchanges,"[83] finally coming together in a devastating ending. However, the novel's fleeting yet nuanced descriptions of everyday slow violence are no less compelling than the spectacular murders with which it concludes.

Building on the work of transportation justice activists, Viramontes frames transportation infrastructure as a technology for differentiating sensory landscapes: if freeway construction enabled "white flight" to the fresh air, quiet, and relatively open vistas of the suburbs, it also exposed densely populated, disproportionately Black and brown urban communities to noxious fumes, clouds of dust and smog, unsightly walls and overpasses, and constant noise.[84] *Their Dogs* frames East LA's polluted air as a repository for the freeway's externalities. In a materialist rejoinder to Marx and Engels's claim that "all that is solid melts into air" under capitalism, one character ruminates, "Who was it that told her all she had to do was look up at the heavens to see the shapes of things missing? . . . Everything went up into thin air but didn't go away" (*TD*, 14).[85] The heavens might hold what's lost or missing, but, in East LA, they are disproportionately burdened with the atmospheric emissions of demolition, construction, and automobiles.

Their Dogs frequently deploys olfactory language to dramatize the debilitating trans-corporeal effects of transportation racism. The novel begins with an image—a child's feet "blackened from the soot of the new pavement"—that attests to the unfixed nature of asphalt's materiality: the way its particles circulate in the air and provisionally settle on surfaces as soot.[86] As a child named Turtle stands staring at the freeways under construction, Viramontes's juxtaposition of "exhaust" with "tired" eyes associates air pollution with a generalized feeling of exhaustion: "The thick, choking stench of blackened diesel smoke rose from the dump trucks, and bulldozers blew carbon exhaust into a haze. Her eyes were so tired, they squeaked as she rubbed them" (*TD*, 27). Atmospheric fumes are so pervasive that their effects cannot be disentangled from other forces: "The exhaust and confining jacket pressed against Turtle's lungs" (*TD*, 19). Over a decade later, after the completion of the busiest freeway interchange in the world in East LA, Grandmother Zumaya perceives the increased smog: "Only twenty of ten on Monday morning and already the sky was a flat canvas of smog haze pulled taut to its combustible edges as far as the eye could see. The air was too thick to filter through her lungs" (*TD*, 129). Turtle has now developed respiratory symptoms that interweave her breath with the surrounding fumes and particulates: "By Monday, the earthmovers would be running again, biting trenches wider than rivers; the groan, thump and burr noise of the constant motors would weave into the sound of her own breath whistling the blackened fumes of dust and crumble in her nasal cavities" (*TD*, 169). Ben—a neurodiverse aspiring writer who suffers from environmentally induced migraines—is forced to cross the street in order to avoid "noise and [the smell of] firecracking sulfur" (*TD*, 111). Ermila and her group of teenage friends hang out at Concha's Beauty Salon, an "airless basement where the ossified breath of tobacco smoke and Black Flag roach spray intermingled with the chemical stench of hair dye" (*TD*,

184). Ermila's friend Lollie finds it painful to breathe on an overcrowded bus: "A passenger's perfume or hairspray, a blend of heavy funeral carnations, made Lollie's stomach wheezy" (*TD*, 187). When Tranquilina—a young woman who has established a ministry for the poor in an abandoned building—encounters a "street woman" (the phrase suggests that her body has merged with the materiality of the streets), she notices an unnerving smell: "The woman's odor blended many smells into something else altogether . . . something indistinguishable and solid but distinctively hers and sharp enough to cut into Tranquilina's breathing" (*TD*, 211). Throughout the novel, Viramontes renders air as a simultaneously material and affective atmosphere—a "perpetual drowsy fog of gaseous fumes" (*TD*, 313) whose effects are differently corporealized by individual characters. Shot through with references to coughing, wheezing, watery eyes, migraines, lethargy, nausea, and confusion in close proximity to everyday smells, *Their Dogs* conveys what disability studies scholar Jina Kim calls a "disabled somatics of place"—"an aesthetic mode in which disability operates as environmental ambience rather than personal attribute."[87] By juxtaposing smell with physiological symptoms and fleeting moments of "brain fog," Viramontes suggests that some of the characters' chronic conditions—Parkinson's disease, mental illness, anxiety, depression, fatigue—could be either produced or amplified by their prolonged exposure to East LA's debilitating atmosphere. Even as the atmosphere of the freeways makes residents ill, public health authorities stigmatize the entire community as contaminated and contagious: in the novel's only marked departure from historical events, city authorities have established a Quarantine Authority to protect the rest of Los Angeles from a supposed rabies epidemic in East LA.

In one of his scattered yet incisive commentaries on atmospheric colonization, Frantz Fanon writes, "There is not occupation of territory, on the one hand, and independence of persons on the other. It is the country as a whole, its history, its daily pulsation that are contested, disfigured. . . . Under these conditions, the individual's breathing is an observed, an occupied breathing. It is a combat breathing."[88] Under quarantine and stifled by a burdened atmosphere—which in many instances is compounded by other forms of colonial, hetero-patriarchal, and ableist oppression—Viramontes's characters walk a fine line between debility and asphyxiation. As an instance of what Jean-Thomas

Tremblay calls "respiratory drama"—a genre in which "breathing gives the fictional world its shape and the plot its thrust"[89]—the novel is filled with fleeting descriptions of breathing impaired by both the slow violence of air pollution and more direct assaults. When her cousin Nacho forcibly kisses her shortly after she "inhaled the s[c]ent of car upholstery so old, its tales rang full in her nostrils," Ermila's feeling of suffocation responds to both the upholstery smell and Nacho's toxic masculinity: "I can't breathe! She pulled back. It was true. His kiss suffocated her. I can't breathe, open the door" (*TD*, 247).

Their Dogs dramatizes the peculiar environmental vigilance and ambient anxiety that characterize Fanon's "combat breathing" through the character of Turtle, whose gang affiliation, nonbinary gender identity, homelessness, and environmental sensitivity leave her particularly exposed as she wanders the streets. Viramontes's third-person narration, focalized through each character's perspective, frequently draws attention to Turtle's breathing: "She breathed out and then waited"; "she inhaled"; "Turtle heard the winds of her own breathing rushing through the passages inside her head" (*TD*, 22, 24, 233). Turtle is able to breathe easy and attend to her feelings only in rare moments of (apparent) security, as when she hops into a *cholo*'s luxuriously upholstered scented car: "Turtle found herself flexing her nostrils to inhale an almost forgotten sanctuary, and she drew it all in until her chest inflated with maximum memory and it was then that she released a sigh, an exhale so long it resembled sadness" (*TD*, 267–68). Turtle's breathing also relaxes—ironically—when she is intoxicated after smoking a joint laced with PCP: "She howled and then sniffed the air, breathing in all this refreshing bedazzled good fortune" (*TD*, 299). In the novel's concluding scene, however, Turtle's intoxication—combined with her eagerness to prove herself to the young men in her gang—leads her to murder Nacho with a screwdriver in an act of retribution. "Encircled by the McBride Boys, Turtle grew larger and invincible and she had to remind her lungs to exhale so that the suffocation she was now experiencing with the screwdriver in her hand could not render her motionless" (*TD*, 322). This juxtaposition of "suffocation" with what the media would frame as a "gang murder" invites readers to consider the chemical and psychological connections between atmospheric slow violence and the spectacular stabbing and police shootings with which the novel concludes.

However, Viramontes's nuanced depictions of environmental violence do not reduce her characters to mere victims. At times, the atmosphere is transfigured by alternative modes of experiencing air and olfaction: confronting armed police and helicopters in the final scene, Tranquilina reenacts her father's spiritual flight as a *volador*, rising into the toxic skies; when Turtle shelters in a crypt at night, dried flowers she had stuffed into her jacket as insulation fall to the floor: "Old carnations and roses and gardenias and magnolias and baby's breath . . . still carried a trace of transient perfumes. All the bunches together . . . created enough padding for a bed" (*TD*, 236). As Dean Franco notes, this faintly perfumed scene—which recalls the miraculous *tilma* imprinted with the image of the Virgin of Guadalupe—encodes an ontological rupture and a sense of "radical alterity" into an ordinary scene.[90] As Paula Moya and Jina Kim have shown, *Their Dogs* also underscores the vital, necessary role of interdependence as a resource for surviving—even thriving—in the face of slow violence. Focusing on the scenes in which Ermila hangs out with her girlfriends, Moya discerns "a form of mutual acceptance and collectivity that is both discerning and loving"; for Kim, the disabling geography of East LA opens onto "a politics of interdependence" modeled by informal safety nets and "marginal figures and sites that simply make life more possible."[91] Because debility is a product of the atmosphere, mutual assistance frequently manifests through a perception of shared exposure apprehended through respiratory impairment. For example, Ray—a Japanese American who commutes to his East LA grocery store from Monterey Park—offers Turtle a job in spite of her sooty hands and "lingering stink," connecting Turtle's toxic exposures to his own experience as an internee at Manzanar who had "breathed in the dust storms like smoke" (*TD*, 262, 260). Despite her consuming desire to get home, Ermila gives up her place in the quarantine line to a mother with a child "struggl[ing] to breathe" (*TD*, 289). And at the end of a novel whose every scene conveys the fragility and preciousness of breath, Tranquilina "emptied her lungs to repeat, Don't shoot! Don't shoot!" as unseen police fire on Turtle (*TD*, 324). Such moments present the improvisation of mutual support as a kind of *conspiracy* originating from the sensory awareness of shared breath. If, as Sloterdijk argues, modernity originates in the discovery and technological exploitation of the "defenselessness of breathing,"[92] *Their Dogs* attends to the racially uneven impositions on breathing that drive large-scale patterns of air conditioning, as well as the modes of resilience and resistance that emerge when shared atmospheric predicaments are rendered perceptible.

* * *

Anticipating contemporary modes of olfactory inquiry such as neighborhood "smell-walks," crowdsourced smell maps, and olfactory art,[93] naturalist smellscapes deploy smell to frame atmospheric disparities as a matter of affective immersion and visceral response. While Petry and Viramontes build on the naturalist aesthetics of smell that figures so prominently in *Vandover and the Brute*, their investment in documenting and resisting environmental racism distinguishes them from Norris and his contemporaries. Whereas *Vandover* frames unhealthy smells as a pivotal element in the decline of white manhood (at times through the atmo-orientalist representations of Asiatic smells that I discuss in chapter 4), Petry and Viramontes depict prolonged, everyday encounters with modernity's racialized atmospheres. In doing so, they detail specific ways in which environmentally induced debility is corporealized: whereas Vandover's lycanthropy allegorizes naturalism's post-Darwinian obsession with the human brute,[94] Petry and Viramontes document how slow violence manifests in respiratory ailments as well as a range of physiological and psychological conditions linked to chemical exposure. They also attend to emergent forms of resistance and resilience within the domains of uncertainty imposed by environmental risks: *The Street* depicts Min's efforts to assert some control over her everyday atmospheres by using hoodoo powders and candles—along with ritual dusting—to counteract her domestic partner's violent rages; Viramontes's novels detail how migrant agricultural laborers and Chicanx communities targeted by urban redevelopment employ folk remedies (the most prominent being pungent garlic), collective memories, expansive forms of kinship, and networks of mutual aid to sustain one another in the face of environmental violence.[95] These environmental justice novels leverage naturalism's aesthetic concern with smellscapes to depict lived experience in unevenly distributed conditions of environmental debilitation, illuminating critical intersections between environment, race, and disabling geographies across the twentieth century.

In addition to tracing the influence of early naturalists on twentieth-century fiction concerned with environmental injustice, reading these diffuse, uncertain treatments of toxic atmospheres calls attention to the role of air—and airborne risks—across a range of twentieth-century neo-naturalist texts. The environmental threat posed by bad air looms over the sump holes, toxic dumps, and polluted streets of hard-boiled crime fiction (see chapter 1); it appears in the cloud of steam and reek of cooking grease that envelops the protagonist of Shoson Nagahara's "naturalist noir masterpiece" *Lament in the Night* (1925);[96] it takes the form of "the smell of hot dust"[97] in the opening chapters of Steinbeck's protest novel *The Grapes of Wrath* (1939); it haunts the narrator of Don DeLillo's *White Noise* (1985)— which Frank Lentricchia and Paul Civello have characterized as a postmodern "naturalist" novel—with the smell of death in the wake of a toxic airborne event;[98] and it perfumes Cormac McCarthy's dystopian speculative novel *The Road* (2006), with the toxic "smell of earth and wet ash in the rain."[99] Across a range of novelistic genres that critics have traced back to turn-of-the-century naturalism, noxious air suffuses narratives of environmental constraint with problems of risk and unknowability. It thus intensifies elements of uncertainty and open-endedness already at play in texts like *Vandover*, while also drawing attention to the daily transformations of body, mind, and mood experienced most acutely by vulnerable communities inhabiting modernity's uneven geographies of risk.

* * *

The patterns of differential deodorization I have traced across the genres of detective fiction, MCS memoirs, naturalism, and environmental justice narratives take on an architectural form in the "white cube" design of modern museums and galleries. Nowhere have odors been suppressed with more care than in conventional gallery spaces. The climate-controlled atmosphere of the white cube gallery has played a pivotal role in sustaining and (by making air a matter of no concern) dissimulating processes of differential deodorization. Like the literary forms I have analyzed—which mobilize olfaction to explore the uneven distribution of odors—the olfactory artworks discussed in the following chapter transgress the inodorate protocols of contemporary art, making space for embodied encounters with the trans-corporeal, embodied consequences of everyday odors.

3

Olfactory Art and Museum Ecologies

One of the most widely publicized works of airborne, trans-corporeal art was an unintentional one. In 2010, Ai Weiwei's *Sunflower Seeds*—a vast expanse of almost a hundred million hand-painted ceramic sunflower seeds ironically commissioned by the hygienic product corporation Unilever—was deemed too toxic for visitors to touch. The installation was intended to present ceramic simulacra of "Nature": cool, hard, inert, and relatively stable objects that could be touched with no risk of chemical reactivity. Although it was designed to be interactive, curators at the Tate Modern soon noticed that *Sunflower Seeds* was *too* interactive, threatening to permeate the gallery's air and visitors' bodies with airborne ceramic dust. Soon after the piece was installed, the museum prohibited visitors from interacting physically with the seeds in order to prevent the proliferation of dust particles that could endanger respiratory health.

The unforeseen risk of ceramic dust inhalation gives a new spin to the Tate Modern's interpretative text for *Sunflower Seeds*: "what you see is not what you see, and what you see is not what it means."[1] While this interpretation refers to the fact that what look like millions of sunflower seeds are actually individually hand-painted ceramic artworks, it also echoes sociologist Ulrich Beck's discussion of the disqualification of vision as an adequate means of interpreting our increasingly toxic world. In contemporary risk society, Beck writes, "Everything must be viewed with a double gaze, and can only be correctly understood and judged through this doubling. The world of the visible must be investigated, relativized, and evaluated with respect to a second reality, only existent in thought and yet concealed in the world. The standards of evaluation lie only in the second, not in the visible world."[2] The museum's response to the possibility that Ai's artworks could materially penetrate and harm visitors' bodies was to curtail interaction—to restore the exclusively visual relation between visitors and artworks that has played a profound role in the design, curation, and conservation practices of modern museums and galleries. If visual apprehension tends to frame bodies as separate from the art objects they view, the ceramic dust scare precipitated by *Sunflower Seeds* exemplifies Alaimo's argument about the potentially unruly, trans-corporeal nature of all matter. By foregrounding our bodily exchanges with airborne particulates, *Sunflower Seeds* unwittingly transformed the gallery from a spectatorial space filled with (supposedly) inert artworks into "a mobile space that acknowledges the often unpredictable and unwanted actions of human bodies, nonhuman creatures, ecological systems, chemical agents, and other actors."[3]

Whereas the airborne, trans-corporeal qualities of Ai's installation were unintended, this chapter focuses on contemporary olfactory artworks that intentionally draw attention to one of the most invisible, unnoticed, yet carefully controlled materials in the museum environment: air. In doing so, these works push visitors not only to experience the conceptual, erotic, affective, and ideological implications of smell but also to reconceptualize museums as spaces of environmental enmeshment. As an inherently trans-corporeal form, olfactory art defies the spectatorial logic that organizes both art galleries and commonsense perceptions of "Nature" as a space that is distinct from the human.[4] Insofar as it activates museum air as an aesthetic medium and highlights the manifold ways in which our bodies literally incorporate that air, olfactory art is especially effective in dramatizing airborne environmental risks. Unlike Ai Weiwei's unintentionally risky installation, however, artists working with scent employ "safe" and controlled concentrations of chemicals to simulate the smells and corporeal responses associated with environmental toxins.[5]

This chapter contextualizes the environmental significance of contemporary olfactory art by underscoring how it intervenes in the visual and atmospheric dynamics of museum galleries. To articulate what is at stake in olfactory art, I begin by discussing how the careful regulation of air serves to establish modern museums as spaces of conservation and visual consumption. I argue that there is a conceptual relay between the conservation of artworks and conservationist approaches to "Nature" that frame the environment as a space that should be preserved from the transformations wrought by human interaction. The museum's aesthetic and ideological functions as an architecture of deodorization contextualize the stakes of artworks that solicit the sense of smell. After detailing the synthetic turn in olfactory art enabled by technologies of scent analysis and synthesis, I consider the work of olfactory artists (Boris Raux, Sean Raspet, Anicka Yi, and Peter de Cupere) who challenge conservationist assumptions concerning the safety and stability of bodies and artworks by staging trans-corporeal predicaments of environmental risk. Because the pace of olfactory art production and curation has been slower in the United States than in Europe (likely as a result of the United States' political and cultural commitments to imperatives of deodorization that sustain boundaries of race, class, and gender), my readings of olfactory art center both the US-based artists, Sean Raspet and Anicka Yi, and European artists—like Boris Raux and Peter de Cupere—whose works explore other contexts of differential deodorization.

Conservation Environments

In November 2018, when smoke from the Camp Fire posed a serious threat to respiratory health through much of Northern California, several of San Francisco's museums—including the San Francisco Museum of Modern Art (SFMOMA) and the Asian Art Museum—opened galleries to the public to provide free access to filtered air. This resulted in uncanny juxtapositions of art spectatorship and postapocalyptic skies, aesthetic contemplation and atmospheric peril: at SFMOMA, for example, visitors seeking refuge from smoke could view Wayne Thiebaud's solo show, which featured his colorful, nostalgic paintings of diner foods conserved behind glass vitrines. While this provided an important public service—particularly for visitors without access to clean indoor air at home—it also accentuates the cultural and socioeconomic conditions that have historically excluded most communities of color from art museums. In "The Case for Arts Institutions as Sites of Refuge from Environmental Injustice," Nia McAllister—a visitor experience associate at the Museum of the African Diaspora—notes that there is a fourteen-year difference in life expectancy between residents in the affluent neighborhood of Russian Hill and the majority Black and brown Bayview and Hunters Point neighborhoods: "It is no coincidence that the same low income communities of color missing from museum spaces are disproportionately vulnerable to environmental injustices such as food deserts, the redlining of neighborhoods, proximity to toxic facilities, and the resulting impacts of poorer air quality."[6] If museums are to provide the public with a refuge from debilitating air, McAllister reasons, they should do so not only during a spectacular event like the Camp Fire, but at all times for residents of "sacrifice zones" like Bayview and Hunters Point who are regularly deprived of access to safe air.[7]

As McAllister's commentary demonstrates, the temporary opening of museums as refuges from outdoor smoke underscores the city's entrenched atmospheric disparities. With its carefully regulated air, the museum is an exemplary instance of the hermetically sealed, air-conditioned spaces that Sloterdijk sees as modernity's defining architecture. According to Sloterdijk, "breathable air had lost its innocence" after the discovery of humans' vulnerability to atmospheric manipulation: "Where there was 'lifeworld,' there must now be air conditioning technology."[8] Microclimatic bubbles like the museum, the shopping mall, and the air-conditioned apartment give spatial form to a historically unprecedented imperative of environmental separation:

> If everything could be latently polluted and poisoned, everything potentially deceptive and suspicious, then whole and being-able-to-be-whole can no longer be derived from external circumstances. Integrity can no longer be envisaged as something gained through devotion to something benevolently enveloping, only as the individual contribution of an organism that actively sees to its separation from the environment. This allows the idea to unfold that life is determined not so much by opening and participation in the whole as by self-closing and a selective refusal to participate. For the organism, the largest part of its social surroundings is poison or meaningless background; it therefore settles in a zone of strictly selected objects and signals that can now be articulated as its own circle of relevance—in short, its environment.[9]

Here, Sloterdijk describes a practice of self-curation that is both atmospheric and semiotic: cut off from the outside, the organism inhabits a carefully maintained atmosphere amid "strictly selected objects and signals." Because this bubble's infrastructure devotes so much attention to maintaining air quality, air no longer needs to be an object of concern for those inside. The museum environment is one from which atmospheric impurities have been cleansed and (in the form of ventilation exhaust or soiled air filters) removed into the impure outside. For Sloterdijk, this principle of filtering is both material and metaphoric: modernity's isolated environments exclude not only airborne toxins but senseless or disorganized "signals." These filtering processes shape the exclusionary art world critiqued by McAllister, wherein an institution like SFMOMA excludes not only the dirty air of poor, racialized neighborhoods, but also (through the siting of museums, admission fees, and curatorial practices) the bodies and cultural perspectives of their residents.

But the museum's atmosphere is only coincidentally comfortable for humans. In reality, the careful practices of atmospheric surveillance and purification that make the art museum an ideal atmospheric refuge are oriented not toward human visitors or the outside environment, but toward conserving artworks. In his ethnographic study of conservation practices at New York's Museum of Modern Art, sociologist Fernando Domínguez Rubio describes the museum as "an 'objectification machine' that endeavors to transform and stabilize artworks as meaningful 'objects' that can be exhibited, classified, and circulated."[10] By emphasizing the unstable materiality of artworks and the quandaries that multimedia installations pose to conservationists, Rubio details an "ongoing effort to control the unrelenting process of physical degradation that threatens to undermine the specific relationship between material form and intention that defines artworks as meaningful and valuable objects."[11] Whereas art historians typically approach artworks as fixed objects presenting themselves for interpretation, Rubio's materialist perspective draws attention to both the volatility of artworks and their continual molecular interactions with the museum environment. Such a materialist reassessment of exhibition spaces is crucial in a moment when artists are experimenting with installations, materials, and concepts that challenge the modernist ideal of the art gallery as an inert "white cube."[12]

Because air threatens to contaminate, deteriorate, or otherwise destabilize artworks, it is a crucial element in museums' conservation efforts. Although the air in museums generally goes unnoticed by visitors, its temperature, humidity, and particulates have been carefully monitored and controlled by conservationists for over a century. Explicit standards were established in the mid-twentieth century, when the United Nations Educational Scientific and Cultural Organization (UNESCO), the International Council of Museums (ICOM), and the International Institute for the Conservation of Museum Objects (IIC, founded in 1950) led efforts to research and improve conditions for the preservation of museum collections.[13] In the years following World War II, conservators adopted "a uniform climate control mantra: Keep everything in the museum at approximately 70 degrees Fahrenheit and 55 percent relative humidity."[14] As Rubio writes, "The development of HVAC systems over the last century has enabled museums to engineer highly controlled environments specifically designed to create the particular climatic conditions that [oil] paintings require for their display and stabilization."[15] A contemporary advertisement for the DustBug—a dust monitoring technology used by many museums—elaborates the risks of cumulative damage that airborne dust could pose to art objects: "On a microscopic scale, dust includes tiny, possibly acidic or sharp mineral particles which can be damaging to materials. Consequent cleaning erodes fragile surfaces, such as textiles and gilding. Dust attracts moisture during periods of high humidity, contributing to staining, corrosion and biological growth. Accumulating dust also provides food for insect pests and bacteria, and high humidity can encourage the growth of moulds."[16] Climate control through heating, ventilation, air conditioning, and monitoring devices such as the DustBug helps stabilize artworks as apparently fixed objects of visual perception. Viewers are prohibited from interacting too closely with these objects: for mixing with human breath, touch, or dust particles could undermine the artwork's stability and jeopardize the gallery's conservation mission.

Thus, art conservation colludes with the "bureaucratization of the senses"—to cite Caroline Jones's phrase for a process of segmenting and organizing the human sensorium that "came to some kind of apogee" in the art world of 1950s Manhattan and, particularly, in Clement Greenberg's art writings.[17] This sensory bureaucratization at once denigrated smell (in an effort to enforce the rational order of vision) and made use of it as a tool of social differentiation and a means of calling forth new consumerist desires. In liberating (or abstracting) visitors from any concern with the air they're breathing, the museum's engineered atmosphere solicits an optical (and, in rarer cases, acoustic or tactile) apprehension of putatively stable artworks. "In fact," writes Sloterdijk, "the museum can be described as a general isolator for objects: whatever there is to see or experience in it appears as an insulated artifact whose presence seeks interaction with a specialized form of aesthetic attention."[18] This "specialized form of aesthetic attention" requires the fiction of separation: not only is the museum's air hermetically sealed off from the outside, but its unnoticed atmosphere serves to insulate bodies and artworks from one another so that visitors can experience the art in contemplative, ocularcentric terms. As Drobnick explains in his critique of "anosmic" museum architectures, "Being inodorate permits the white cube to define itself as a zero-degree status of display, the mythic fundament out of which art objects emerge *ex nihilo*."[19] Under these conditions, both the nonhuman world and the experience of atmospherically marginalized communities may be represented to the so-called higher senses of sight and hearing, but not taken in by the nose or lungs. By maintaining conditions of sensory calm and disinterestedness, the "white cube" gallery sustains the bureaucratized sensorium constitutive of white masculinity.

There are striking parallels between the priorities of art conservation, the bureaucratization of the senses, and environmental conservation. Efforts to stabilize visual art objects developed alongside Western environmentalists' endeavors to demarcate and stabilize wilderness environments untainted by human activity, and these two processes of conservation share key assumptions about the need to keep environments pure of contamination. Thus, the proximity of chimneys, "the problem of solid dirt in the air of cities," and "the acid vapours which belched out of furnaces with the smoke" of London present significant problems for museum conservators as well as for environmentalists; in his classic manual *The Museum Environment*, Garry Thomson draws on research about how air pollution affects plants, explaining, "The attack on plants by air pollution, including ozone, is not the concern of antiquities conservators, but the misfortunes of lichens and mosses can be made use of as sulphur dioxide pollution indicators."[20] In addition to shared concerns about preserving purity, museum environments— along with the oil paintings and visual consumption practices they are designed to sustain—have influenced the governance of environments *outside* the museum by helping to forge an ideology that opposes the "Natural" to the social. From landscape paintings to natural history dioramas, nineteenth-century visual culture played a pivotal role in establishing the ideology of "wilderness" that has fueled efforts to imagine and preserve "Nature" as a space purified of human inhabitation and interaction.[21] Thus, the sublime landscape paintings of Caspar David Friedrich, Thomas Cole, and Frederic Edwin Church reduce humans to cosmic insignificance, while the museum habitat dioramas of Carl Akeley blend taxidermy, staged landscapes, and painted backgrounds with the explicit aims of conveying ecological knowledge and inspiring conservationist values. Donna Haraway's incisive commentary on the dioramas in the Museum of Natural History's Akeley African Hall highlights the fundamental separation of humans and nonhuman animals that links these displays to conservationist ideals: "The glass front of the diorama forbids the body's entry, but the gaze invites his visual penetration. The animal is frozen in a moment of supreme life, and man is transfixed. No merely living organism could accomplish this act. . . . The animals in the dioramas have transcended mortal life, and hold their pose forever."[22] These nineteenth-century genres share the illusion of a subject-object split that Bruno Latour diagnosed in still life paintings, which gave Enlightenment philosophers the misguided notion "that it actually makes sense to stop an object."[23] The imperatives of conservation in both environmentalism and art galleries—*Look, but don't touch! Leave no trace!*—may help sustain the putative insularity of visually discrete bodies, but they are impracticable at the molecular scale of transcorporeal material exchanges.

The problems with such a conservationist view of the environment are well documented. In his classic essay "Radical American Environmentalism and Wilderness Preservation: A Third World Critique," historian Ramachandra Guha explains not only how American environmentalism's emphasis on nature conservation avoids addressing the environmental effects of overconsumption and militarization but also how conservationism exacerbates environmental and economic injustice in the Global South: "Because India is a long settled and densely populated country in which agrarian populations have a finely balanced relationship with nature, the setting aside of wilderness areas has resulted in a direct transfer of resources from the poor to the rich."[24] In the US context, Ray argues that environmentalism's idealization of a pure, uncontaminated wilderness has relied on the "ecological-othering" of bodies constructed as environmentally alienated: not only forms of "racial, sexual, class, and gendered othering" but, more fundamentally, the figuration of "the disabled body [as] the quintessential symbol of humanity's alienation from nature."[25] In addition to reinforcing a range of geographic and social inequities, the conceptual separation of humans from "Nature" obscures the central environmental problems of the Anthropocene: the proliferation of trans-corporeal entanglements, hybrid "nature-cultures," and anthropogenic risks such as climate change and radiation.[26]

If the recent convergence of new materialism and environmental research inspired by thinkers such as Barad, Latour, Alaimo, and Jane Bennett has helped shift the attention of environmental humanities scholars to questions of material agency that refuse the idea of a separation between humans and "Nature," this material turn has only begun to unsettle the field's long-standing focus on visual texts and epistemologies. Thus, in addition to literature, ecocritics have attended to the ways in which photography, painting, film, television, video games, and other primarily visual (and occasionally sonic) eco-media represent mutually transformative material exchanges between humans and the nonhuman world. Even as he considers formal strategies for "render[ing] slow violence visible," Nixon pauses to consider the limits of visual epistemologies for conveying environmental violence: "What, then, in the fullest sense of the phrase, is the place of seeing in the world that we now inhabit? What, moreover, is the place of the other senses? How do we both make slow violence visible yet also challenge the privileging of the visible?"[27] In developing a framework and preliminary archive for an olfactory ecocriticism, I hope to demonstrate both the representational and nonrepresentational (chemical and/or affective) potentialities of scent as a vehicle for communicating atmospheric risks.

A Trans-corporeal Medium

Before the 1960s, artists and critics generally went along with Western philosophy's rejection of smell as an aesthetic medium. More recently, however, experimental artists have become intrigued by the very qualities of olfaction that Kant, Condillac, Freud, and others saw as limitations. Artists and critics are drawn to smell not only for its immersive qualities but also for its capacity to evoke memories and embodied affects by acting upon the brain's limbic system.[28] As anthropologist

Mark Graham explains, smell has striking affinities with postmodern aesthetic values: "Sight has been described as the modernist sense par excellence (Levin 1993). It is the sense that discriminates, divides and orders the world into mutually exclusive categories. Smell, by contrast, has been dubbed the sense of the postmodern (Classen, Howes and Synnott 1994: 203–5), the sense that confuses categories and challenges boundaries. It is difficult to localize, hard to contain and has the character of flux and transitoriness."[29] Transitory, mobile, and trans-corporeal in nature, air cannot function as a "pure" aesthetic medium: to be perceived, smells must enter and interact with our bodies and surroundings in ways we cannot fully control. Air can be a medium of toxicity as well as a medium of sensation; moreover, the intoxicating capacities of airborne particles may not be fully understood, or even noticed. Insofar as its transmission involves such risky, trans-corporeal exchanges, smell violates the ideal of purity that governs both visual perception and conventional attitudes about environmental conservation.

"Olfactory art" encompasses a range of aesthetic practices, from the exclusively olfactory work of synthesizing perfumes to multimedia artworks that juxtapose scents with other (usually visual) media.[30] Following the olfactory artist Peter de Cupere's discussion of the olfactory medium, I use the term "olfactory art" to refer to both artworks consisting entirely of smell and visual representation that "concerns smell concepts and/or works of art in which smell is a context or gives a context."[31] De Cupere distinguishes between works in which smell provides context ("Olfactism") and more visually understated works in which it is the primary actor ("Olfactorism"—a term intended to frame smell as a dynamic *actor* rather than a contextual "fact").[32] Beyond providing contextual information for other (usually visual) media, works of Olfactorism aim to make the perceiver "conscious of [their] environment" in olfactory terms.[33] In these works, smell functions as neither a substitute nor a footnote for visual perception: instead, smell transforms vision by altering the viewer's body, mind, and mood. Whether through semiotic or chemical channels—or both—smells can intensify, interrupt, or unsettle visual and auditory elements of artworks. In addition to provoking unsettling and embodied sensory experiences, olfactory art refuses the notions of permanence that have oriented not only art curation but the art market: as artist Brian Goltzenleuchter notes, "Through its volatility and immateriality, olfactory art inherently challenges commodification, collection, and archiving."[34]

In his overview of "Olfactory Art," curator and cofounder of the Scent Culture Institute Ashraf Osman traces the medium to Duchamp's use of coffee and perfume aromas in the 1938 and 1959 International Surrealist Exhibitions in Paris. In the 1960s and 1970s, artists associated with Fluxus, Arte Povera, Land Art, and feminism incorporated scent into their works.[35] These works explored themes such as our visceral responses to food smells,[36] corporeal scents, and environmental pollutants. Among the most striking of these early works are Judy Chicago's *Menstruation Bathroom* (1972)—which challenges the social marginalization of menstruation by introducing the smell of blood into an otherwise deodorized bathroom installation[37]—and Richard Wilson's *20:50* (1987), which viscerally conveys Western modernity's dependence on petroleum by exhibiting a pungent reservoir of sump oil. According to Drobnick, the 1990s saw the beginnings of a concentrated "olfactory turn" marked by artists' experiments with scent in an effort to "strategically counteract the increasing virtualization of experience and the hegemony of visual media, as well as concentrate on everyday experiences and the actuality of materials."[38] Food, rot, pollution, and sex have continued to play prominent roles in these recent works: for example, Damien Hirst's *Black Sun* (1997) consists of thousands of dead, rotting bluebottle flies stuck together into a dark circle;[39] in an aromatic challenge to discourses of olfactory orientalism (see chapter 4), Sita Kuratomi Bhaumik applies curry powder directly to gallery walls in several pieces, such as *MCDXCII* (2010) and *To Curry Favor* (2011); and Peter de Cupere's *The Deflowering* (2014) presents a statue of the Madonna made of a frozen liquid that releases a scent synthesized from real women's vaginal scents as it melts. Many of these works deploy minimalist visual elements to provide a background for their olfactory components, inverting our conventional, ocularcentric tendency to relegate smell to the background of our sensorium.

While twenty-first-century olfactory artists have continued to explore smell's intimate ties to memory, food, sex, and environment (often through works that feature culinary, botanical, and corporeal scents), their work is distinguished by a growing interest in technologies of olfactory analysis and synthesis such as the gas chromatograph and mass spectrometer.[40] Collaborating with geneticists, perfumers, and other scent experts, contemporary artists have moved beyond organic and found smells to explore the potentialities of synthetic scents.[41] In 2000, for example, Helgard Haug "collaborated with Karl-Heinz Burk, a professional from the industrial aroma-producing factory H and R in Braunschweig," to produce *U-deur*—a perfume based on the scents of Berlin Alexanderplatz.[42] Sissel Tolaas has utilized Headspace (gas chromatography) technology and other perfuming equipment provided by International Flavors and Fragrances (IFF) to sample and exhibit scents from cities around the world.[43] The high cost of scent technologies has resulted in numerous collaborations between olfactory artists and corporations endeavoring to explore new ways to commodify scent: IFF—the world's leading scent-engineering corporation, which was recently sued for exposing workers to diacetyl in microwave popcorn—regularly partners with artists and designers "to expose our perfumers to new and uncharted creative territories, to stretch their minds and fuel their creative energy."[44] While IFF has supported groundbreaking work, the corporation has an interest in downplaying questions of chemical toxicity: for example, although Tolaas has frequently sampled scents in polluted sites in cities like Mexico City and Detroit, she espouses liberal values of olfactory "tolerance" and "optimism" that overemphasize the semiotic aspects of smell while downplaying its potential toxicity: as she puts it, "nothing stinks but thinking makes it so."[45] The idea of approaching cross-cultural olfaction with tolerance and optimism erroneously assumes that affect and thought precede and determine olfaction, when in fact smells can modulate both affect and thought through involuntary memory and chemical agency.

The growing prestige of olfactory art has given rise to institutions that aim to provide noncorporate channels for artists interested in accessing scent technologies and perfuming expertise. Since 2013, the Institute for Art and Olfaction (IAO) in Los Angeles has fostered interdisciplinary art projects "by building an archive of contemporary perfume releases, by creating an accessible laboratory for scent experimentation and—most importantly, by inciting cross-genre collaboration between perfumers and folks on the cutting edge of other fields."[46] Air Variable, a company founded by the artist Sean Raspet (whose work I discuss below), has been providing scent fabrication services to artists and designers since

Figure 3.1. Boris Raux, *The Swimming Pool* (*La Piscine*), 2005. Soupline fabric softener, 1.4 × 3 m, depth unspecified. VKS Art Center. Image courtesy of the artist.

2014.[47] Institutions like these—along with individual olfactory artists such as Klara Ravat and Frank Bloem—offer artists and other culture workers access to perfuming workshops, ingredients, and tools such as distillation and Headspace equipment while also making space for public conversations about the stakes of olfactory aesthetics.[48] The increasing availability of scent fabrication technologies has laid the groundwork for a synthetic turn in olfactory art—as well as a range of artworks that explore synthetic scents as a medium for conveying anthropogenic and potentially risky phenomena.

The Swimming Pool (2005; Figure 3.1), an installation by the French artist Boris Raux, exemplifies olfactory art's potential for staging atmospheric toxicity—as well as its refusal of Enlightenment concepts of autonomy, embodiment, and nature—in both representational and nonrepresentational terms. A luminous blue pool filled with Soupline fabric softener sited in the center of a gallery space, the work blends a captivating appearance with a cloying chemical scent. Visually, the installation presents only "a simple blue rectangle of impenetrable depth . . . minimal and rather ordinary"; yet the exhibition space is also filled with "an invisible presence—just a smell, at first reassuring, but [one that] quickly brings on a headache [*entêtante*]."⁴⁹ Captivating, reassuring, yet eventually intoxicating, *The Swimming Pool* presents an artificially scented version of the myth of Narcissus—or, as one curator puts it, "a fragrant mirror."⁵⁰ This draws attention to the smell of the narcissus flower—a heady fragrance that had been noted in texts such as *The Homeric Hymn to Demeter* and the *Cypria* fragment long before Ovid's spectatorial rendering of the Narcissus story. The *Homeric Hymn*, for example, recounts how Persephone was ensnared by the flower's smell: "From its root a hundred-fold bloom sprang up and smelled so sweet that the whole vast heaven above and the whole earth laughed, and the salty smell of the sea."⁵¹ If *Swimming Pool*'s luminous yet reflective surface invites the visitor to approach and look, its heady scent induces discomfort, if not a stronger allergic and/or psychosomatic reaction.

Although *The Swimming Pool* does not feature scents analyzed or synthesized by the artist, it exemplifies Raux's interest in "found" fragrances as well as his interdisciplinary practice (Raux holds degrees in physics, chemistry, engineering, design, and the arts and previously worked as a "trainee for L'Oréal or Reckitt Benckiser (the makers of Dettol, Veet, Vanish)").⁵² Confronting visitors with olfactory discomfort and potential intoxication, *The Swimming Pool* reframes the body as porous, vulnerable, and always already materially entangled with its surrounding atmosphere. The visual appeal of the liquid—the desire to gaze upon the reflection in its surface as well as into its luminous depths—is in tension with a smell that many visitors would experience as unpleasantly intense, as well as the risks posed by unknown chemical exposure. Rather than presenting a stabilizing ideal ego, this reflecting pool underscores the ontological uncertainty precipitated by everyday risks. Beck theorizes risk society as the product of "reflexive modernization"—a process by which the risks (such as air pollution, radiation, and toxic waste) produced in the course of modernization themselves become a central concern of modernity. Raux's Soupline mirror may offer a stabilizing visual reflection, but getting close enough to see it exposes the viewer to problems of reflexivity: What chemicals constitute the scent of Soupline, what do we know about them, what *don't* we know about them, how do they make us feel upon inhalation, how do they bioaccumulate in bodies over time? Is it safe to exhibit *The Swimming Pool* at all?

This enhanced risk awareness relativizes the visible world, undoing the specular misrecognition that Lacan associates with the mirror stage. As Jones writes in her account of the Narcissus myth's ocularcentrism, "Were he to try to activate [the] other senses, the mythic illusion would be shattered (the mirrored 'self' destroyed). To produce the I/Eye, to become modern, the narcissistic subject must subordinate nonocular senses and attend rapturously to that emergent self-reflective ego."[53] For Lacan, the "Ideal-I" presented in the mirror is linked with "the statue onto which man projects himself": it initiates a series of fantasies "that proceed from a fragmented image of the body to what I will call an 'orthopedic' form of its totality—and to the finally donned armor of an alienating identity that will mark his entire mental development with its rigid structure."[54] Feeling their own body to be fragmented and disorganized, the infant identifies with an alienating image of corporeal "totality"—an image that Lacan associates with fortresses, statues, and ostensibly impenetrable "armour." By contrast, olfactory perception of *The Swimming Pool* conveys a sense of the body immersed in a risky atmosphere, inhabited by intoxicating chemicals. Rather than visual alienation, smell stages material interrelation and environmental intimacy. By reintroducing smell into our conception of narcissistic identification, *The Swimming Pool* insists upon a material understanding of human embodiment as well as an awareness of the risky environmental implications of the scented personal care products that play such a widespread role in olfactory self-fashioning. However, the olfactory consequences of atmospheric disparities reach far beyond the individual body. The following section turns to olfactory artworks that bring the trans-corporeal nature of smell to bear on processes of differential deodorization that extend across architectural, urban, and transnational scales.

Olfactory Art and Environmental Risk

While art critics have begun to consider the potential of scent as an aesthetic medium linked to food, memory, corporeality, and place, there has been little work on scent's capacities for staging the trans-corporeal environmental predicaments presented by contemporary risk society. As Drobnick explains in a generative study of spatially oriented olfactory art, "Contemporary artists are at the forefront of exploring the dynamics of toposmia, which implicate a number of disciplines, namely geography, cultural history, sociology, and urban studies, as well as aesthetics."[55] Toposmia, or "mapping by smell," encompasses place-based scents such as Haug's *U-deur* (discussed above) as well as olfactory geographies such as Tolaas's compendia of urban scents and collaborative urban smell walks designed by artists such as Caitlin Berrigan and Michael McBean (*The Smelling Committee*, Brooklyn, 2006), de Cupere (*Scent City Walk*, Palermo, 2015), Tolaas (*Incomplete City Walk: Smell Scape*, Singapore, 2016), and Beatrice Glow (*Lenapeway and NYU Native Plant Gardens Walking Tour*, 2016).[56] Whereas Drobnick provides a lucid account of the ways in which olfactory art can convey and destabilize place-based memories, I focus on the trans-corporeal dimensions of toposmia: how place literally enters and affects our bodies through volatilized scent molecules.

Drawing attention to the fact that air is a necessity of life as well as a vehicle for scent, olfactory art frequently explores the theme of environmental risk. As Drobnick notes in a discussion of his experiences as an olfactory art curator, "Olfactory artworks are . . . visceral, since the act of breathing compels the absorption of airborne particles into one's inner being, where some scents will interact with a person's body chemistry and perhaps even influence their emotional state, heart rate, and other physiological functions."[57] Insofar as it is inextricable from air as a geographically differentiated medium of life itself, scent is an inherently biopolitical aesthetic medium. Under the conditions of risk society, air has become a vital site of political struggle: the distribution of airborne pollutants produces uneven and highly contested geographies of health, profit, and power.

Recent olfactory artworks draw attention to air as a heterogeneous and frequently risky medium, presenting breathers (a term I borrow from Choy to contrast the material intimacy of olfactory apprehension with the sight- and hearing-based terms "viewer" and "audience") with the scents of cigarettes, chemical deodorants, city streets, air pollution, decomposition, and garbage.[58] Such works draw on the nineteenth-century understanding of airborne "miasmas" as agents of disease.[59] Although miasma theory was supplanted by the germ theory of disease in the late nineteenth century, its focus on polluted or unhealthy air as a cause of disease provides an antecedent for understanding the harmful effects of hazardous airborne materials such as smog, radiation, mold, dust, and chemicals vapors. In contrast with the white cube's ocular-centric, conservationist framing of "Nature" discussed above, olfactory art explores postnatural ecologies in which human activity is inextricably intermeshed with environmental processes. Insofar as it engages in the synthetic modification of air, olfactory art is an ideal medium for provoking breathers to reflect on what, if anything, environmental risk smells like. The works considered below demonstrate a range of approaches to the smell of risk: Sean Raspet and Anicka Yi disrupt the putatively "pure" atmospheres of gallery spaces in order to sensitize breathers to the intoxicating possibilities of aesthetic experience; recent pieces by Peter de Cupere offer critical yet intimate engagements with geographically uneven flows of airborne risk. While these artists deploy olfaction to strikingly different ends, they share a fascination with smell as a visceral yet uncertain index of environmental toxicity.

The curation of the art gallery's *atmosphere* is the subject of the LA-based artist Sean Raspet's *Micro-encapsulated Surface Coating* (2014–15), part of his *Residuals* exhibition at the Jessica Silverman Gallery. Visually indistinguishable from a white gallery wall, the installation piece takes the form of a scratch and sniff emulsion. As the gallery notes explain,

> The work starts with a process in which the air of Jessica Silverman Gallery is analyzed using a "SUMMA canister." The stainless steel vessel initially contains a vacuum and collects air from the surrounding environment over the course of a week. Raspet then sends the accumulated air to a lab to determine its molecular composition and then creates a liquid mixture that is a many thousand-fold condensation of the chemical signature of the gallery's air. The artist then sends this liquid to be "micro-encapsulated" into a "scratch-and-sniff" emulsion that is spray coated on the gallery's surfaces. The background smell of most interior environments often comes from their construction and cleaning materials. This chemical signature corresponds to the gallery's ambient scent profile, a kind of condensed olfactory background noise.[60]

Like the detective stories and MCS memoirs discussed in chapter 1, *Micro-encapsulated Surface Coating* simulates hyperosmia, artificially enhancing visitors' olfactory sensitivity to the gallery air. The installation

Figure 3.2. Sean Raspet, *Atmospheric Reformulation (Reconstituted Atmosphere with 4-Point Resolution)*, from *Residuals* (2014). Nitrogen (78.08 percent), oxygen (20.95 percent), argon (0.93 percent), and carbon dioxide (0.04 percent) dimensions variable; flow rate 100 mL per minute. Cylinders supplied by Praxair, Dixon regulators set to 5–25 psig, and each output to a four-gas parallel inlet/common outlet flowmeter that emits the gases in the above mL/min proportions. Image courtesy of the artist and the Jessica Silverman Gallery.

gives material form to Drobnick's observation that "no space . . . is without a scent of some kind, as all indoor and outdoor atmospheres carry olfactory vestiges of human activity and natural processes. Museums are no different, notwithstanding their efforts to provide the conditions for a pure visual experience. Cleaning products can leave traces of their use, the aromas of restaurants and cafes can waft around corners, and over-perfumed visitors can trail clouds through the galleries."[61] Instead of being exhibited "in" the gallery, Raspet's process of analysis, multiplication, and synthesis exhibits the gallery's environment itself—the "chemical signature" produced by its particular blend of architecture, bodies, objects, and cleaning materials. By exaggerating and thus making perceptible the artificial nature of the gallery air, Raspet provokes questions about how that air might affect or even harm visitors. At the same time, the scratch and sniff format demands both intimacy and complicity: touching the walls to release the encapsulated chemicals into the air, mixing one's own corporeal scents with the emulsion on the wall, and leaving with material traces of the exhibit rubbed into one's fingertips.

Micro-encapsulated Surface Coating was accompanied by air canisters that continually renewed the gallery's signature composition of primary gases as well as a "negative air machine, which . . . continually filter[ed] out stray odor compounds and reinstate[d] the background chemical signature of the gallery."[62] The removed odor compounds were then synthesized into a solvent mixture that, at the end of the exhibition, was "used to clean the scratch and sniff coating off the walls and return the gallery to its original state"—an atmosphere filled with airborne human residues (Figure 3.2). By foregrounding the continuous inputs and outputs necessary to reproduce the gallery's not-quite-pristine air—what we might call the curation of curation's atmosphere—Raspet provokes critical questions about the considerable environmental externalities imposed by carefully controlled gallery environments: Whose labors in proximity with cleaning and construction particulates have produced and maintained the spaces in which we encounter works of art? What is the cost of the "pure" gases with which Raspet's exhibition continually renews the air's chemical signature, and how are they sourced? What happens to the impurities filtered out of gallery spaces? Finally—following Latour's account of the proliferation of nature-culture hybrids—does the Western museum's deodorization of aesthetic interaction enable the proliferation of trans-corporeal toxics everywhere else by maintaining a (fictive) separation of humans from "Nature"? These questions resonate with an emerging discussion among museum conservators, who are revisiting expensive climate control standards that require environmentally unsustainable emissions.[63] By staging an elaborate apparatus for maintaining a gallery's "original" atmosphere while simultaneously exposing the extent to which that air is already suffused with cleaning and construction chemicals, *Residuals* challenges the assumptions about purity and environmental ethics that underlie all gallery environments.

If Raspet's work draws attention to residual yet potentially risky aspects of the museum environment, the Korean American artist Anicka Yi pushes breathers to rethink the culturally constructed elements of our olfactory associations. *You Can Call Me F* (2015), a solo exhibition at New York's Kitchen gallery, is structured by a gendered opposition between the manufactured sterility of gallery spaces and olfactory and visual artworks grounded in (conventionally feminized) processes of lively fermentation. Near the gallery entrance, a glowing Plexiglas vitrine displays the title of Yi's exhibition inscribed on a living bacteria culture. The artist collaborated on this bacterial artwork with the MIT synthetic biologist Tal Danino, cultivating microorganisms from cheek swabs donated by one hundred women in Yi's social network. The exhibition blends the "nutty and musky" scent of this collective bacterial culture (described by one critic as "Parmesan cheese or rancid butter with sour floral accord up top") with the "antiseptic" scent of the Gagosian Gallery on Madison Avenue, which Yi analyzed and reproduced with assistance from Sean Raspet's scent fabrication company, Air Variable.[64] In addition to providing an olfactory "[response] to a phallogocentric privileging of the eye as the organ responsible for knowledge and domination,"[65] *You Can Call Me F* contrasts modernity's efforts to eradicate undesirable smells in the name of hygiene with the irrepressible productivity of women's bodies and social networks. As Yi's press materials explain, three rotating diffusers capped with motorcycle helmets "release a scent that synthesizes the all-female network of the collective bacteria with the almost imperceptible odor of the ultimate patriarchal-model network in the art world—Gagosian Gallery."[66] The result is what Drobnick would call a "dialectical odour"[67]—a complex smell that dramatizes the frictions between two ideologically opposed atmospheres as the scent of female networks invades and contaminates the art world's purified, patriarchal gallery space. If the helmets visually evoke the fantasies of autonomy that underlie Western aesthetics and environmental relations—the armored body, the rational head disentangled from corporeality, the lower senses sealed off from the world, a state of purity free from material entanglements, the motorcyclist detached from the machine's environmental externalities—their function as scent diffusers undercuts those fantasies by interpellating visitors through scent and breath.

You Can Call Me F invokes and repurposes the visual iconography of quarantine and contagion: as one press release puts it, "The Kitchen's gallery will function as a forensic site in which the artist aligns society's growing paranoia around contagion and hygiene (both public and

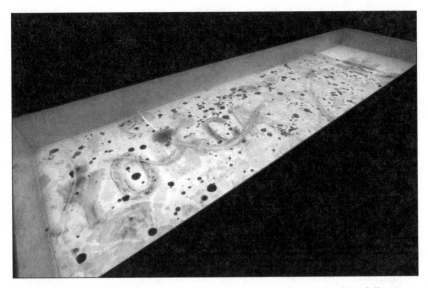

Figure 3.3. Anicka Yi, *Grabbing at Newer Vegetables*, 2015. Photo: Jason Mandella. Courtesy of the Kitchen, New York.

private) with the enduring patriarchal fear of feminism and potency of female networks. . . . In the gallery, viewers will enter an environment evoking the anxious isolation in the aftermath of a pandemic."[68] Yi's inscription of the exhibit's title in an illuminated bacterial culture in a piece called *Grabbing at Newer Vegetables* (Figure 3.3) is borrowed from a publicity gimmick for Steven Soderbergh's outbreak film *Contagion* (2011), in which the film's title was spelled out by bioluminescent fungi on two billboards in Toronto; elsewhere in the gallery, transparent quarantine tents display objects referencing personal (socks and mouthwash) and ethnically distinctive (dried shrimp and seaweed) scents.[69] Instead of either avoiding or containing risk factors, however, Yi's critical depiction of "anxious isolation" urges visitors to dwell in trans-corporeal exchanges: after all, breathers could not experience the exhibit without inhaling and corporealizing the scent and "culture" of women's networks. Art critic Caroline Jones contrasts Yi's lively "biofictional colloids"—which seem to embody speculative scenarios of biosocial ferment—with "nineteenth-century bohemian [creators of glass flowers] who sought to fix biology in a permanent realm, stopping death itself in hardened silica with a bloom of brown."[70] Challenging Western patriarchy's tendency to stigmatize and eradicate volatile phenomena such as disease and fermentation, Yi's nuanced engagement with airborne risk recalls Priscilla Wald's trenchant analysis of communicable disease narratives: "Communicable disease compels attention . . . not only because of the devastation it can cause but also because the circulation of microbes materializes the transmission of ideas. The interactions that make us sick also constitute us as a community. Disease emergence dramatizes the dilemma that inspires the most basic of human narratives: the necessity and danger of human contact."[71] While musky scents and lively "miasmas" are conventionally associated with the risk of disease,[72] Yi repurposes the language of "virality" and contagion as indices of communicable feminine potential.[73] Rather than viewing trans-corporeality solely in terms of toxicity and disease, *You Can Call Me F* aestheticizes bacteria, mold, and feminine ferment while gesturing toward the unpredictable and potentially transformative possibilities of olfactory intoxication: in Mel Chen's formulation, this shift from toxicity to intoxication "prioritizes a queer reach for toxicity's 'worlding.'"[74] Yi's attention to the vital links between bacterial proliferation and human "culture" challenges modernity's tendency to stigmatize microbes—as well as environments and populations associated with them—as health risks. The implicit argument of *You Can Call Me F* resonates with recent work on the material relations between humans and bacteria by feminist materialist scholars such as Deboleena Roy. "In addition to playing a crucial role in the genesis of this planet and all of its inhabitants including humans," Roy writes, "bacteria have a great deal to teach us not only about changefulness and nonhuman becomings but also about desire, response, experimentation, and communication through language, writing, and text."[75] If bacteria are vital agents in environmental, biological, and cultural becomings, then perhaps the true environmental and social hazards are located not in the bacterial scent of fermentation but in the antiseptic atmosphere of the deodorized gallery.

Whereas Raspet and Yi mobilize smell to critically challenge our assumptions about the rarified air of art galleries, the Belgian artist Peter de Cupere brings olfactory aesthetics to bear on problems of environmental risk at geographic scales that extend well beyond the gallery environment. Since the 1990s, De Cupere has produced a remarkable range of olfactory artworks that experiment with the scents of materials such

Figure 3.4. *Smoke Cloud.* © Peter de Cupere, www.peterdecupere.net, 2014. Image courtesy of the artist.

as sweat, genitals, candy, toothpaste, urine, garbage, pollution, grass, cardamom, and peppermint; in 2018, he received the Institute for Art and Olfaction's Golden Pear award for his lifetime contributions to scent culture, and he is currently organizing the Art Sense(s) Lab (https://pxl-mad.be/en/art-senses-lab)—the first Master in Arts program focusing on the lower senses (smell, taste, and touch)—at PXL University College in Hasselt, Belgium. According to critics Larry Shiner and Yulia Kriskovets, De Cupere "has created an artistic identity that is a cross between artist and olfactory chemist that may become a model for other olfactory artists in the future."[76] Two works that De Cupere recently exhibited in Havana exemplify how olfactory art can viscerally convey the environmental distinctions propagated by geographically uneven development. *Smoke Cloud* (2014; Figure 3.4), which appeared in the 2015 exhibition *The Importance of Being* in Havana,[77] consists of a ladder placed beneath a fabricated cloud suspended from the gallery ceiling. Visitors ascend the ladder one at a time, placing their heads inside the cloud and inhaling the scent of air pollution. This installation interacts with visitors both visually (by presenting to others the incongruous spectacle of a body with its head in a cloud) and trans-corporeally (by introducing the scent of air pollution into the breather's lungs). While the idiom *having one's head in the clouds* generally refers to a tendency toward fantasy or idealism, De Cupere's cloud immerses breathers in the materiality of smog: through chemical or psychosomatic channels, the scent of smog could physically affect a breather's mood or health. The resulting frictions between the work's visual and olfactory dimensions— contemplation vs. smog inhalation, ascent vs. intoxication, visual beauty vs. invisible harm—interrupt the ocularcentric order of the art gallery: one at a time, visitors' heads disappear into the sculpture; for those who ascend, the gallery space itself vanishes as the smell of smog sets in. De Cupere's decision to fill the cloud with the scent of air pollution was inspired in part by his encounter with Havana's poor air quality, and specifically "the powerful scent of gasoline that the old Chevys and Buicks spit out."[78] The polluted air presented by *Smoke Cloud* thus references not only urban air pollution in Cuba but also its transnational origins in the Cold War trade embargo, which has been in place since 1960.

If *Smoke Cloud* implicitly positions the US trade embargo as a mechanism of differential deodorization, *The Smell of a Stranger* (2015) frames the Obama-era "Thaw" in US-Cuba relations as another likely context for atmospheric violence. This installation was De Cupere's contribution to the Havana Biennial, exhibited outdoors at the High Institute of Technology and Applied Sciences at the University of Havana. Blending scent engineering, bioengineering, and the ethos of speculative fiction, *The Smell of a Stranger* offers a cautionary allegory about both bioengineering and the "opening" of Cuba to US commerce and diplomacy. Working with scents provided by IFF, De Cupere genetically modified nine local Cuban flowers and plants. While the results appear identical to natural specimens, De Cupere's flora emit a range of incongruous odors including the scents of "American New Dollars, Blood, Sperm, Vagina, Dead Body, Gun Powder, Sweat (smell of fear), Air Pollution, and Geraniums" (Figure 3.5).[79] By contrasting the beauty of local plants with smells associated with sex tourism, labor exploitation, military violence, pollution, industrial food production (the artist originally intended to include the smells of hamburgers and Belgian fries, but these were omitted for tech-

Figure 3.5. *The Smell of a Stranger* (with the artist). © Peter de Cupere, www.peterdecupere.net. Photo: Frederick Buyckx, 2015.

nical reasons), and death, De Cupere suggests that the opening of US-Cuba trade and diplomacy under the Obama administration could have devastating effects upon Cuba's people and environment.[80] As the artist explains, "Western culture is slowly creeping [into Cuba] and the capital automatically follows. . . . Cuba has a lot of nature and a lot of cultural aspects which can be exploited with bad intentions."[81] Despite its somewhat reductive assumptions about the prior purity of Cuba's "nature" and "cultur[e]," this statement helpfully associates the artwork's postnatural, bioengineered flowers with the threat of increased capitalist incursions on Cuba's atmosphere. *The Smell of a Stranger* upturns the expectation that flowers and plants will offer up refreshing "natural" fragrances, leaving breathers disturbed—if not disgusted—by a range of visceral or unnatural scents. Different breathers could find the scent of sperm, sweat, money, and food physically arousing or repulsive; as with *Smoke Cloud*, the chemical components of these scents may be literally toxic for chemically sensitive visitors. Such physical responses viscerally convey how the environments we produce affect our bodies, minds, and moods through trans-corporeal exchanges. Siting this work outdoors at once underscores the plants' visual continuities with Cuba's "natural" environment and sidesteps the curatorial problems—such as unwanted exposures and scent mixing—that would be more likely to occur in an indoor exhibit.

The title of De Cupere's installation alludes to the cultural specificity of scent: the way in which perceptions of attractive and repulsive scents vary across cultural boundaries as well as the ways in which scent is mobilized to delineate and reproduce those boundaries.[82] If smell demarcates cultural and social boundaries, "the smell of a stranger" invokes the idea of an ethical encounter with the Other—a cross-cultural scenario in which Cubans and foreigners could become more comfortable with each other. But rather than delivering on this promise of cross-cultural olfaction, De Cupere presents visitors with another sort of "stranger" altogether: postnatural plants that exude anthropogenic odors. Many of these scents—sperm, money, dead bodies, gunpowder, and air pollution—would not be "strange" to either Cubans or visitors from the United States; instead, their strangeness lies in their juxtaposition with each other and with the installation's apparently "natural" plants. Although the scents of American and Belgian food may be interpreted as a "funny reference to our Western culture with the scent of hamburgers,"[83] the references to hamburgers and fries take on darker connotations when placed alongside the scents of money and dead bodies. If hamburgers and Belgian fries symbolize US and Belgian culture,[84] they are also foods that, when eaten or smelled, have trans-corporeal effects upon people's bodies. Industrially produced fast food is a vehicle of malnutrition, obesity, and what Lauren Berlant calls "slow death" on a global scale;[85] the circulation of hamburgers can be mapped as an exchange of money for premature death across unevenly developed terrains. Whether conveyed through fast food, sex tourism, capitalist exploitation, or militarization,[86] uneven development and economic imperialism threaten to bring new health risks to Cuba's human and more-than-human inhabitants. The "stranger" here is not American culture but the plundered, contaminated, and commercialized dystopia that Cuba is in danger of becoming. Rob Nixon's identification of "temporal dispersion" as a central component of slow violence clarifies the stakes of De Cupere's dystopian scents: because the health effects of fast food, militarization, and rampant capitalism could take decades to emerge, De Cupere turns to a speculative—yet still material and vis-

OLFACTORY ART AND MUSEUM ECOLOGIES | 111

cerally trans-corporeal—tactic of temporal condensation as a formal means of manifesting future threats.[87] *The Smell of a Stranger* thus offers a powerful cautionary allegory of the stark possibilities opened up by the intensified neoliberalization of Cuba's economy. Where Raspet's *Residuals* highlights the chemicals already present in the gallery's air, *The Smell of a Stranger* proleptically dramatizes Cuba's future vulnerability to uneven transnational flows of desire, risk, and exploitation. Like the literary mode of magical realism, De Cupere's bioengineered Cuban plants register the dislocating effects of transnational contacts and capital circulation upon local reality; yet the more-than-real aspects of *The Smell of a Stranger*—which include their trans-corporeal interactions with breathers' bodies—actually exist as material products of genetics, biotechnology, and scent fabrication.

* * *

Despite the innovative, trans-corporeal experiments with risky substances discussed in this chapter, even olfactory art is a limited medium for engaging with the ethics of environmental toxicity. As the fate of Ai Weiwei's *Sunflowers* installation demonstrates, galleries are obligated to protect visitors from hazardous levels of exposure delineated by institutions such as the US Occupational Safety and Health Administration (OSHA). And while the establishment of "acceptable levels" of exposure is shot through with problems and contradictions, olfactory art is unlikely to present scents whose concentrations of toxic substances exceed acceptable levels. For most visitors, even these trans-corporeal installations work primarily as simulations of toxicity: they pose no immediately evident health risks, even if they present low levels of potentially toxic substances.

Yet to the extent that olfactory art engages with questions of toxicity, it raises vital questions about how "acceptable levels" are determined, what it means to agree to a *"permissible extent* of poisoning,"[88] and for whom these acceptable levels are valid (not, presumably, for people afflicted with multiple chemical sensitivity or idiopathic environmental intolerance). The tensions between visible forms and invisible scents—or the broader tension between perceptible forms and unknown risk factors—at play in olfactory artworks also draw attention to the politics of risk perception: Who has access to the technological tools of risk analysis? Who decides which risk factors should be researched and which neglected? Which populations are regularly exposed to more toxic particulates than what visitors voluntarily and temporarily sample in art exhibitions? By introducing even "acceptable" levels of potentially toxic substances into breathers' bodies, olfactory art activates—and opens to political consideration—the rarefied air of conventional art galleries, as well as the air outside those galleries. In doing so, it confronts the "white cubes" and conservationist values of gallery spaces with other, trans-corporeal modes of environmental engagement.

The discussions of hyperosmic narratives of detection, naturalist novels, air-conditioned galleries, and olfactory artworks presented so far have considered a range of approaches to incorporating olfaction into aesthetic forms as well as the particular ways in which these forms internalize and/or challenge the dynamics of differential deodorization. Building on these readings of olfaction's formal affordances, the following chapters turn to race, colonialism, and Indigeneity as key sites of olfactory differentiation. Both real and imagined odors—as well as the sensory suppression of olfaction—have played powerful roles in sustaining racialization and colonization. For example, North American discourses of deodorization have long associated Asiatic populations with modernity's noxious odors. In addition to documenting this long-standing discourse of "atmo-orientalism," the following chapter considers how works of Asian North American fiction and olfactory art have mobilized smell to stage more nuanced encounters with diasporic bodies and spaces.

4

Atmo-Orientalism

Olfactory Racialization and Environmental Health

Kate McLean's widely circulated map of *New York's Smelliest Blocks* (2011; Figure 4.1) indiscriminately combines potentially toxic chemical odors such as "perfume" and "car oil" with organic odors—like "five-spice" and "dried fish"—whose "smelliness" has more to do with cultural preferences than environmental health. Although the map—which incorporates information gathered through interviews with local residents—appears to present an objective perspective on the distribution of unwelcome smells, it simultaneously reproduces ethnocentric ideas about smell by stigmatizing the smells of Chinese and Southeast Asian cuisine in Manhattan's Chinatown neighborhood. Did McLean's interviews with local residents include immigrant laborers and long-term residents (many of whom may not have been available for English-language interviews), or did they solicit data only from visitors and newer arrivals in this gentrifying neighborhood? As anthropologist Martin Manalansan documents in his study of olfactory experience in New York City's Asian American communities, Asian culinary smells simultaneously resist "the displacement and fragmentation of migrant experiences" by evoking culturally specific memories "and, at the same time, constitute many quotidian dilemmas and struggles around immigrant embodiment" as immigrants struggle with imperatives of deodorization.[1] Because smells must enter and transform the body in order to be perceived, they have historically figured prominently in discourses of environmental health: even common culinary odors "become part of grids that speak to issues of hygiene, disgust, and aspirations."[2] However, the subjective and uncertain nature of olfactory perception—the difficulty of defining a "bad" smell or of documenting the toxicity of specific airborne particulates—makes smell a fuzzy medium for determining what counts as a public nuisance or environmental hazard.

Figure 4.1. Kate McLean, *New York's Smelliest Blocks*, 2011. Digital media, 169 × 257 mm. ©Kate McLean. Used with permission.

The fuzzy, indeterminate zone in which cultural "otherness" over-laps with environmental toxicity has given rise to a complex and flexible discourse that I term *atmo-orientalism*—a discourse that frames Asiatic subjects (and particularly the Chinese) in terms of noxious atmospheres. Environmental studies scholars have introduced the term "environmental orientalism" to describe imperialist depictions of non-western environments as "strange and defective" and therefore in need of Western intervention—or "forms of environmental conservation that simultaneously seek to protect nature and to vilify Third World poor today."[3] While these scholars highlight orientalist depictions of environments in need of protection, I emphasize the racializing effects of atmo-orientalism—a term that encompasses not only how Asiatic subjects are framed in association with atmospheric toxicity, but also how Asiatic atmospheres are perceived as biochemical threats to the integrity of white bodies and minds. While it sometimes legitimizes state interventions in Asian diasporic communities, households, and laws, atmo-orientalism primarily functions as a form of "environmental exclusion" through which "the environmental movement deploys cultural disgust against various communities it sees as threats to nature."[4] This emphasis on racially distinctive relations to space, environment, and air distinguishes atmo-orientalism from other modes of olfactory racism grounded in beliefs about biologically distinctive odors: whereas historians have documented a pattern of discourses asserting the capacity to detect racial Blackness by smell (particularly in contexts of passing where Blacks are present in "white" spaces),[5] the racialization of Asiatics tends to target modern practices and spaces such as the opium den, the Chinese quarter, commercial squid drying, the overcrowded apartment, and the unregulated factory.

Atmo-orientalism does the work of racialization on two levels: as a discourse and as a strategy for producing space.[6] As a discourse, it organizes political and cultural power by tethering olfactory perception to racial difference. As Corbin writes, "Abhorrence of smells produces its own form of social power. Foul-smelling rubbish appears to threaten the social order, whereas the reassuring victory of the hygienic and the fragrant promises to buttress its stability."[7] Ostensibly instinctive responses to smells reinforce the legitimacy of the state as an agent of hygiene and deodorization. At the same time, they perpetuate ideas of racial difference that effectively blame the victims of environmental racism (which unevenly allocates noxious air) by construing them as atmospheric threats. As a strategy for producing space, atmo-orientalism both orchestrates and disavows the dispersed, atmospheric materiality of racism—its capacity to be embodied not just in physiognomic or genetic terms but through the ways in which geographically differentiated atmospheres enter and chemically transform racialized bodies. In her provocative discussion of the always changing, always incomplete discursive, material, and affective nature of racial atmospheres, Renisa Mawani argues for "rethinking race and racism in ways that are no longer anthropocentric. The atmosphere . . . forges an expansive, limitless, and mobile field. It is a force that is not visible or even palpable but one that remains vital and necessary to biological and social existence. Like the air we breathe, the racial atmosphere provides the very conditions of life and death."[8] Mawani's formulation helps bring into focus the dual nature of atmo-orientalism as both a process that disproportionately exposes Asiatics to noxious air and a discourse that naturalizes those exposures by racializing noxious air as Asiatic. The racialization of atmospheric inhalations offers an important site for "reading *orifically*"—to borrow Kyla Tompkins's phrase for an approach that moves beyond the focus on skin and surface ("the intellectually limited inheritance of the epidermal ontology of race") that has oriented much of the scholarship on race and embodiment.[9]

This chapter traces the development of atmo-orientalist discourses from nineteenth-century medical geography and miasma theory to contemporary Yellow Peril narratives and nuisance complaints targeting Asian immigrants. I focus on the sense of smell, which functioned in nineteenth-century medicine and health discourses as a visceral and culturally variable, yet notoriously elusive mode of apprehending and representing racialized atmospheres. Alongside the racialized figure of the "coolie," atmo-orientalism emerged as a response to massive shifts in environment and spatial scale as industrial capitalism consolidated global markets, railroad and steam transportation, and the intense horizontal and vertical stratifications held in proximity by modern cities. In addition to contextualizing the atmospheric representation of Asian groups across a range of US health campaigns and cultural narratives, this genealogy of atmo-orientalism illuminates the stakes of Asian diasporic aesthetic projects that set out to reconfigure their audience's perceptions of Asiatic smells: writing in the Exclusion era, Edith Maude Eaton / Sui Sin Far deploys motifs of fragrance and fresh air in an effort to discursively deodorize Chinese immigrants; the contemporary olfactory artist Anicka Yi produces cross-racial and transpacific conviviality by deploying the immersive and combinatory qualities of scent. Along with the genealogy of atmo-orientalism presented in the first section of this chapter, these aesthetic works indicate how olfactory racialization has persisted and a powerful mode of sensory conditioning from the earliest decades of anti-Asian agitation in the United States to the xenophobic climate of the 2010s. As illustrated by these case studies, theorizing olfaction provides a critical hermeneutic for analyzing the atmospheric interventions that frequently go unnoticed in the background of antiracist cultural productions.

Yellow Miasmas

Sensory anthropologists and historians have documented how communities that have come to valorize "deodorization" mobilize beliefs about olfactory difference to shore up social boundaries.[10] As Constance Classen notes, "It is evident in most such cases that the stench ascribed to the other is far less a response to an actual perception of the odour of the other than a potent metaphor for the social decay it is feared the other . . . will cause in the established order."[11] Another sensory historian, Andrew Kettler, explains that such menacing odors are often perceived on the level of "tacit knowledge [that] exists within the body and can be transferred between persons through forms of social consciousness that are not always explicitly linguistic."[12] What distinguishes atmo-orientalism from many other forms of olfactory racialization is that, rather than emphasizing the odors of "uncivilized" bodies and exotic cultural practices, it underscores odors and environmental risks associated with modernity: industrial production, urban crowding, and global commerce. As Colleen Lye and Iyko Day have noted, Asiatic racial form made the Asian immigrant a figure of "dehumanized economism" by underscoring "the inorganic quality of the Asiatic body."[13] In *Alien Capital: Asian Racialization and the Logic of Settler Colonial Capitalism*, Day frames Asian racialization as a key element of "romantic anti-capitalism"—a critical but misguided response to capitalism that posits a false antinomy between the concrete and the abstract: "Expressing the antinomy of concrete and abstract, nature . . . personifies concrete, perfected human relations against the social degeneration caused by the abstract circuits of capitalism."[14] Capitalism's depredations are attributed to "the abstractness of money and finance," which are given biological expression in racial representations of Asians.

If Asian racial form gives form to social anxieties about perceived shifts from the natural and concrete to the inorganic and abstract, then atmosphere is an optimal medium for staging those anxieties. Atmo-orientalism is preoccupied with the denaturalization of air—an element characterized by indistinct boundaries between the abstract and the material, the "natural" and the anthropogenic. On the one hand, air is abstract, invisible, and putatively "natural" (as Whitman insisted prior to the onset of risk society, "The atmosphere is not a perfume, it has no taste of the distillation, it is odorless");[15] on the other hand, air is materially differentiated, chemically volatile, and at times intoxicating. Critic Mark Jerng has analyzed the powerful role played by "the incoherence and fogginess of abstractions" in Yellow Peril narratives, as race is delinked from visual and corporeal qualities and represented in atmospheric terms.[16] Floating in the background of public health discourses and literary representations of Asian immigrants, atmo-orientalism blends these foggy abstractions with anxieties about trans-corporeal inhalations and Asiatic miasmas. Following Ann Laura Stoler, we might say that real or imagined Asiatic atmospheres embody the *molecular intimacies of empire*:[17] the threats posed to both individual and national bodies by the transpacific circulation of volatile airborne chemicals and microorganisms. Spanning two centuries and an eclectic range of discourses, atmo-orientalism insistently associates olfaction with feelings of repulsion and fear of contagion, while both materially and rhetorically displacing odors propagated by modernization and capital accumulation onto racial "others." If this displacement functions through figurative language (for example, metaphors of contagion and pollution), it nevertheless makes the atmospheric risks of global modernity—the infrastructures and labor regimes that make Asian immigrants disproportionately vulnerable to airborne pathogens and toxins—a key feature in the olfactory racialization of Asians.

Representations of toxic Asiatic atmospheres have their origins in nineteenth-century miasma theory. Health experts believed that diseases were spread through airborne miasmas released by decomposing matter. In their view, one of the most serious urban health threats was "vitiated air," or air thick with human exhalations of "carbonic acid."[18] One of the most widely circulated examples of the dangers of carbonic acid was the story of the "Black Hole of Calcutta," in which the Nawab of Bengal allegedly crowded British prisoners of war into a small cell in 1756. Presuming that most of these prisoners died from suffocation, nineteenth-century ventilation manuals framed the common urban conditions of overcrowding and poor air quality as an Asiatic health condition—one that implicitly legitimized British imperialism as a sanitary and humanitarian project. Yet imperialism and migration to the West brought their own forms of suffocation: one commentary on the ventilation of *Hospitals, Infirmaries, and Dispensaries* cites the Black Hole of Calcutta alongside "the fearful mortality on board Coolie ships" as preeminent cases illustrating the dangers of poorly ventilated spaces.[19]

In the 1870s, even as medical experts were embracing the germ theory of disease, anxieties about vitiated air circulated widely in representations of Pacific Coast Chinatowns as public health threats. As the historian Nayan Shah has documented, San Francisco public health officials accused Chinese immigrants of "willful and diabolical disregard of our sanitary laws" and represented Chinatown as a "plague spot" and "cesspool" characterized by poor hygiene and disease risk.[20] Widespread anxieties about the quality of "Chinese" air were legally encoded in the Sanitary Ordinance passed by San Francisco's Board of Supervisors in 1870. Popularly known as the "cubic air law" or the "pure air law," this ordinance "made it a misdemeanor for anyone to let rooms or apartments that should contain less than five hundred cubic feet of air for each adult person sleeping or dwelling in them and made it a crime as well for any tenant to dwell or sleep in such a room or apartment."[21] As historians have noted, this ostensibly color-blind law was exclusively enforced against the Chinese;[22] in 1877, a white landlord who had rented rooms to Chinese tenants objected that the law was "applied simply and entirely to molest and drive out the Chinese; but if applied to all classes, nearly every block in the city would be found defective. The law is violated by whites as well as Chinese."[23] In 1876, the California legislature passed a statewide version of the law, and New York City enacted a similar law requiring six hundred cubic feet of air space per person in 1879. Planning scholar Ellen Pader explains that "their justification for establishing highly restrictive occupancy limits touted the best scientific evidence of the day—scientific evidence long since disproven. They believed that exhaled breath contained poisonous carbonic acids that created miasmas (impure air). This then created a potentially deadly environment in which people could drown in their own breath if there were insufficient air space to dilute the poison."[24] Despite this medical rationale, experts disagreed as to both the precise cubic footage of air necessary to sustain a healthy life and whether ventilation, rather than air volume, was the critical factor for ensuring health. There were also problems with implementation, as "hundreds of Chinese immigrants were rousted out of beds and jailed for violating this law, [then] packed in jail to the point where they had scarcely 100 cubic feet of air apiece."[25] Anticipating that the jails would not be able to accommodate so many prisoners, Chinese community leaders advised tenants to opt for jail time rather than pay a fine. As Jean Pfaelzer writes, "Many Chinese refused to pay the fines and announced that they would crowd the jail rather than fill the city's coffers—turning the codes into an ironic form of mass civil disobedience."[26] Through these "cubic air" ordinances, the law apprehended Chinese immigrants not as discrete racialized bodies, but as deviant constellations of bodies and air.

In "Monterey-by-the-Smell: Odors and Social Conflict on the California Coastline," historian Connie Chiang details how atmo-orientalism played out in a very different context, among a coastal settlement of Chinese squid fishermen working in Monterey, California. After the Chinese in Monterey were pushed out of conventional fisheries by hostile competitors, accusations of unsustainable fishing, and a series of racially targeted regulations (including a ban on the Chinese bag net and California's 1880 prohibition of fishing by "aliens incapable of voting"), they turned to the business of harvesting and drying squid.[27] Chiang documents how local residents, newspapers, and businesses stigmatized the odors of drying squid, framing these "Chinese" smells as both aesthetically offensive and a threat to public health. Determined to protect the city's property values and burgeoning tourist economy (which attracted visitors who believed the coastal air had health-enhancing effects), city officials declared squid drying a nuisance and ordered the Chinese fishermen to relocate. Racially discriminatory complaints and regulations continued until 1907, when the city of Monterey prohibited squid drying within city limits altogether and effectively terminated an important means of employment for Chinese migrants. By contrast, Chiang observes that in subsequent decades cannery owners and their predominantly white employees successfully responded to complaints about the odors of sardine processing by framing them as a distinctive feature of Monterey's economy and history. The divergent outcomes of these odor complaints demonstrate the efficacy of olfactory racialization, as "those with superior resources and political authority were able to define odors and use them to exercise power over people and their environment."[28]

San Francisco's cubic air ordinance and Monterey's regulations of squid drying gave legal force to diverse health reports, travelogues, political cartoons, and fictional narratives associating Chinese immigrations with unhealthy air and noxious odors. Despite their ostensibly scientific basis in theories of miasma and vitiated air, these accounts of "Chinese" smells are characterized by rhetorical excess in the form of a compulsive and never-quite-successful effort to describe the indescribable. For example, an 1885 municipal report on Chinatown's health conditions renders the popular stereotype of the "inscrutable" Chinese in olfactory terms: "The intermingling odors of cooking, sink, water-closet and urinal, added to the fumes of opium and tobacco smoke and the indescribable, unknowable, all-pervading atmosphere of the Chinese quarter, make up a perfume which can neither be imagined nor described."[29] Although this characteristic description of Chinatown's smells lists numerous details that can be traced to faulty infrastructure, poor building maintenance, and the legacies ("opium and tobacco") of the plantation system, global commerce, and the Opium Wars, the notions of promiscuous "intermingling" and inscrutability frame the odors in terms of deviant practices and anti-Chinese stereotypes. The report goes on to stage a virtual tour of a Chinatown basement, but the tour itself is forestalled by another thick description of the basement's atmosphere:

Now follow your guide through a door, which he forces, into a sleeping-room. *The air is thick with smoke and fetid with an indescribable odor of reeking vapors.* The atmosphere is tangible. Tangible—if we may be licensed to so use the word in this instance—to four out of the five human senses. Tangible to the sight, tangible to the touch, tangible to the taste, and *oh, how tangible to the smell!* You may even hear it as the opium-smoker sucks it through his pipe bowl into his tainted lungs, and *you breathe it yourself as if it were of the substance and tenacity of tar. It is a sense of a horror you have never before experienced, revolting to the last degree, sickening and stupefying.* Through this semi-opaque atmosphere you discover perhaps eight or ten—never less than two or three—bunks, the greater part or all of which are occupied by two persons. . . . Before the door was opened for your entrance every aperture was closed, and here, *had they not been thus rudely disturbed, they would have slept in the dense and poisonous atmosphere until morning, proof against the baneful effects of the carbonic acid gas generated by this human defiance of chemical laws, and proof against all the zymotic poisons that would be fatal to a person of any other race* in an hour of such surroundings and such conditions.[30]

The visual conventions and second-person address of a tenement tour are here interrupted by the trans-corporeal inhalation of a poisoned "atmosphere of horror."[31] Olfaction induces a shift from the rational descriptive voice of the health expert to a sudden exhalation that draws attention to the activity of breathing: "oh, how tangible to the smell!" The momentum of the passage becomes bogged down when "you" are confronted by the affective ("revolting"), physical ("sickening"), and cognitive ("stupefying") effects of breathing a mixture of opium and "carbonic acid gas." The report suggests that the Chinese are biologically distinguished by their putative immunity to this noxious atmosphere, whose poisons "would be fatal to a person of any other race in an hour."

Even the Methodist missionary Otis Gibson, who was known for his sympathy and support for Chinese immigrants, registers a visceral and racialized response to "the Chinese smell" in *The Chinese in America* (1877):

The Chinese smell is a mixture and a puzzle, a marvel and a wonder, a mystery and a disgust; but, nevertheless, you shall find it a palpable fact. The smell of opium raw and cooked, and in the process of cooking, mixed with the smell of cigars, and tobacco leaves wet and dry, dried fish and dried vegetables, and a thousand other indescribable ingredients; all these toned to a certain degree by what may be called a shippy smell, produce a sensation upon the olfactory nerves of the average American, which once experienced will not soon be forgotten.[32]

Gibson's "Chinese smell" consists of an indiscriminate mixture of food and psychoactive drugs, but its most distinctive feature is its inscrutability: a "puzzle," a "mystery," "a thousand other indescribable ingredients." Gibson also assumes a physiological (even if environmentally conditioned) distinction between "the olfactory nerves" of Chinese immigrants and those of "the average American." Yet he tempers these implications of foreignness with more positive affective responses: the smell is unforgettable, "a marvel and a wonder" as well as "a disgust." Along with the smells of cigars and opium the vague "shippy" smell invokes global commerce rather than autochthonous "Chinese" products. The smell of Chinatown, in Gibson's rendering, derives not just from China, but from tobacco plantations (likely located in the United States), Indian opium farms, and transpacific ships (including overcrowded "coolie" ships). Gibson thus attempts to destigmatize atmo-orientalism in the very act of invoking it: for him, the Chinese smell is as alluring as it is repulsive, as cosmopolitan as it is "Chinese." He concludes this paragraph by invoking the ease with which we adapt to new smells: despite his claim that this smell "will not soon be forgotten," he writes, "But never mind, we shall not notice the smell so much when we get a little further into it, and have become a little more accustomed to it."[33]

For those who viewed the Chinese as a health threat, however, to become accustomed to Chinatown's smells would be to neglect important warning signs of a potential disease outbreak. In 1880, the Workingmen's Committee of California published a sixteen-page pamphlet titled "Chinatown Declared a Nuisance!," which cited Chinatown as an atmospheric threat to surrounding neighborhoods: "That this laboratory of infection—situated in the very heart of our city, distilling its deadly poison by day and by night, and sending it forth to contaminate the atmosphere of the streets and houses of a populous, wealthy and intelligent community—is permitted to exist is a disgrace to the civilization of the age."[34] The figuration of Chinatown as a "laboratory" in which poisons are distilled frames Chinese odors not as premodern emanations but as distinctive expressions of a dystopian modernity. Alfred Trumble's *The "Heathen Chinee" at Home and Abroad* (1882) depicts Chinatown's air as a greater and more intractable threat than the notorious London smoke: "Over this blighted heart of a great American city a tainted atmosphere broods like the smoke bank upon the spires of London, or rather like the fever fog that rises over a tropical river when the sun goes down. Only, unlike the fog, it defies the sun, and remains ever in place. This pestilential air wraps Chinatown about in a shroud as deadly as the shirt of Nessus. Born of the foul earth and the fouler living things beneath it, it can only vanish when the last house in Chinatown is razed and the last clod of its corrupted soul purified by [sentence unfinished]."[35] With an atmosphere tainted by industrial, "tropical," subterranean, and monstrous (in Greek mythology, the shirt of Nessus contaminated Heracles with the venom of the Hydra and the blood of a centaur) elements, Chinatown posed a mythic threat to the bodily and racial integrity of white Americans.[36]

Writing in the *Medical Sentinel* in 1903, Oregon-based physician Woods Hutchinson cited overcrowding and poor ventilation as health threats reminiscent of the Black Hole of Calcutta: "There are rooms not to exceed 10x12 feet, which have neither windows nor air shafts, nor connection with the outside air of any sort or description, save a door opening into a dark passage barely thirty inches wide and thirty feet long, which opens into a very moderately lighted hallway. In such a Black Hole of Calcutta as this, from five to seven Chinamen will live, cook, eat and sleep."[37] Hutchinson blamed the Chinese inhabitants—rather than landlords, economic conditions, and the widespread purges that led many Chinese to migrate to urban settlements in the first place[38]—for these conditions, and contrasted their "greed for space" with the deodorization measures of city officials:

> The roosts which have been built from the back wall of one biulding [sic] to the back wall of the next by the Chinese in their greed for space, absolutely shutting off what little air penetrated to the already squalid courts below, have been torn out bodily, new ventilators and plumbing are being put in, cellars are being filled up, and everything is being dusted, where dryness will avail, with chloride of lime, and drenched, where moisture is

more suitable, with strong solutions of carbolic acid and bichloride. The seven and thirty separate smells of Chinatown have all been drowned in one grand olfactory delirium of chloride of lime and carbolic acid. Never was Chinatown so free from vermin.[39]

Despite these successes, Hutchinson echoes Trumble in affirming that there is only one way to eradicate the "problem of Chinatown" for public health: "It is my profound conviction from a careful daily inspection of the district covering nine consecutive days, that Chinatown can never be cleaned except by fire. Sterilization by dry heat at 400 degrees Fahrenheit is, in my judgment, the only cure for its filthy condition."[40] Hutchinson likely had in mind the 1900 conflagration that burned down Honolulu's Chinatown, which began as a controlled fire ordered by public health officials in an effort to control a bubonic plague epidemic.[41] Following the 1906 San Francisco earthquake and fire (which destroyed much of Chinatown), city officials proposed to move the Chinese settlement to Hunter's Point, "an industrial district of slaughterhouses and tenements south of downtown." Although it was prevented by the intervention of China's consul-general, this planned relocation was based on the assumption that the malodorous Chinese would not suffer greatly from being moved to a distant, noxious neighborhood.[42] Throughout the Pacific region, anti-Chinese activists mobilized rhetorics of nuisance and contagion against Chinese residents and businessmen, at times calling for the institution of an official "smelling committee."[43]

In addition to legitimizing laws intended to discipline and displace Chinese immigrants, public health discourses racialized them as an environmentally insensitive population. These discourses built on scientific and popular accounts of "Asian unimpressibility"[44] that represented the Chinese as impassive, insensitive to pain, and indifferent to environmental conditions such as poor ventilation and overcrowding. For example, the American Board of Commissioners for Foreign Missions missionary Arthur Henderson Smith's influential book *Chinese Characteristics* (1894) claims that Chinese bodies are able to tolerate the most filthy and toxic surroundings: "The Chinese race, though apparently in a condition of semi-strangulation, seems to itself comparatively comfortable, which is but to say that the Chinese standard of comfort and convenience, and the standard to which we are accustomed, are widely variant. . . . The Chinese has learned to accommodate himself to his environment."⁴⁵ Although it was immiseration and inequality that constrained Chinese immigrants to inhabit substandard and often noxious spaces, public health discourses frequently reframed harmful environments resulting from structural inequality as racial characteristics. This effectively blamed the victims of racial and environmental inequality for living in overcrowded, unventilated spaces, just as the state attempted to ameliorate environmental harm by punishing individual tenants rather than regulating faulty spaces and infrastructure.

At once echoing and inspiring public health discourses about Asiatic atmospheres, literary representations of the Yellow Peril mobilized atmospheric representation—as well as supposed physical and moral attributes—to depict racial difference as an insidious threat to environmental health. Alongside the visual signs of poor hygiene—such as worn clothing, stains, and the presence of vermin—that appear throughout this literature, olfaction plays a subtle yet powerful role in evoking readers' repulsion. Whereas vision preserves a sense of distance, smell calls forth feelings of vulnerability and terror at the specters of contagion and uncontrollable material intimacy. Frank Norris—whose fascination with noxious smells was discussed in chapter 2—repeatedly associates Chinese sailors with discomfiting odors in *Moran of the Lady Letty* (1898). In her groundbreaking critique of the novel's racializing representations of "Asiatic coolieism," Lye underscores Norris's depiction of "coolie" physiognomy and swarming masses.⁴⁶ These racializing techniques are enhanced by the novel's olfactory horrors. Descending into the forecastle, the novel's protagonist is struck by the noxious air surrounding the "Chinamen": "A single reeking lamp swung with the swinging of the schooner over the centre of the group, and long after Wilbur could remember the grisly scene—the punk-sticks, the bread-pan full of hunks of meat, the horrid close and oily smell, and the circle of silent, preoccupied Chinese."⁴⁷ In a novel that moves from perfumed drawing rooms to a gas explosion, to a "rancid" schooner bent on harvesting reeking "yellow oil" from shark livers, to an interracial battle over an aromatic lump of ambergris, the "horrid" smell of the foc'sle puts Chinese laborers on a continuum with industrial accidents, class stratification, environmental depredation, and brutal extraction processes characteristic of the capitalist economy. Through a proleptic reference to Wilbur's remembrance of this moment "long after," Norris both acknowledges and leverages olfaction's powerful hippocampal connections with memory; the passage's lurid olfactory details endeavor to make this "grisly scene" just as unforgettable for the novel's readers.

If other literary evocations of Chinese immigration are less obsessed with smell, they nevertheless invoke Asiatic atmospheres at pivotal moments. Susan Lanser and Erica Fretwell have suggested that Charlotte Perkins Gilman's "The Yellow Wallpaper" (1892) draws on a broad cultural pattern associating the color yellow with disease and degeneration.[48] The wallpaper's troubling "yellow smell"—which could literally be making the narrator ill as a result of dust or pigment inhalation—thus invokes multiple anxieties about race and immigration, including Yellow Peril discourses prevalent "in California, where Gilman lived while writing 'The Yellow Wallpaper.'"[49] "Chun Ah Chun" (1910), Jack London's rags-to-riches story based on the life of the Hawai'i-based merchant and coolie importer Chun Afong, deploys olfactory memories to mark Ah Chun's unassimilability: "As the years came upon him, he found himself harking back more and more to his own kind. The reeking smells of the Chinese quarter were spicy to him. He sniffed them with satisfaction as he passed along the street, for in his mind they carried him back to the narrow tortuous alleys of Canton swarming with life and movement."[50] Despite his status as a member of the Hawaiian Yacht Club, a millionaire, and a parent of mixed-race children educated at elite US colleges, Ah Chun's exposure to these "reeking smells" inspires an irresistible atavistic "desire to return to his Chinese flesh-pots."[51] Even the 1897 Broadway production of Francis Powers's *The First Born*—a romantic, yellowface melodrama set in San Francisco that was intended to depict Chinese characters in sympathetic terms—enveloped its audience in the smell of Chinese "punk"; as the *New York Journal*'s critic reported, "The theatre was bathed in this hideous tinkative [*sic*] odor of incense, and during the long overture, you sat there getting fainter and fainter."[52]

Twentieth-century Yellow Peril fictions imagine a striking range of atmo-orientalist plots. Sax Rohmer's *The Insidious Dr. Fu-Manchu* (1913; Figure 4.2), which introduced the twentieth century's most notorious serial Asiatic villain, begins with a corpse murdered through the agency of an envelope perfumed with the essential oil of a rare Burmese orchid. Later, a sarcophagus emits a "green mist" that "seemed to be alive," kill-

Figure 4.2. *The Insidious Dr. Fu Manchu* (1913; New York: Pyramid, 1970). The scenes depicted on this cover image are connected by the ominous gas that appears to emerge from Fu Manchu's mouth and nostrils.

ing two men and debilitating another. Doctor Petrie and detective Nay-land Smith themselves are almost killed by the same means—"a sort of yellowish-green cloud—an oily vapor."[53] After escaping the mist, Petrie explains, "'It is a poisonous gas!' I said hoarsely; 'in many respects iden-tical with *chlorine*, but having unique properties which prove it to be something else—God and Fu-Manchu, alone know what! It is the fumes of chlorine that kill the men in the bleaching powder works. We have been blind—I particularly. Don't you see? There was no one in the sar-cophagus, Smith, but there was enough of that fearful stuff to have suffo-cated a regiment!'" (*FM*, 157). If Petrie understands this murderous mist through an analogy with chlorine gas, he also insists on its difference—a difference that can be comprehended only by "God and Fu-Manchu." These mysterious "unique properties" simultaneously invoke and am-plify a common cause of industrial sickness and death ("the fumes of chlorine that kill the men in the bleaching powder works"). Fu Manchu's Asiatic atmosphere both spectacularly stands in for and displaces ev-eryday occupational health hazards. Both this "yellowish-green cloud" and industrial chlorine fumes share an insidious and nearly invisible materiality indicated here by the terms "blind" and "see": after killing and dispersing, the gas leaves "no clew remaining—except the smell" (*FM*, 158). Smell thus turns out to be the most perceptible quality of "the ghastly media employed by the Chinaman" (*FM*, 148). Rohmer fills his later Fu Manchu novels with noxious and "miasmatic" smells, framing the detective's work as a project of racial deodorization.[54] If, according to Peter Sloterdijk, the introduction of gas warfare in 1915 precipitated a new ontological understanding of humans as continuous with and dependent on a "breathable" surrounding atmosphere, it is notewor-thy that Yellow Peril narratives had begun imagining such scenarios of "atmo-terrorism" by the late nineteenth century.[55]

Cherie Priest's critically acclaimed steampunk novel *Boneshaker* (2009) attests to atmo-orientalism's persistence in twenty-first-century genre fiction. *Boneshaker* is set in an alternate nineteenth-century time-line in which Seattle has been devastated by the release of a toxic under-ground gas called the Blight, unwittingly released by a massive drilling machine. Possibly inspired by the Asiatic zombification gas featured in Victor Halperin's *Revolt of the Zombies* (1936),[56] the Blight transforms those exposed to it into "rotters"—hordes of fast-moving zombies who traverse the ruins of the city's downtown. Seattle's central blocks have been walled off, and only a few intrepid outcasts—along with a settlement of "Chinamen"—have chosen to remain in ventilated underground areas beneath the contaminated zone. The novel has been praised for its "superb world-building," which produces dynamic steampunk scenarios in which air pumps, airtight curtains, and a panoply of stylish gas masks keep the reader's attention focused on the fragility of breath.[57] However, *Boneshaker*'s world making turns out to be entirely dependent on its marginalized "Chinamen," who with few exceptions appear as deindividualized hordes surrounded by dirty air.[58] When the protagonist, Briar, first encounters them,

> It felt like a dozen men, but it was only three or four.
> They were Asian—Chinese, she guessed, since two of the men had partially shaved heads with braids like Fang's. . . .
> Even through the charcoal filter in her mask, she could sense the soot choking the air. It smothered her, even though it couldn't really be smothering her, could it? And it watered her eyes, though it couldn't really reach them.[59]

Here, the undifferentiated Chinese working the furnaces are immediately contiguous with soot-filled air and its uncertain ("real," imagined, or psychosomatic?) effects on Briar's body. In an interesting departure from atmo-orientalist conventions, it turns out that the Chinese are actually responsible for purifying the interior air of the Blight. That is, they immerse themselves in soot and dirt so that everyone in the sealed-off areas can breathe easier: "Those are the furnace rooms and the bellows. The Chinamen work them; they're the ones who keep the air down here good and clean, far as it ever gets good and clean. They pump it down here from up top, by these big ol' tubes they made" (*B*, 128). On the one hand, these "Chinamen" sustain the novel's world by maintaining the breathability of its setting. On the other hand, Priest's characterization of these plural "Chinamen" renders them analogous to the novel's hordes of atmospherically produced zombies. As Briar and her son escape a zombie attack near the end of the novel, they see a group of "masked men who cared nothing for whatever fight still raged beneath the station" impassively lighting bonfires to keep the zombies away from the Chinese quarter (*B*, 389). Even as they cleanse the air and protect their settlement from zombies, the mechanical behavior of these faceless "Chinamen" already approximates that of the zombies. Both their furnaces and their bonfires evoke the plight of "reflexive modernity" diagnosed by Beck:[60] in the course of cleansing the air and repelling the zombies, they fill the air with smoke and soot. Not surprisingly, when polarized lenses make it possible for Priest's characters to see the Blight, its appearance recalls that of Fu Manchu's fatal mist: "Even in trace amounts it would appear as a yellowish-greenish haze that oozed and dripped" (*B*, 45).

Atmo-orientalism continues to play a powerful role in contemporary public discourse. In *Animacies*, Mel Chen argues that 2007 US media reports about toxic lead in Chinese toys racialized the substance as a foreign threat to the integrity and normativity of white children's bodies. This racialization of Chinese lead sustained an "exceptionalist" view of the United States as victim while obscuring the health threats that toy factories pose to workers and neighboring communities in China.[61] As Chen explains, "Mass media stories pitched Chinese environmental threats neither as harmful to actual Chinese people or landscapes, nor as products of a global industrialization that the United States itself eagerly promotes, but as invasive dangers to the U.S. territory from other national territories. These environmental toxins were supposed to be 'there' but were found 'here.'"[62] A similar dynamic occurs in media accounts of noxious air. For example, Michael Ziser and Julie Sze have critiqued the fascination with "Chinese smog" that characterized US media coverage of the 2008 Summer Olympics in Beijing. While smog certainly posed a serious health risk in many Chinese cities, Ziser and Sze incisively observe that coding that smog as "Chinese"—particularly when a vast proportion of Chinese carbon emissions are a byproduct of production for export to the United States and Western Europe—"[displaces] Western responsibility for historical carbon emissions onto a convenient geopolitical scapegoat and rival."[63] A 2009 headline announcing that "Toxic Chinese Drywall Turns U.S. Homes into Smelly Cancer Traps" illustrates how environmental risk continues to be racialized through perceptions of Asiatic odors transgressing the boundaries of American homes and bodies.[64] Atmo-orientalism also animates neighbors' disproportionate hostility toward Asian restaurant and factory smells throughout the United States. Recent nuisance complaints against Chinese restaurants,[65] the Wat Mongkolratanaram Buddhist temple in Berkeley (which hosts a Thai brunch on weekends to raise funds), and Huy Fong Foods in Irwindale, California (the manufacturer of Sriracha Sauce), register "resentment of the presence of Asianness . . . through a refusal of the visceral and purported offensiveness of Asian odors."[66] While it is vital to take such nuisance complaints as potential indicators of environmental health risks, the genealogy of atmo-orientalist discourse that I have traced raises questions about the subjective (and racializing) aspects of odor and risk perception as well as the complex ways in which risk perception interacts with the ongoing production of racial difference on both material and representational levels. The following sections consider how Asian diasporic artists have mobilized olfactory metaphors and materials in efforts to reshape public perceptions of race and risk.

Edith Maude Eaton / Sui Sin Far's Deodorization Narratives

Atmo-orientalism provides a crucial context for understanding the hitherto overlooked motifs of fragrance and fresh air in the writings of mixed-race Asian North American author Edith Maude Eaton / Sui Sin Far. A stenographer, journalist, and fiction writer who spent her career working in various cities in Canada, Jamaica, and the United States, Eaton was the first North American author of Chinese descent to publish a collection of short stories. Best known for her "Chinatown" stories collected in *Mrs. Spring Fragrance* (1912), Eaton's writings thematized air quality and its health effects across diverse geographies, including Jamaica, urban North American Chinatowns, and a range of sites in the US and Canadian countryside. Although descriptions of air appear to linger in the background of Eaton's Chinatown writings as signs of exoticism and "local color," her writings about Chinese immigrant communities and the North American countryside subtly reorient public perceptions of Chinese immigrants' olfactory experiences and desires. Judith Fetterley and Marjorie Pryse have persuasively framed Eaton as a writer whose critical, placed-based practice aligns with the category of "regionalism"; however, her writings have not to date been engaged by scholars of the environmental humanities.[67] Attending to Eaton's literary atmospherics—and particularly her appeals to olfaction—illuminates

Figure 4.3. *Mrs. Spring Fragrance* cover (Chicago: A. C. McClurg, 1912).

the ecocritical stakes of her work as well as the vital ways in which her representations of urban and rural environments convey critical perspectives on immigration, race, and empire. By mapping the racially uneven distribution of breathable atmospheres across urban, national, and transnational scales, Eaton directs readers' attention to political questions concerning mobility and access that are occluded by atmo-orientalist discourse.

Racializing descriptions of Chinese smells provide an environmental health context for interpreting Eaton's deployments of floral iconography. Whereas critics tend to associate the flowers imprinted into the spine, title page, and every page of *Mrs. Spring Fragrance* as signs of Eaton's auto-orientalist and self-feminizing "exoticizing aesthetic,"[68] Eaton's prolific flower imagery would have appealed to turn-of-the-century readers on an olfactory level as well as a visual one (Figure 4.3). As Melanie Kiechle has documented, middle-class American women in the nineteenth century were well versed in the use of aromatic flowers to improve indoor air quality. Domestic manuals instructed women in the arts of potpourri, planting flowerbeds as "olfactory buffers" against urban odors, and sweetening domestic air by placing flowers near doors and windows.[69] Because miasma theory's associations between smell and disease persisted even after experts embraced germ theory, "pleasant smells were not merely an aesthetic preference, but healthful agents," and "sweet plants released a fragrance that improved the air of the home and helped women protect their families' health."[70] According to Classen, Victorian writers extended these putative health effects to character traits, "associat[ing] floral odors with virtue and traditional values."[71] In the 1870s and 1880s, when the young Eaton attended Sunday school and socialized with missionaries, philanthropic middle-class women organized Flower Missions to distribute fragrant bouquets to impoverished inhabitants of urban hospitals, prisons, asylums, schools, and tenement houses.[72] For the Flower Missions, "The benefit of flowers was as obvious as that of day excursions to the shore or mountains: a change of air improved health."[73] Eaton's pen name, Sui Sin Far—which literally translates as "water fragrance flower" or the narcissus flower—underscores the notion of "fragrance" invoked by her book's title. Although it is most commonly associated with visual seduction in the myth of Narcissus, the narcissus flower has long been celebrated for its sweet scent.[74] Widely used in the production of perfumes, the fragrant narcissus situated at the figurative threshold of *Mrs. Spring Fragrance* announces the book's project of discursively deodorizing Chinatown. Eaton's authorial pseudonym and floral iconography strategically leverage the common floral imagery of nineteenth-century sentimental fiction in the service of her stories' critical reframings of smell and inhalation. These floral motifs—which extend across many of Eaton's stories— may be visually self-orientalizing, but the scents they invoke challenge atmo-orientalism's tendency to blame environmental health risks on the Chinese. Like many racializing discourses, atmo-orientalism is a binary formation: it encompasses both the stigmatization of "bad" odors and the fetishization (and plundering) of exotic Asian scents. If Eaton strategically appropriates the latter in her appeals to the idea of feminized, Asian "fragrance," she tempers these with references to nationalist (and, as I show below, settler colonial) ideas about pure wilderness air.

Eaton's most extensive deployment of air as a plot element occurs in her 1898 story "Away Down in Jamaica" (which she did not include in *Mrs. Spring Fragrance*).[75] Written over a decade before the publication of *Mrs. Spring Fragrance* and one of the few stories Eaton published under her own name, "Away Down" draws on the author's experience working as a court stenographer and reporter in Jamaica from 1896 to 1897. The story's plot traces the erotic relations and frustrations of four characters: the domineering white businessman Wycliff Walker, his reluctant fiancée Kathleen Harold, a court stenographer named Everett who is hopelessly in love with Kathleen, and Walker's jilted mulatta lover Clarissa. The story culminates with the deaths of Everett and Kathleen: just after Everett succumbs to a constitutional disease attributed to Jamaica's climate, Kathleen is killed by her repeated exposures to toxic flowers gifted by Clarissa. Assisted by a local "Obi man" or Obeah practitioner, Clarissa's revenge against both Walker and Kathleen—the story's embodiments of US neoimperial commerce—has been persuasively interpreted as an act of anti-imperial resistance.[76] However, Eaton's allegory of resistance on the part of racialized women, Obeah practitioners, and Jamaica's climate relies on colonial traditions of geographical determinism and "moral climatology" that attributed racial and moral differences to the effects of tropical climates.[77] In this story written early in her career as a fiction writer, Eaton depicts Jamaica's "tropical climate" and "hot, dusty

streets" as health hazards: long before Clarissa's poisoned flowers kill
Kathleen, Everett has contracted a tropical fever figured as a "poison" in
his veins.[78] In depicting Jamaica's atmosphere as a source of anticolonial
resistance, Eaton perhaps unwittingly reinscribes beliefs concerning the
racialized toxicity of tropical atmospheres as well as criminalizing associations of Obeah with the use of poisons.[79]

Mrs. Spring Fragrance takes a different approach to atmospheric
representation. The collection's title echoes Eaton's earlier sketch titled
"Spring Impressions" (1890), which describes a time of year "when the
spring fragrance and freshness fill the air; when all nature rejoices in
returning life."[80] While such a passage might sound like a naïve description of an idealized "nature," associating the Chinese with fresh air and
its associated health effects quietly undercuts the demonization of urban
Chinese atmospheres. Eaton, who suffered from rheumatic fever and
writes in her memoir that she was "ordered beyond the Rockies by the
doctor, who declare[d] that I will never again regain my strength in the
East,"[81] was acutely aware of medical beliefs associating climatological
differences with health and disease. Eaton's deodorization of Chinatown
is most evident in her omission of the olfactory and atmospheric conventions of Chinatown description: while she occasionally describes
characters smoking and burning incense, her stories about the Chinese
seldom describe unpleasant smells.

"'Its Wavering Image'" (1912) is unique among the stories in presenting
an account of Chinatown's unpleasant atmosphere. This story, however,
subtly inverts the atmo-orientalist demonization of Chinese interiors by
describing a white journalist moving from Chinatown's public spaces
into the pleasant atmosphere of a Chinese home: "After the heat and
dust and unsavoriness of the highways and byways of Chinatown, the
young reporter who had been sent to find a story, had stepped across the
threshold of a cool, deep room, fragrant with the odor of dried lilies and
sandalwood, and found Pan."[82] Whereas the Chinese home is "fragrant"
with the smells of nature, the "dust and unsavoriness" of Chinatown's
streets are products of municipal neglect: as Shah notes, "The municipality did have responsibility for street cleaning, but often it blatantly ignored the condition of Chinatown streets. Both the influential physician
Dr. Arthur B. Stout and the special police officer George Duffield testi-
fied that the city superintendent of streets ignored Chinatown streets

despite tax contributions by Chinese residents."[83] When the reporter
later publishes a sensationalistic article exposing Chinatown's mysteries,
he presumably omits this sensory distinction between the municipality's
stink and the fragrance of the Chinese home.

Whereas "Away Down" underscored the toxicity of Jamaica's climate,
Mrs. Spring Fragrance emphasizes Chinese immigrants' restricted access
to the invigorating influence of fresh air. Eaton offers a lyrical account
of the countryside in the story "Tian Shan's Kindred Spirit" (1912). Here,
her prose uncharacteristically echoes turn-of-the-century wilderness
discourse: "The air was fresh, sweet, and piny. As Tian Shan and Fin
Fan walked, they chatted gaily . . . of the brilliant landscape, the sun
shining through a grove of black-trunked trees with golden leaves, the
squirrels that whisked past them, the birds twittering and soliloquizing
over their vanishing homes, and many other objects of nature."[84] Eaton's choice of names—another idiosyncrasy that critics have framed as
a self-exoticizing tactic—associates her protagonists with their desires
for fresh air: "Tian Shan" evokes the Chinese for "heavenly mountains,"
where "tian" is the Chinese word for sky; "Fin Fan" invokes the English word "fan," along with associations of air flow and ventilation. Soon
after this idyllic scene, Eaton reminds us that access to mobility, public
space, and fresh air was racially uneven when Fin Fan reads that her
beloved Tian Shan has been captured: "A Chinese, who has been unlawfully breathing United States air for several years, was captured last
night crossing the border" ("TS," 124).[85] Whereas the phrase "unlawfully
breathing United States air" might pass as another instance of Eaton's
self-exoticizing prose (in which such metaphors indicate the difference
of Chinese speech without rendering it as dialect), it also suggests that
if Chinese immigrants frequently lived amid unhealthful urban air, it
was in part because their capacities to reside and move around outside
of urban enclaves were severely curtailed by both legal restrictions and
extralegal violence.[86] Before Chinese immigrants (many of whom had
arrived as miners and railroad laborers) were forced out of the countryside and smaller towns by the Foreign Miners' Tax, racial purges,
vagrancy laws, and Alien Land Laws,[87] they had considerably greater
access to fresh air: as a Chinese "Forty-Niner" interviewed by Eaton recounts, "The new life [in California] brought with [it] renewed health
and strength. In the old California days the Chinese lived and worked

in the open air . . . the sunshine and freshness of this western country transformed me both physically and mentally."[88] For Chinese workers driven from outdoor work and countryside settlements to urban enclaves, the problem of noxious air stems not from any racial propensity for poor hygiene but from the racial violence that has driven them out of "physically and mentally" salubrious environments.

If "Tian Shan's Kindred Spirit" critiques legal and extralegal restrictions on Chinese immigrants' access to fresh country air, it nevertheless relies on the "romantic anti-capitalist" and settler colonial ideology of wilderness as an invigorating retreat from the vitiating influence of urban spaces and industrial production.[89] When Tian Shan makes a daring crossing at the US-Canadian border "in an Indian war canoe" ("TS," 121), the repurposed (and pacified) war canoe works to indigenize and masculinize the Chinese immigrant as a skilled outdoorsman. Eaton's "Wing Sing of Los Angeles on His Travels" (1904), a fictionalized travelogue recently recovered by Mary Chapman, stages the entanglements of fresh air and settler colonialism by depicting a Chinese merchant on a transcontinental railroad trip across Canada and the United States. Apparently unaware of the histories of anti-Chinese purges and exclusion legislation in both nations, Wing repeatedly expresses his appreciation for the freshness of the western air. "I hear the men in the next [*sic*] speak of the air—how clear and how sweet it is—of the forests, how grand and how beautiful of the rivers and streams, of the birds and the fish, big game and small game, of all the sport to be had in this region— and I think how excellently beneficial to the mind and the body must be the days that are passed by the shores of this lake."[90] In passages like this, Wing's explicit mimicry of white travelers' identifications and desires underscores his complicities and limitations as a narrator. Wing's exuberant accounts of western air support his blithe speculations about a future in which Chinese farmers settle throughout the prairies: "He [an Irish traveling companion] say plenty room for poor people to come and take farm and grow rich in this and, so I think when I go back to China I tell some of my countrymen to come. My countrymen good farmers, make things grow in all land they touch. I think the wheat land the same to the white man as the rice land to the Chinaman" ("WS," 209). If Wing's fantasy of Chinese settlement elides the history of anti-Chinese violence and land-owning prohibitions directed against Chinese settlers in the western United States, it nevertheless participates in settler fantasies of uninhabited land and inexhaustible clean air.[91]

At times, Wing's assimilationist desires for farmland and fresh air give way to critical insights about the imperial nation's enclosure of salubrious atmospheres. In addition to eliding ongoing settler colonial violence, the conception of nature as a pure and invigorating "wilderness" is also conscripted into sustaining imperial wars abroad. The section titled "Why American Soldier Is Nurtured" condenses complex and multifaceted histories of race and empire: "Much exhilarated am I by the pure, rare atmosphere. . . . There is also a fort call Fort Harrison now occupied by United States colored troops. Hot water springs for the good of the people that cold water spring not suit are situate in convenient position and I am inform that the American government think to buy them out for a soldiers' sanitarium, for the American government want try hard to keep soldiers alive for the foreign governments to kill" ("WS," 236). Named after president William Henry Harrison—who was best known for his prominent role in battles against Native Americans—Fort Harrison was built to consolidate military forces that had been more dispersed during the American Indian Wars. In 1902, the First Battalion of the African American Twenty-Fourth Infantry Regiment was housed at the fort after serving in the Philippine-American War and before being redeployed to the Philippines in December 1905.[92] Eaton's account of this fort underscores how both wilderness and racialized populations could be incorporated into projects of imperial violence: Black soldiers fought in both American Indian Wars and the Philippine-American War; and according to Wing's source, the government was interested in instrumentalizing the "natural" hot springs and mountain air near the fort as tools for rehabilitating and recreating imperial soldiers. If imperial violence might recreate African Americans as valued elements of the national body, then settler colonialism (at least in the imagined absence of anti-Chinese immigration and land ownership laws) seems to Wing a promising strategy for incorporating Chinese farmers into Canadian and US national narratives. The shift from "clean" air to "pure, rare atmosphere" here is telling: here the atmosphere is not an infinite and freely available resource but a "rare" commodity available only to those deemed deserving. The air's healthful "purity" invokes eugenic ideas associating wilderness experiences with racial purity: as Bruce Braun writes in his groundbreaking analysis of American articulations of nature, race, and risk, "Nature . . . served as a purification machine, a place where people became white."[93] For Wing, the deodorizing influence of the countryside's "pure, rare atmosphere" promises to render Chinese immigrants useful to the imperial settler nation.

Eaton's deodorized representations of Chinatown and Chinese immigrants' excursions into the countryside combat "romantic anticapitalism" by refuting its opposition between Asiatic abstraction and settler colonial "nature." In Eaton's stories, Chinese households are suffused with carefully curated fragrance, and Chinese immigrants yearn for the physical, mental, and emotional health benefits afforded by access to fresh air. Yet the ironic tensions between antiracism and settler colonialism in "Wing Sing" point to the limitations of this deodorizing strategy: namely, its complicities with settler colonialism and overseas imperialism. If Wing undoes the whiteness of "wilderness" by depicting Chinese bodies in the countryside, he does so by simultaneously reinscribing fantasies of the unsettled frontier as a freely available space for the deodorization and invigoration of settler bodies corrupted by urban modernity. The following section considers how olfactory artist Anicka Yi mobilizes atmospheric promiscuity—as opposed to notions of atmospheric purity—to formulate a convivial aesthetic response to atmo-orientalism. Whereas Eaton frequently deploys deodorized, middle-class spaces and bodies in an effort to represent the Chinese as assimilable subjects, Yi employs discomfiting odors to stage assimilation as a multidirectional hybridizing process that transgresses the boundaries of race, class, gender, and species.

Atmospheric Conviviality

Underlying atmo-orientalism's racial stigmatization is an anxious awareness of the risky, trans-corporeal exchanges of matter between bodies and environments theorized by Alaimo. Olfaction necessarily puts the smeller's body at risk: to smell something is to become vulnerable to it. Historically, this vulnerability has been distributed along the lines of race, class, and gender: as Neel Ahuja writes, "Atmosphere names a space of unpredictable touching, attractions, and subtle violences—a space at once geophysical and affective, informed by yet exploding representation, a space where the violences of late-carbon liberalism subtly reform racialized sensoria through shifting scales of interface."[94] But what if olfaction's capacities for violence and vulnerability are also occasions for transformed capacities of perception and empathy—for the reconception of bodies in terms of molecular exchanges and the expansion of material and ethical relations across racial and geographic lines? What if empire's molecular intimacies could be experienced not only in terms of toxic menace but also as emergent and experimental modes of conviviality? As Mawani notes in a nuanced reading of Fanon's comments on atmosphere, "The racial atmosphere may be weighted, but its shifting properties open spontaneous possibilities for resistance and change."[95] Ahuja, too, suggests that atmosphere materializes queer intimacies as well as environmental violence: "In ever more precarious intimacy with the shrinking number of living species, we inhabit a queer atmosphere in which the ether of the everyday is marked by senses of transformation and crisis."[96]

The perceptual and ethical intimacies enacted by shared atmospheres lie at the heart of Anicka Yi's olfactory artworks, which deploy smell to make an irresistible claim on our bodies—a claim that is no sooner perceived than inhaled and internalized. For Yi, even strange or unpleasant smells have a seductive edge: "Growing up in a Korean-American household, I was immersed in pungent kitchen aromas. The smell of fermenting kimchi and *doenjang* [soybean paste] seemed to sink into our furniture, clothing, and hair. As a child, I often felt ashamed of my family's olfactory world. I wanted to smell American, which I imagined would involve becoming perfectly odorless. But shame works in mysterious ways: the strongest odors disgusted but also excited me, eliciting a tingling response."[97] As a Korean American artist, Yi is conscious of atmo-orientalism's flexibility—its capacity (shared with many other anti-Asian discourses) to expand from its earlier focus on (primarily) Chinese immigrants to a pan-ethnic framing of olfaction applied to new waves of Asian immigrants and refugees across the twentieth and twenty-first centuries. Yi's artistic production frequently reframes expectations about Asian diasporic odors by drawing out the seductive, "tingling" qualities of scent. Yi's works have leveraged olfaction to convey—in material, sensuous terms—a striking range of subjects, including the personal experience of the exiled Japanese Red Army founder and leader Fusako

Shigenobu (Anicka Yi and Maggie Peng, *Shigenobu Twilight*, 2008), the sensory dissonance of beautiful yet pungent tempura-fried flowers (*Sister*, 2011), and the blended olfactory signatures of the Gagosian Gallery and bacterial cultures sampled from a network of one hundred women in Yi's social circles (*You Can Call Me F*, 2015, discussed in chapter 3). In works such as these, Yi explores "a growing curiosity about alternative paths, about other senses. . . . I want to shift perception through the other senses and influence the forces that compose the field in which perception occurs. We've lost our empathic core. It's through the other senses that I believe we can try to rebuild this core."[98] Whereas vision has been privileged within a post-Kantian aesthetics of disinterestedness and autonomy, smell's immersive and visceral qualities make empathy unavoidable.

But Yi is also acutely aware of smell's capacities for menace and estrangement. As she concluded a meeting with Johanna Burton, the artist shared that she was "headed to the Abercrombie & Fitch around the corner to place a stink bomb and watch the place clear out (she does not consider this activity artwork, but a social service)."[99] Whether or not she followed through on this plan, the stink bomb frames the olfactory as a powerful site of social intervention. Until 2017, when it was replaced with a gender-neutral bergamot scent, Abercrombie & Fitch stores were all scented with "Fierce"—an overstated "generation-defining scent" that, according to *Vice* writer Amanda Arnold, epitomized "teen masculinity."[100] A stink bomb set off at one of these stores would have undercut an atmospheric brand that targeted teenagers with images and smells of toxic masculinity. As Burton remarks, "If you want to challenge the prevailing social order, mess with its eco-system."[101] For Yi, olfaction's power lies in its capacity to convey both menace and seduction, thus reorienting breathers' ideas about beauty, risk, and intimacy.

Yi's work with olfaction frequently intersects with her interest in bacteria. She notes that bacteria first entered her practice spontaneously, when it took over an installation involving raw tofu; subsequently, she became interested in its capacities as a material whose emergence and transformations require not artistic control but accommodation.[102] Yi speaks of bacteria as a companion species that is profoundly enmeshed with human embodiment and experience: "The human body contains one hundred trillion microorganisms in its intestines. The level of microbial activity in the gut is like a forgotten organ. The microbes can teach me what I am, what we are."[103] Working with bacteria—and inhaling it when experiencing Yi's art—puts one's microbiome, and thus one's body, mind, and mood, at risk of unpredictable transformations. Identity, or "what I am," can be fully realized only through this process of engaging and accommodating trans-corporeal exchange. In her illuminating commentary on Yi's works, critic Rachel Lee theorizes the artist's interests in foods, odors, and microbes in terms of metabolic processes that have profound and strikingly varied geographical, bodily, and genetic consequences: "As the arena of biochemical processes that translate cues from the environment into subcellular activities (e.g., tightening or relaxing chromatin, blocking or leaving accessible promoter genes), metabolism bespeaks the molecular choreography that produces a variety of phenotypical patterns out of relatively stable (conserved) genetic material."[104]

Life Is Cheap (2017), Yi's Hugo Boss Prize installation at the Solomon R. Guggenheim Museum, deploys olfaction's potentialities for estrangement and empathy against entrenched discourses of atmo-orientalism. Whereas culturally specific culinary smells such as kimchi and *doenjang* exemplify broad patterns of olfactory "othering," Yi's installation centers hypermodern, dystopian scenarios of urban stench, fumigation, and factory labor that are more distinctive of atmo-orientalist discourse. *Life Is Cheap* consists of three interlinked works that incorporate the intermingled scents and bacterial cultures of carpenter ants and the Asian diaspora. The installation begins in an entryway, where three gas canisters release the blended scents of Asian American women (sampled from Manhattan's Chinatown and Koreatown) and carpenter ants. By sourcing scents from Asian American women, Yi moves her earlier exploration of feminist ferment (in *You Can Call Me F*) into intersectional terrain; this acknowledges Asian women's particular vulnerabilities to olfactory stigmatization as well as to labor exploitation and occupational and environmental toxins. Along with the fumigation canisters, a metal gate gives this piece the appearance of a detainment facility, evoking both contemporary and historical patterns of racial xenophobia, detention, and deportation leveled against immigrants of color: as Lee suggests, the mise-en-scène alludes to "late 19th and early 20th century sanitary techniques of delousing the presumed 'dirty' immigrant

Figure 4.4. Anicka Yi, *Immigrant Caucus*, 2017.
Powder-coated steel and powder-coated aluminum
expanded mesh, stainless steel insecticide sprayer with
brass fittings, ultrasonic diffuser, fragrance dimensions variable. Image courtesy of the artist and 47 Canal, New York.

at the Mexican border."[105] But the centerpiece here is the smell, which
Yi synthesized in collaboration with perfumer Barnabé Fillion, forensic
scientist Kenneth Furton, three Columbia University PhD students spe-
cializing in the biological sciences, and olfactory artist Sean Raspet.[106]
Yi describes the "Asian-American part of the fragrance" as "vegetal and
floral, with notes of cedar, hay, cumin, and cellophane" and the ant fragrance as "citrusy and meaty."[107] The combined scent, according to Yi,
is "sweaty and herbacious until the garlicky note of the ant kicks in. . . .
People have described it as delicate, but they also seem unsure of how to
talk about it."[108] Visitors are exposed to this unsettling trans-species and
(for many) cross-racial scent—as well as its physiological, cognitive, and

affective consequences—prior to encountering the other two pieces in Yi's exhibition. By introducing this odor into the conventionally deodorized "anosmic cubes" of the modern art museum, Yi endows the odors of ants and Asians with the cultural capital of the Guggenheim.[109]

The title of this initial work, *Immigrant Caucus* (Figure 4.4), has a similarly unsettling effect. Who are the "immigrants" here—the Asian American women, the carpenter ants, or the museum's visitors whose own odors blend with Yi's synthesized scent? If a caucus is a meeting of a political party frequently oriented toward choosing a representative, then what does it mean to bring these three heterogeneous groups together in a multispecies, multiracial caucus? The term "caucus" immediately frames the olfactory—in this case a scent produced through bacteriological and chemical means—in political terms. Is the material, trans-corporeal blending of scents already a powerful form of political deliberation, a mode of olfactory conditioning that contests the politics of differential deodorization while predisposing ants, Asian Americans, and diverse gallery goers toward transformed political views and social practices?

Whereas Eaton pauses at the moment of "step[ping] across the threshold" in order to highlight the pleasant fragrance of Chinatown's middle-class interiors, Yi mobilizes the exhibition's threshold to confront visitors with a peculiar, potentially unsettling scent. *Immigrant Caucus* inverts the usual logic of prophylaxis that governs "air conditioning" in museums: instead of immunizing visitors and art objects from each other, the work is itself a mechanism of air conditioning that gets into breathers' bodies. As Burton notes, Yi "sees her work as operating most directly when it is so very physical as to literally enter the person there to 'see' it."[110] For Burton, Yi's olfactory works "suggest that there are affectively charged modes of intelligence and critical thinking available to, and by way of, the other senses. We have simply been encouraged and trained to use and rely on these much less."[111] In her insightful discussions of Yi's practice, Jones also argues that sensory experiences can disclose new modes of relationality. She frames Yi's artworks through the concept of "biofiction"—a practice of material speculation in which "fiction [is] released even from text and allowed to play in haptic and olfactory domains."[112] Through both its spatial presentation and its inhaled scent, *Immigrant Caucus* draws visitors into a "biofiction" that explores what it might be like to perceive and feel as an Asian woman, an ant, a bacterium—or some combination of all three. As the exhibition's wall text notes, "Yi posits the scent as a drug that manipulates perception, offering humans the potential to experience the installation with a new hybridized perspective."[113]

After participating in *Immigrant Caucus* (by both inhaling it and contributing their own scents to it), visitors enter a space in which two opposing dioramas are on display, "each providing a view into a self-contained biosphere."[114] While the form of the diorama invokes the ocularcentrism, timelessness, and nature/culture demarcation that Donna Haraway diagnosed in the Museum of Natural History's African dioramas (the artist "consulted . . . with diorama experts at the Natural History Museum"),[115] Yi's immersive displays present multiscalar spaces, hybridized *naturecultures*, and living specimens to visitors who have just inhaled what they're observing. On one side, *Force Majeure* (Figure 4.5) features agar tiles, framed artificial flowers, and illuminated sculptures resembling biomorphic chairs displayed behind a vitrine, all overgrown with colorful bacterial cultures sampled from Manhattan's Chinatown and Koreatown. According to the exhibit's curators, this living composition looks "as if an invasive life force has overrun the environment."[116] Because Yi obtained the bacterial samples for this work by swabbing surfaces such as toilet handles and door handles, these bacterial cultures index racialized spaces rather than Asian bodies: thus, they draw attention to how geography, rather than biological essence, materializes racial disparities (even as these disparities often manifest in biological forms such as microbes, metabolisms, disease, and epigenetic inheritances). The title of this piece alludes to the *force majeure* clause found in most contracts that (at least temporarily) releases both parties from their obligations when a "greater force" or extraordinary circumstance prevents one or both parties from fulfilling the contract.[117] Framing these visually striking bacterial cultures as a manifestation of *force majeure* underscores how conceiving of agency in material terms (constantly shifting masses of bacteria and chemical scents) shakes up the idea of contract that forms the basis of liberal society. Noting that "the installation of this diorama caused upset among museum workers bothered by the stench," Lee suggests that *force majeure* may allude to museum protocols that would have prohibited the odors of these bacteria from being

Figure 4.5. Anicka Yi, *Force Majeure*, 2017. Plexiglas, aluminum, agar, bacteria, refrigeration system, LED lights, glass, epoxy resin, powder-coated stainless steel, light bulbs, digital clocks, silicone, and silk flowers. Dimensions variable. Image courtesy of the artist and 47 Canal, New York.

exhibited in the exhibit proper, rather than in the entryway.[118] If we are physically, mentally, and affectively transformed by microbes, smells, and other trans-corporeal materials, then even something as apparently insignificant as an odor can undercut our capacity to freely enter and fulfill contracts. Already transformed (and perhaps intoxicated) by the odor of *Immigrant Caucus*, the exhibition's visitors must relinquish any claim to occupy the status of liberalism's deodorized, disinterested, and fully rational subject. As Ahuja puts it in his incisive theorization of atmospheric intimacies, "Liberalism thrives on masking violence through ruses of the individual's transcendence, the refusal of the 'promiscuous' interspecies connections that make bodies, according to Donna Haraway, 'constitutively a crowd.'"[119]

On the far side of the room is another diorama that takes the form of both an intricate ant farm and an arrangement of reflective metal sheets, pathways, mushroom-shaped forms, and LED lights resembling a massive electrical circuit board. Titled *Lifestyle Wars* (Figure 4.6), this diorama incorporates a colony of twenty thousand living ants that have

Figure 4.6. Anicka Yi, *Lifestyle Wars* (detail), 2017. Ants, mirrored Plexiglas, Plexiglas, two-way mirrored glass, LED lights, epoxy resin, glitter, aluminum racks with rackmount server cases and Ethernet cables, metal wire, foam, acrylic, aquarium gravel, and imitation pearls. Dimensions variable. Image courtesy of the artist and 47 Canal, New York.

been exposed to the scent of *Immigrant Caucus*. Yi explains that her fascination with ants is inspired by "their matriarchy, industry, and powerful sense of smell, which they use to recognize the caste of other colony members."[120] More attuned to smell than humans, the ants perform the olfactory disorientation that Yi hopes to have inspired—albeit on a subtler level—in the exhibition's human visitors: "At times," observes Yi, "groups of [the ants] have appeared confused by the scent, seeming to interrogate a single ant as though they were prosecutors cross-examining a witness. What do they make of the invisible stranger in their midst?"[121]

Yet viewed from even a short distance, the ants *are* the "invisible stranger[s]" inhabiting *Lifestyle Wars*. When first approached, the diorama's play of mirrored and luminous surfaces resemble an enlarged electronic circuit board, "evoking a massive data-processing unit."[122] The ants' initial invisibility—along with their industrious behavior, their appearance as an undifferentiated plurality, and Yi's decision to title the exhibition *Life Is Cheap*—evokes the socially invisible status of marginalized Asian laborers. Historically, anti-Asian agitators represented the Asiatic as an "indissociably plural" mass of undifferentiated, dehumanized laborers;[123] today, Asian laborers continue to be dehumanized and exploited in both Asia and the United States. Yi's ants dramatize the invisibility of Asian laborers—particularly those who manufacture the electronics that we generally assume to be odorless and nontoxic (at least for the consumer). For laborers involved in the extraction, production, and disposal processes of the tech economy, toxic exposure is an everyday affair.[124] Framing these transnational exchanges of toxic debilities and technical capacity in atmospheric terms, Ahuja writes, "The everyday activities of carbon-dependent industrial living connect one's bodily consumption and waste to the 'stranger intimacies' of a shared atmosphere, slowly threatening other far-flung bodies, human and nonhuman."[125] *Lifestyle Wars* thus assembles—on both visual and olfactory levels—ants associated with transpacific productive labor, an enlarged image of that labor's product (the electronic circuit board), and the reflected image of the product's consumers (the gallery's visitors reflected in the metal sheets).

The structural violence of differential deodorization is sustained by atmo-orientalist "lifestyle wars" in which middle-class subjects avoid and stigmatize the smells of the labor conditions that enable their technologically mediated lifestyle. Rather than disavowing and displacing the odors associated with the transnational flow of bodies and commodities, Yi makes the visitor chemically intimate with those smells. Along with the hybridized smells of ants and Asian women, the mushroom forms in *Lifestyle Wars* allude to the airborne dissemination of fungal spores as a model of material kinship and "cultural" (fungal, bacterial) reproduction. Spores may extend kinship networks not only by reproducing fungi but by entering and materially altering the composition of bodies. For Yi, these molecular intimacies of empire may be productive and intoxicating as well as toxic or debilitating. Yi's conception of her work as exploring a "biopolitics of the senses"[126]—an atmospheric biopolitics in which bacterial and molecular flows overrun the visual and conceptual lines that racism draws between populations—marks a departure from Foucault's theorization of racism as introducing and enforcing a biopolitical "break between what must live and what must die."[127] *Life Is Cheap* instills olfactory empathy not through melodramatic imagery or psychological structures of identification, but by incorporating into the aesthetic experience a process of trans-corporeal becoming that crosses geographic, racial, and species boundaries.[128] Yi's work thus enacts the concept of "conviviality" theorized by Jasbir Puar: "As an attribute and function of assembling," Puar writes, "conviviality does not lead to a politics of the universal or inclusive common, nor an ethics of individuatedness, rather the futurity enabled through the open materiality of bodies as a Place to Meet. . . . There is no absolute self or other, rather bodies that come together and dissipate through intensifications and vulnerabilities, insistently rendering bare the instability of the divisions between capacity-endowed and debility-laden bodies."[129] *Life Is Cheap* literally instills in its visitors an experience of the multiscalar (chemical, bacterial, corporeal, and global) circulations disavowed by atmo-orientalism: here, bodies and minds materially imbibe one other through the affective channels of olfaction.[130]

* * *

While their strategies of discursive deodorization and trans-corporeal conviviality vary widely, Eaton and Yi provide suggestive historical and conceptual bookends for studying a broader archive of Asian diasporic engagements with smell. Atmo-orientalism clarifies the stakes of other olfactory experiments that have (with the exception Larissa Lai's work) received little attention from scholars of Asian diasporic culture, such as Sadakichi Hartmann's critically panned scented performance "A Trip to Japan in Sixteen Minutes" (1902);[131] Lai's speculative, erotic accounts the smells of salt fish and genetically mutated durian in *Salt Fish Girl* (2002);[132] Sita Kuratomi Bhaumik's innovative deployments of curry as a compositional material in *To Curry Favor* (2010); and Beatrice Glow's artworks investigating the transpacific colonial geographies produced in the wake of Europeans' desires for Asian scents and spices.[133] Atmo-orientalism also clarifies connections between such Asian North American works and works by Asian artists—such as Korean artist Lee Bul's *Majestic Splendor* (consisting of sequinned rotting fish, and pulled from display at the New York MOMA in 1997 as a result of visitors' complaints about its smell)[134] and Chinese artist Yuan Gong's *Air Strikes around the World* (2013), in which drones released scented clouds of yellowish gas in Venice and Shanghai.

More broadly, the genealogy of atmo-orientalism traced in this chapter illustrates the vital stakes of atmospheres frequently perceived as mere "background" in literary plots and art museums. The cases of ol-factory contestation I have considered—from one of the earliest books of Asian North American fiction to the most critically acclaimed work of Asian American olfactory art to date—demonstrate the critical need for practices of "atmospheric reading" that are attentive to the racial dy-namics of "air conditioning."[135] Atmospheres—in the later nineteenth century and increasingly today—call for a material and ontological analysis of race that attends not only to discourses or assumptions about biologically fixed essences but to environmentally induced transforma-tions of individuals and populations. Bringing atmospheric geography into conversation with race studies provides new contexts and methods for cross-scalar analysis (from the molecular to the transnational), for thinking in material terms about unevenly distributed geographies of debility and capacity, and for considering the potentialities activated by molecular trans-corporeal intimacies such as those conveyed by Yi's hy-brid gases and bacterial cultures.

Like the Asian diaspora, Indigenous people have also been racialized through smell—not as malodorous, but as primitives who supposedly overvalue olfactory experience. It is not their bodies but their noses that have to be deodorized. Colonialism stigmatized olfactory modes of knowing and relating to the world at the same time that it transformed Indigenous smellscapes into unrecognizable, disproportionately toxic atmospheres. The following chapter considers how racial atmospheres are deployed, critiqued, and decolonized under conditions of settler co-lonial and postcolonial slow violence. If atmo-orientalism's tendency to associate Asians with dystopian, hypermodern smells exemplifies a ra-cial atmospherics that simultaneously includes and marginalizes Asian laborers within modernity, colonialism's atmospheric engineering is oriented by a logic of elimination that directly targets Indigenous life as well as Indigenous sovereignty, sensoria, and environmental relations.[136]

5

Decolonizing Smell

In their introduction to a *Social Text* dossier on *Decolonial AestheSis*, Walter Mignolo and Rolando Vazquez theorize decolonial modes of perception that have been excluded from the canon of "modern aestheTics." Distinguishing between *aesthesis* as sensory practice and aesthetics as a canon of sensory norms, they write, "Decolonial aestheSis starts from the consciousness that the modern/colonial project has implied not only control of the economy, the political, and knowledge, but also control over the senses and perception."[1] If Western modernity and coloniality are built upon subjectifying institutions of aesthetic regulation, then undoing these projects will require not only political, economic, and epistemological transformations but also the decolonization of the senses. As Jarrett Martineau and Eric Ritskes put it in their introduction to a special issue of *Decolonization* on "Indigenous Art, Aesthetics, and Decolonial Struggle," "Indigenous art disrupts colonial hegemony by fracturing the sensible architecture of experience that is constitutive of the aesthetic regime itself—the normative order, or 'distribution of the sensible'—that frames both political and artistic potentialities, as such."[2] In her groundbreaking monograph on decolonial (and primarily visual) alternatives to colonial capitalism's "extractive view," Macarena Gómez-Barris writes that "decolonial thinkers put into motion a range of methods and epistemologies that give primacy to renewed perception."[3]

While decoloniality has been the subject of considerable scholarship in visual culture and sound studies, there is much less research addressing these issues in connection with the so-called lower senses.[4] Yet smell's very position at the bottom of the Enlightenment hierarchy of the senses is a product (and producer) of racial and colonial thinking. Olfaction is also deeply bound up with material atmospheres and trans-corporeal ecologies and thus conveys embodied engagements with issues of geographic inequity and environmental health. Because smell is conditioned and inflected through material smellscapes, decolonizing smell is not just a metaphor for changing how one thinks or perceives:[5] it requires material transformation of both land and air. Thus, both the philosophical derecognition of olfactory knowledge and the geographically uneven distribution of material odors present important, interconnected sites for the work of decolonization: at the same time that settler colonialism has proliferated atmospheric disparities, colonial education has endeavored to invalidate olfaction as a mode of knowledge and relation. At stake in the decolonization of smell is a powerful medium for accessing and communicating sensory knowledge of "the coexistence and imbrication of human and nonhuman lives"—to invoke Cajetan Iheka's articulation of an "aesthetics of proximity" evident in African environmental representation.[6] Indigenous engagements with olfaction are not only struggles over environmental violence but also struggles to revivify a vital mode of knowing and connecting with nonhuman kin. This chapter works through the problems posed by olfactory decolonization by first synthesizing discussions of atmospherics and smell in settler colonial studies and Indigenous studies, then turning to three Indigenous writers—Albert Wendt (Samoa), Haunani-Kay Trask (Hawai'i), and Robin Wall Kimmerer (Potawatomi)—who challenge the ways in which colonialism orchestrates both the perception and the material distribution of smells.

Colonial Smellscapes

Before considering efforts to decolonize smell, we must first attend to the diverse ways in which smell has been conscripted as a colonial resource—and, in some cases, a repressive weapon.[7] The colonization of smell functions on numerous levels: (1) the perceptual level that determines whether smells are acknowledged, valued, or suppressed; (2) the environmental level that encompasses how different atmospheres are unevenly distributed across space, scale, and populations; and (3) the trans-corporeal level where smells and other atmospheric materials are absorbed by bodies, often resulting in either slow or spectacular environmental violence. Together, these overlapping registers of olfactory experience mobilize both deodorization and noxious atmospheres to reproduce colonial power relations while extracting profit from colonized spaces and Indigenous bodies. This section establishes a framework for the close readings that follow by surveying a range of theoretical and aesthetic works that articulate the vital stakes of colonialism's olfactory transformations.

Deodorization played an important role in "the civilizing process" documented by Norbert Elias, whereby Europeans developed notions of middle-class manners and civility.[8] Civilization required the suppression of embodied sensations, including the rejection of smell as an involuntary sense incompatible with Kantian ideals of disinterestedness and autonomy. Colonialism introduced this osmophobic (smell-fearing) worldview to Indigenous societies throughout the world, often imposing systems of education intended to eradicate Indigenous olfactory cultures. Across a vast range of Indigenous societies, the perception and manipulation of smells provides embodied modes of environmental knowledge and relationality. Some examples of olfactory traditions that have been threatened or suppressed by colonial education include Native American smudging (which will be discussed in more detail below); the "aromachology"—or olfactory healing practices—performed by Amazonian shamans and *perfumeros*;[9] Indigenous knowledge of botanical smells that, according to Kettler, were vital for European botanists in the Americas in the eighteenth century (even as those botanists published visually oriented, deodorized accounts to satisfy the ocularcentric biases of Europe's scientific community);[10] the Hawaiian *honi*, or nose press, which J. Kēhaulani Kauanui notes was denigrated by Europeans as an atavistic olfactory practice; the use of olfactory knowledge in traditional Oceanic seafaring;[11] the cosmology of the Ongee people of the Andaman Islands, for whom all "living beings are thought to be composed of smell";[12] forms of existence such as the *tjelbak* fog snake encountered by Elizabeth Povinelli and her colleagues in the Karrabing Indigenous Corporation, which apprehend and are apprehended through smell;[13] and the spiritual and reverential associations of scent in Chamorro culture noted by Vicente Diaz, who explains that *ñgiñgi'* or sniffing is the traditional way to show reverence for elders and that "the sudden whiff of certain smells, especially of flowers where none are found, is understood to be a sign of otherworldly presence."[14] In her study of decolonial cosmogonies in contemporary Hawaiian literature, Brandy Nālani Mc-Dougall (Kanaka Maoli) suggests that we think of aesthetics in terms of 'ala, or fragrance. "He inoa 'ala" (A fragrant name) is used to describe an ali'i, or chief, whose good deeds may continue to be felt and remembered. Smells are central to descriptions of goodness and evil throughout the Pacific and are often thought of as signs or warnings. Smell can be useful to articulate aesthetics in terms of legacy or memory, as they often indicate presence despite absence or invisibility. . . . Consequently, thinking of aesthetics as the 'ala of a literary text allows us to make textual, cultural, and historical connections and associations grounded in legacy and memory, to actively genealogize layers of meaning across contexts—and to think of these intellectual challenges as pleasurable.[15]

In Oceanic culture, smell serves to make connections across space and time: it is both a navigational tool grounded in knowledge of the smells of particular islands and a mode of connecting with personal and collective memories. By cultivating olfactory shame and installing a hierarchy of the senses that denigrates olfaction, colonizers did much more than discourage Indigenous attentiveness to odors—they eroded Indigenous spiritual life, collective memories, cultural geographies, and kin relations with land and air. In "Sniffing Oceania's Behind," Indigenous studies scholar Vicente Diaz situates smells as ephemeral yet historically meaningful phenomena that have generally been excluded from written and visual archives.[16] He responds to the deodorization of historical archives and methods by proposing that we "[learn] to smell Islander cultural and political pasts as a form of politicized historiographical practice."[17] Reading the thematics of smell (in particular, olfactory accounts of the anus) in the writings of Tongan author Epeli Hau'ofa alongside traditional Indigenous olfactory practices throughout the Pacific, Diaz suggests that olfaction offers historians access to decolonized modes of lived experience.

While deodorization aptly describes the olfactory ideology of Western modernity, it does not provide an accurate account of modernity's actual effects on material atmospheres and smellscapes. Indeed, the institutions and ideology of deodorization have helped sustain a notion of air as an empty and uniform commons—*aer nullius*, ready to receive settler culture's atmospheric embellishments and externalities.[18] If colonial educators introduced hygienic practices and olfactory aversions that targeted particular odors, settler colonialism's ecological domination also imposed widespread transformations in Indigenous smellscapes.[19] Because olfactory perception is neurologically linked to deep-rooted memories and sense of place,[20] the changes to Indigenous smellscapes brought about by physical displacement, the decimation of indigenous species, the introduction of nonindigenous species, monocrop agriculture, urbanization, militarization, industrial waste, and Western infrastructure and architecture profoundly affected Indigenous experiences of place, environment, spirituality, and identity. These transformations of the smellscape reconfigured the atmosphere itself into a medium for settler colonialism's elimination of Indigenous modes of embodiment and environmental knowledge.[21] In tracing a range of analyses and responses to the toxic entanglements that constitute settler colonialism, I build on Michelle Murphy's (Métis) reflections on the "words, protocols, and methods that might honor the inseparability of bodies and land, and at the same time grapple with the expansive chemical relations of settler colonialism that entangle life forms in each other's accumulations, conditions, possibilities, and miseries."[22]

In her autobiographical accounts of her deracinating colonial education at White's India Manual Labor Institute, Zitkala-Ša (Gertrude Bonnin; Yankton Dakota) contrasts the fragrance of prairies traditionally managed with controlled burns ("the perfume of sweet grasses from newly burnt prairie") with her feeling olfactory repulsion while mashing turnips in the school kitchen: "I hated turnips, and their odor which came from the brown jar was offensive to me."[23] Zitkala-Ša's aversion to the smell of turnips—a staple food imported to the United States from Europe—impels her to mash them so fiercely that she crushes the bottom of the glass jar. Rather than merely alienating her, the unfamiliar smellscape of the boarding school moves Zitkala-Ša to perform an act that she experiences as a "triumphant" assertion of "the rebellion within me."[24]

Similarly, John Dominis Holt's On Being Hawaiian (1964)—a foundational work for the Second Hawaiian Renaissance—critiques the "urban industrial way of life" imposed by colonialism by recalling ancestral olfactory experiences. Prior to colonization, he writes, Kānaka Maoli "did not suffer in the spiritually crippling morasses of the world's great cities: the slums of London, Paris, Calcutta, Chicago, New York or Naples.

Even around the crowded shacks of Kakaako, of a few years ago, gardens flourished and the night air was filled with a ginger pungence of scented night-blooming flowers, instead of the reek and stink of urine soaked tenement hallways in the dead heat of mid-summer."[25] Elaborating on his Hawaiian cultural identity, Holt underscores the importance of a spiritual "collective ethos of centuries of culture, and the shape this has taken under the subtle influences of environment."[26] According to critic Otto Heim, breath has special significance in Hawaiian culture as a metaphor for "relational values" and sovereignty: "Attention to breath . . . literalises a reckoning with the presence and precedence of other agents."[27] Colonial olfactory transformations introduced air conditioning's processes of "microclimatic splintering" to an atmosphere whose shifting scents have oriented Hawaiian culture for centuries.

In her ethnographic study of olfactory experiences of air pollution by members of the Indigenous Aamjiwnaang First Nation residing on ancestral lands in Canada's "chemical valley" (a fifteen-square-mile area in Sarnia, Ontario that contains 40 percent of Canada's petrochemical industry), anthropologist Deborah Jackson coins the term "dysplacement" to convey the transformation of olfaction from something that "reinforce[d] a sense of positive emplacement" in the past to a field of experience that "is now instilling . . . a profound sense of alienation from the ancestral landscape."[28] Drawing on olfactory references across numerous memoirs and interviews, Jackson notes that in the earlier twentieth century smells evoked "positive emotions" associated with local plants, animals, and seasonal activities: "Each fragrance, in its time and season, characterized particular parts of the reserve and connected those places with specific events and practices important to community life."[29] She contrasts the traditional inhalation of "protective and healing fragrances from sacred plants" with the ubiquitous odor of air pollution emitted by the petroleum plants that have proliferated in the area since the 1960s: "In a stench-filled environment such as Aamjiwnaang, place integrates with body in sinister and destructive ways, as the simple act of breathing entails an unintended embodiment of the smelled (toxic) substance."[30] Jackson's concept of "dysplacement" evokes how Indigenous communities like the Aamjiwnaang can be at once deeply attached to their environment and profoundly disturbed by invisible odors and their associated environmental risks. More broadly, dysplacement draws attention to diverse experiences of anxiety and harm precipitated by an entire spectrum of environmental changes, ranging from colonialism's long history of ecological transformations to the environmental slow violence spread by toxic industries and military projects sited on or near Indigenous land.

In "Settler Atmospherics," anthropologist Kristen Simmons (Southern Paiute) argues that the atmospheric manipulation of the "collective and unequally distributed" conditions of breathing is a vital component of settler colonialism.[31] Noting that Indigenous nations suffer from vastly disproportionate exposures to air pollution and Superfund sites, Simmons observes that "the settler colonial project of U.S. Empire is, after all, to place indigenous nations and bodies into suspension."[32] In the struggle over the Dakota Access Pipeline at Standing Rock, efforts to block the oil pipeline's threats to water and air on Indigenous land were met with tear gas and pepper spray. At the Oceti Sakowin camp, Simmons writes, "we experienced various suspensions: of time, bodies, affects. Anticipation of state violence became a rhythm, with constant low-flying helicopters, floodlights, and a large militarized police presence creating a tension that settled deep into muscles."[33] Settler colonialism engineers the atmosphere in order to transform the very conditions of embodiment, feeling, and perception. As Puar has argued, understanding debility in colonial and postcolonial contexts calls for a shift from approaching disability primarily as an identity category to an analysis of "the biopolitics of debilitation" focused on understanding debilitation as a calculated "distribution of risk" and "a tactical practice deployed in order to create and precaritize populations and maintain them as such."[34] Simmons's account of settler atmospherics demonstrates the manifold ways in which the settler colonial state deploys air itself as a medium for either slowly or spectacularly debilitating Indigenous populations. Disproportionately exposing Indigenous communities to substances whose components and long-term effects are not always well understood or even inquired about, settler atmospherics imposes the "*loss of sovereignty* over assessing the dangers" that, according to Ulrich Beck, is one significant consequence of environmental risk awareness.[35]

Among the most nefarious examples of settler atmospherics is Skunk Water, an olfactory anti-crowd weapon designed in consultation with Israeli police and tested without consent on (primarily Palestinian) protestors by the Israeli firm Odortec. Odortec advertises Skunk Water as a humane weapon responding to "an acute dilemma in confrontations with violent civil unrest: the need for effective riot control and the duty to preserve the health and safety of all, including the protestors themselves. . . . Using 100% food-grade ingredients, the Skunk is 100% eco-friendly—harmless to both nature and people."[36] Geographer Marijn Nieuwenhuis, however, notes that "the IDF . . . regularly uses designated Skunk trucks to soak Palestinian streets, gardens, homes, schools; equipped with water cannons, these trucks can turn entire neighborhoods rancid."[37] In 2012, police sprayed a Muslim funeral possession with the malodorant; in 2018, Israel introduced a new "Shoko drone" designed to drop Skunk Water directly on crowds.[38] Nieuwenhuis argues that the liberal media's depiction of Skunk as a humane and ethical weapon is grounded in an "insensitivity to the truly debilitating power of smell," noting that the malodorant lingers on clothing, furniture, and bodies for days (in one case, a reporter's camera smelled for nearly half a year) and suggesting that its social and affective consequences are profound.[39] "Under the liberal pretext of non-lethality," he concludes, "Skunk forges lines of racial division according to a hierarchy of smells, between the stench of bestial savagery and the deodorized fragrance of civilization. It authorizes the state to violently cleanse its lands along racial lines."[40] Skunk Water is a powerful tool for the everyday "disrupt[ion of] the distribution of the senses" that, according to Palestinian legal scholar Nadera Shalhoub-Kevorkian, "turns the colonized neighborhoods into a blinding, putrid space, making room for the colonizer, while denying space and access—but also sight, hearing, and smell—to the colonized."[41] Although the weapon was designed and most frequently used to target Palestinians, Skunk Water has since been used against Ethiopian-Israeli protestors, tested (unsuccessfully) in India, and purchased by several local US police agencies in the wake of the 2015 uprisings in Ferguson and Baltimore. Skunk Water's circulation as a settler and antiblack weapon attests to how, as Simmons observes, settler atmospherics produces the breathing conditions for new solidarities: "In a porous relationality—attuning to how others (cannot) breathe, our haptics are enhanced and we develop capacities to feel one another otherwise."[42]

In an effort to build sensory and affective connections between audiences in Britain and an Indigenous community affected by both climate change and the North Alaska oil fields, geographer and anthropologist Julia Feuer-Cotter collaboratively produced *Smell of Change* (2015) with an Inupiaq women's group in Kaktovik. The work is intended to convey "the Kaktovik community's experience of perceived changes as they want to emphasize them for others located outside of Kaktovik" by distilling, analyzing (with gas spectrometry), and synthesizing a series of local scents.[43] Feuer-Cotter recounts that "the group collected and sent me pieces of blown-out tires, tools, mud, fur, rocks, and plants over several months, so that the odor would capture the seasonal change in the Arctic."[44] After synthesizing the scents of the objects shared by the Inupiaq women, Feuer-Cotter blended them "according to the design that was agreed upon by the group" and sent the vials of fragrance to Kaktovik for feedback. The result was a synthetic scent that evokes Kaktovik's changing and increasingly polluted smellscape:

> Top note: muddy, dirty laundry, wet dog, puddle, compost, hint of red berries
>
> Middle note: heavy oil note, locker room, coins, wet leather
>
> Base note: rotting blueberries, cloudberry, sandstone dust, iron[45]

Like the olfactory artworks discussed in chapter 3, *Smell of Change* aims to affect breathers directly through biochemical means, enabling them to experience the changing smellscape of Kaktovik without the mediations of language or visual representation. The work endeavors to present the polluted Arctic not as an image or story, but as an affect conveyed through trans-corporeal communion.

Warren Cariou, a Canadian author of Métis descent, stages both odor's insidious violence and its resistance to representation in "Tarhands: A Messy Manifesto" (2012). In what is ostensibly a photo essay on Athabasca oil sands mining in Canada, Cariou dwells on the problem of communicating toxic odors:

> What I remember most about the tar sands is the stink. We stood there with our cameras, trying to capture a record of that obliterated landscape, but I could hardly even see. The fumes were like hammers: sulfur and

benzene and diesel and something else—a dead smell, a charnel residue on the back of my tongue. I had a migraine in half a dozen breaths. I breathed into my shirtsleeve, trying not to retch. How could people work in this, day after day? How could the Cree, Metis and Dene people of Fort Mackay live in it?[46]

Disturbed that people appear to have become accustomed to such debilitating smells, Cariou proposes the establishment of a "stink-tank" that would foster olfactory modes of knowledge production: "How do you point out that the air smells, when everyone's already used to it? By making more stink. . . . Stinking as thinking" ("T," 21). Cariou then proceeds to reframe Western philosophical and literary traditions in olfactory terms, noting "that some forms of thought create a noxious atmosphere, a stink, sometimes subtle and other times overwhelming" ("T," 28) and rewriting a passage from *Paradise Lost* in a pungent poem titled "Satan Rouses His Legions on the Shores of Syncrude Tailings Pond #4" ("T," 29).

Works like Feuer-Cotter's *Smell of Change* and Cariou's "Tarhands" leverage the visceral force of olfaction to communicate the embodied effects of air pollution in the "extractive zone"—to adapt Gómez-Barris's term for majority-Indigenous areas in South America suffering the environmental effects of natural resource extraction.[47] But decolonizing the smellscape requires more than the documentation of environmental violence: a decolonial approach aims to transform our modes of sensing and relating to the atmosphere, and ultimately to transform the atmosphere itself. To decolonize smell is not to position decolonization as a mere metaphor for transforming consciousness, foregoing decolonial activists' emphasis on land, bread, and water in favor of "decolonizing the mind";[48] rather, I would suggest adding the increasingly stratified atmosphere to the material stakes of decolonization: land, bread, water, and air. In asking what it would take to decolonize smell, I take inspiration from what Sarah Wald, David Vázquez, Priscilla Solis Ybarra, and Sarah Jaquette Ray have theorized as a "recovery model [that] demonstrates the myriad ways that communities excluded from the dominant environmental and national imaginary have long held environmental values and continue to create new ways of thinking about environmental issues."[49] The imposed forgetting, persistence, and resurgence of Indigenous olfactory experience is a central concern for the texts to which

I will now turn: Albert Wendt's "I Will Be Our Saviour from the Bad Smell" (1984) and Haunani-Kay Trask's poetic meditations on Hawaiian colonization and self-determination. Together, these texts attest to the intimate continuities between olfaction and spirit in Oceanic cultures documented by Diaz and McDougall, as well as the diverse modes of atmospheric violence (missionaries' denigration of smell, plantation agriculture, nuclear and other weapons testing, military installations, and tourist infrastructures) imposed across Oceania's colonized and postcolonial spaces.

"Air-Conditioned Coffins"

Among the most influential and prolific figures in Oceanic literature, Wendt is best known for his groundbreaking cultural manifesto "Towards a New Oceania" (1976) and his award-winning epic novel about a family struggling to thrive in the midst of colonial and postcolonial pressures, *Leaves of the Banyan Tree* (1979). Having grown up in colonial Western Samoa in the decades before the nation gained its independence (and renamed itself "Samoa") in 1962, and having subsequently studied and resided in New Zealand (where he wrote a master's thesis on Samoa's anticolonial Mau movement), Wendt is well positioned to explore the tensions between colonial education, globalization, and Samoa's Indigenous culture. Although the short story "I Will Be Our Saviour from the Bad Smell" (1984) has received much less critical attention than Wendt's novels, it offers a nuanced account of the challenges to decolonization posed by colonialism's atmospheric and sensory legacies.

The moralizing imperative to deodorize public space is at the heart of Wendt's satirical parable. First published in the New Zealand–based journal *Islands* and subsequently collected in *The Birth and Death of the Miracle Man and Other Stories* (1986), "Bad Smell" presents an elliptical allegory of deodorization: when the Samoan village of Saula awakes to a nauseating stench one morning, its community leader appoints the narrator the chairperson of a "committee to explore the land, sea and air."[50] Wendt's plot echoes the histories of nineteenth-century smelling committees convened to detect and mitigate the sources of public odors.[51] But although the narrator directs a systematic search of the island and its environs, neither his Westernized methods nor the local "miracle healer" nor a white scientist from the Agricultural Department in Apia succeeds in tracing or eradicating the smell. Eventually, other villagers adapt to the smell by persuading themselves and the nation "that it was a harmless, non-infectious and healthy odour, a mark of distinction and uniqueness" ("BS," 123). But the narrator remains obsessed with the imperative of deodorization: although he contributes slogans to the public opinion campaign ("OUR SMELL IS THE PERFUME OF THE PACIFIC"), he secretly believes that eradicating the smell is "my struggle, my mission . . . the meaning of my life. I was born for it" ("BS," 123, 125). As critic Paul Sharrad observes, Wendt's plot blends the magical realism of authors like Borges, Márquez, and Calvino with an existential treatment of sickness reminiscent of Albert Camus's *The Plague* (1947).[52]

Although Wendt never discloses the smell's source, critics have associated it with the cultural pollution introduced by colonialism: for example, Sharrad proposes that "if we think of Wendt's repeated denunciations of palagi-imposed images of the Pacific, the smell can be read as the colonial legacies to which most people learn to submit—take for granted or even profit from."[53] At times, the narrator hints that the smell is tied to Christianity when he observes that "the whole area *occupied* (that was the appropriate description) by the Bad Smell was oval-shaped and our church building was its centre" ("BS," 106) and when he notes that the village priest "reminded me of a fit rooster with gas in its belly" ("BS," 106, 110). Here, the italicization and parenthetical commentary on the term "*occupied*" associate the smell with colonial occupation. But the narrator also associates the smell with organic materials: "rotten fruit, decaying flesh, rancid cheese (I've never tasted that), brackish water . . . swamp mud" and "shit" ("BS," 96, 98). With the exception of cheese, these are all elements of the local smellscape—materials that have frequently been targeted by modernity's deodorization campaigns. The "bad smell" is thus fundamentally ambiguous: at once indigenous and foreign, organic and ideological, material and psychosomatic.

The story is structured around the ironic contradiction whereby the narrator's mock-heroic struggles against the smell proliferate colonial thinking and potentially toxic odors. If the smell embodies colonialism's effects on Samoan culture and society, the implementation of euphemisms (such as the term "Bad Smell"), cartography ("Geography had been one of my strong subjects at high school"), and a smelling committee to combat the smell only intensifies colonialism's influence ("BS," 101). Similarly, when the narrator considers deploying "rockets" to shatter the atmospheric boundaries of the smell or using an airplane to release "eighteen tons of perfume" or "fumigation spray" to mitigate the smell, he fantasizes about the proliferation of military, agricultural, and cosmetic products that have had devastating ecological effects throughout Oceania ("BS," 124, 125; Figure 5.1). The narrator's eagerness to lead the deodorization campaign—which persists long after his neighbors have lost interest in eradicating the smell—is entangled with his ambition for power and prestige. Like the national Health Department officials who stop by "to see if we needed some form of inoculation," the narrator's increasingly absurd efforts to mobilize rationality against the noxious smell caricature the public health campaigns that have helped legitimize the modern state ("BS," 122).

Wendt's discussion of colonial architecture in his groundbreaking, frequently anthologized essay "Towards a New Oceania" (1976) provides a helpful context for understanding the atmospheric politics at work in "Bad Smell." Affirming the vitality and importance of Oceanic cultural production as a tool for resisting cultural colonialism, Wendt frames the essay by citing Trobriand poet John Kasaipwalova's indictment of colonialism's atmospheric effects: "Chill you're a bastard. . . . Your history and your size make me cry violently / for air to breathe."[54] Although "Towards a New Oceania" is often cited as a call for Oceania's literary autonomy, architecture provides some of Wendt's most powerful examples of the effects of colonial education:

> A frightening type of papalagi architecture is invading Oceania: the super-stainless/super-plastic/super-hygienic/super-soulless structure very similar to modern hospitals, and its most nightmarish form is the new type tourist hotel—a multi-storied edifice of concrete/steel/chromium/ and air conditioning. This species of architecture is an embodiment of those bourgeois values I find unhealthy/soul-destroying: the cultivation/ worship of mediocrity, a quest for a meaningless and precarious security based on material possessions, a deep-rooted fear of dirt and all things rich in our cultures, a fear of death revealed in an almost paranoic quest for a super-hygienic cleanliness and godliness. ("TNO," 56)

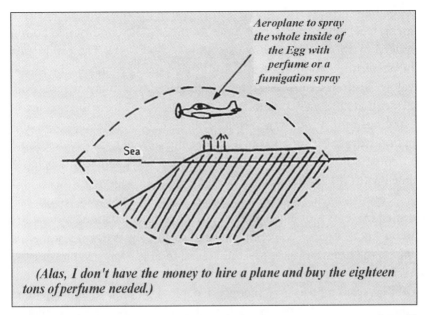

Aeroplane to spray the whole inside of the Egg with perfume or a fumigation spray

Sea

(Alas, I don't have the money to hire a plane and buy the eighteen tons of perfume needed.)

Figure 5.1. Illustration from Albert Wendt, "I Will Be Our Saviour from the Bad Smell," in *The Birth and Death of the Miracle Man and Other Stories* (Honolulu: University of Hawai'i Press, 1986).

This passage inverts the plot of "Bad Smell": the existential threat in Wendt's manifesto for Oceanic cultural independence is not a noxious odor but rather "an almost paranoic quest" for deodorization. Air conditioning and hygienic "education" colonize both the space and the sensorium of Oceania, resulting in an impoverished smellscape and a cultural aversion to smell characteristic of Western modernity. Instead of the environmental continuities afforded by the traditional Samoan *fale*—a thatched hut supported by columns, with no walls—air-conditioned structures with no connection to Oceanic traditions propagate what urban studies scholar Richard Sennett has diagnosed as "the problem of sensory deprivation in space."[55] For Wendt, "The new tourist hotels constructed of dead materials . . . echo the spiritual, creative, and emotional emptiness in modern man. The drive is for deodorized/sanitized comfort, the very quicksand in which many of us are now drowning, willingly" ("TNO," 56–57). With their inert materials, formal uniformity, and complete disregard of the surrounding environment, Oceania's proliferating hotel rooms are "air-conditioned coffins lodged in air-conditioned mausoleums" ("TNO," 57). The production of Westernized, modernist, and deodorized spaces results in "bourgeois values, attitudes, and life-styles which are compellingly attractive illnesses that kill slowly, comfortably, turning us away from the richness of our cultures" ("TNO," 57). Wendt's critique of colonial and postcolonial architecture rejects the biomedical assumptions of hygienic discourse: he equates deodorization with slow death, while implicitly associating smell with "the richness of our cultures."

"Towards a New Oceania" reprises many of the ideas Wendt presented in "A Sermon on National Development, Education, and the Rot in the South Pacific," a speech delivered at the 1974 Waigani Seminar on the topic of Education in Melanesia held in Port Moresby. Drawing on Wendt's own experience as the principal of his former high school, Samoa College, from 1969 to 1973, the speech deploys the extended metaphor of "the rot" to diagnose the social damage resulting from colonial religion, education, and architecture throughout Oceania.[56] The "rot" is a product of greed and elitism exacerbated by colonialism: in an account that looks forward to the political expediency that motivates the narrator of "Bad Smell," Wendt declares that "much of our development has been based, and still is being based, on whim and fancy, on personal advantage, vindictiveness and the desire to maintain oneself in power at all costs."[57] A section titled "Architecture and the Rot"—which includes many of the observations about deodorized tourist structures already quoted from "Towards a New Oceania"—concludes with a bad smell that pervades Pacific societies struggling with colonialism and its legacies:

> The senseless struggle for political power, the whisky flab, the steel and hygienic plastic, the petty empire-builder-hunter and seller of human flesh, the seemingly indestructible colonial Hollywood dream of South Seas paradises, the whispering of pastor and confidence "expert," the unprincipled politician and tourist prophet fingering Joseph's coat of many colours, Papa Docs and their hungry clans, the smiling teeth of sermons and political litanies, the woolen charcoal suits and black ties and mafia sunglasses are upon us. To those who are not yet repressed into passivity, *the stench of the rot is becoming overpowering.* ("S," 377, emphasis added)

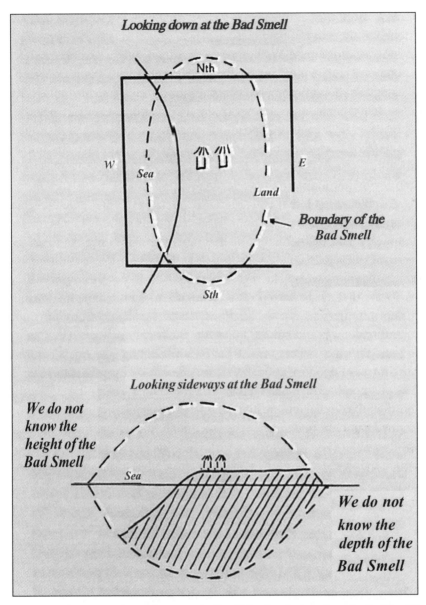

Figure 5.2. Illustration from Albert Wendt, "I Will Be Our Saviour from the Bad Smell," in *The Birth and Death of the Miracle Man and Other Stories* (Honolulu: University of Hawai'i Press, 1986).

This account of Oceania's bad smell explicitly identifies the sources of stench in the cultural tendencies toward individual gain resulting from colonialism's decimation of Indigenous tradition and the architectural and economic incursions of Western modernity and global capitalism. Wendt's catalogue of the rot's components transitions from his architectural criticism to a trenchant critique of colonial education as a mechanism for spreading the stench, transforming students "into tired, middle-aged, young people, very willing wearers of the white-collar noose, chasing the dream of 'respectability' in a dog-kennel-shaped house. . . . Duplicates of ourselves, they in turn perpetuate the rot" ("S," 378).

A subject of colonial education, the narrator of "Bad Smell" recoils from the body and its excretions. Drawing on his training in geography, geometry, and mathematics, he diagrams the shape, size, and boundaries of the smell (Figure 5.2). But when his wife asks what difference these diagrams will make, he comments, "In every community there is always that hard-hearted realist who, whenever our imaginations lift us up into dizzy poetic speculations, drags us back down to our body odour and juices and pain" ("BS," 109). The narrator's aversion to "body odour" indicates perhaps the strongest source of the bad smell: colonial discourses of deodorization. The story's demonized smell (associated at various points with "evil," "Hell," and the "Devil") may simply be the product of colonial and postcolonial health officials and educators who trained Samoans to denigrate the smells of bodies, decaying plants, and swamp water ("BS," 96, 99, 109, 110). The smell emanates from both Samoan living spaces *and* the Christian church because it is the church's deodorizing ideology that frames everyday Indigenous practices in stigmatizing terms. The odor emerges from the friction between Christianity and Pacific cosmologies: as Sharrad notes, "The oval of the smell's area of influence traces the shape of the traditional *fale* building and village layout, and there are Pacific creation myths that begin with a cosmic egg-shape."[58] The majority of the villagers eventually come to "acknowledge our Odour as an essential part of our lives"; only the narrator, with his intense investments in Western education and science, persists in his paranoid and counterproductive plans to fight the smell with militarized rockets, perfume sprays, and chemical fumigation ("BS," 124). As the narrator concocts schemes that would only exacerbate the air's toxicity, the story suggests that the only way to effectively extirpate the "bad" smell would be to decolonize the narrator's sensorium. Wendt's story thus stages the distinction between the postcolonial and the decolonial subject described by Priscilla Solis Ybarra: "The postcolonial is genealogically based on Western theory, taking as a point of departure a modern subject for whom 'knowledge can be objective' (Mignolo, *Darker* xxiv), while the decolonial prioritizes a non-Western theoretical basis and puts the body, a body politics of knowing at its center."[59] Read alongside Wendt's earlier commentaries on colonial architecture and rot, "Bad Smell" emerges as a caustic parable of colonial air conditioning's psychologically and environmentally damaging consequences: in his efforts to eradicate the stench of colonialism, the narrator only proliferates atmospheric violence and the deodorized thinking that dissembles it.

The Smell of Sovereignty

Like Wendt, Kanaka Maoli activist, writer, and political scientist Haunani-Kay Trask has contributed to Indigenous and decolonial movements throughout Oceania and well beyond. Her poetry and nonfiction build on her work as an advocate for Hawaiian sovereignty and the founder and former director of the University of Hawai'i's Kamakakūokalani Center for Hawaiian Studies. "[My] writing is both de-colonization and re-creation," she writes. "It is *creativity against the American grain and in the Hawaiian grain.*"[60] In "The Color of Violence" (2004), Trask draws on Fanon's concept of "peaceful violence" to frame colonization in terms that resonate with Nixon's recent conceptualization of environmental slow violence: "This kind of 'peaceful violence' results in land confiscations, contamination of our plants, animals, and our peoples, and the transformation of our archipelago into a poisonous war zone."[61] In Trask's poetry and essays, critical assessments of colonialism's orchestrations of smell clarify the stakes of her decolonial invocations of Indigenous modes of olfactory knowledge and practice.

Whereas Wendt underscores the psychological and cultural effects of Western ideologies of deodorization, Trask dwells on both the olfactory ecologies occluded by colonization and the unpleasant—and in many cases toxic—odors that it calls forth. Like Wendt, she catalogues the multifarious components of colonialism's stench in *From a Native Daughter: Colonialism and Sovereignty in Hawai'i* (1993). Trask's account, however, emphasizes colonialism's material effects on Hawaiian atmospheres:

> In colony Hawai'i, not only the cruelty but *the stench of colonialism* is everywhere: at Pearl Harbor, so thoroughly polluted by the American military that it now ranks among the top priorities on the Environmental Protection Agency's superfund list; at Waikiki, one of the most famous beaches in the world, where human excrement from the overloaded Honolulu sewer system floats just off shore; at Honolulu International Airport, where jet fuel from commercial, military, and private planes creates an eternal pall in the still hot air; in the magnificent valleys and plains of all major islands where heavy pesticide/herbicide use on sugar plantations and mammoth golf courses results in contaminated wetlands, rivers, estuaries, bays, and, of course, groundwater sources; on the grid-locked freeways, which swallow up more and more land as the American way of life carves its path toward destruction; in the schools and businesses and hotels and shops and government buildings and on the radio and television, where white Christian American values of capitalism, racism, and violent conflict are upheld, supported, and deployed against the Native people.[62]

Conflating the metaphorical and material registers of colonialism's "stench," Trask depicts the US occupation as a process of atmospheric transformation. She documents how air pollution resulting from militarization, tourism, transportation infrastructure, and monocrop agriculture—processes whose benefits accrue to settlers and visitors—disproportionately endangers Kānaka Maoli people, even as cultural institutions and media produce a discursive atmosphere that artfully obscures—and thus upholds—settler colonialism's dependence on structural violence.

Particularly in Oceania, colonialism's stench has been dissimulated (and in many cases exacerbated) by discourses and industries that commodify its exoticized scents. Hawai'i's fragrant sandalwood trees, for example, were decimated in the early nineteenth century by New England merchants who traded it for tea in China. Although sandalwood was once one of the most common upland trees in Hawai'i, "by 1856 the wood had become very scarce."[63] By the time Mark Twain visited Hawai'i in 1866, the notion of the land's "fragrance" was already trite enough to caricature: "I never breathed such a soft, delicious atmosphere before, nor one freighted with such rich fragrance. A barber shop is nothing to it."[64] In his *Natural History of Hawaii* (1915), William Bryan exoticizes the fragrance of the *maile* vine, detaching it from its social and spiritual significance: "It is of the maile that the voyager first hears as he lands in the islands of sunshine and smiles. It is for the maile that he learns to seek on his day-long rambles in the mountains, and it is a braided strand of maile thrown about his neck at the fond parting by the shore that tells with its fresh breath of the enchanted forest, in an enchanted land."[65] As Drobnick has shown, Paul Gauguin's influential memoir *Noa Noa* (1901) overturns Victorian aesthetic norms by indulging in exoticizing and effeminizing representations of Oceania's scents (the book's title means "fragrant" in Tahitian).[66] In a trenchant critique of tourism's effects on Hawai'i, Trask underscores the role of smell in exoticizing, sensuous representations of her land: "Hawai'i—the word, the vision, the sound in the mind—is the fragrance and feel of soft kindness."[67]

Trask's poetry opposes efforts to commodify Hawai'i's "fragrance" not only by exposing colonialism's proliferation of noxious smells, but also by drawing attention to decolonial practices of olfaction. For Indigenous Hawai'ians, many botanical scents are imbued with spiritual significance: for example, "Maile is associated with worship of the gods. Old Hawaiians declare that the subtle pervasive scent of maile still clings to those sites where ancient heiaus stood. Especially is the maile noted among the plants used for decorating the altar to the gods of the hula."[68] Kahu Mikahala Roy articulates her calling as "Kahu (Spiritual Guardian)" of the Ahu'ena sacred site in olfactory terms: "I search for the channel made fragrant by the maile."[69] Moreover, a Kanaka Maoli sensorium would situate fragrance on a continuum with stench, refusing the moralizing opposition between "good" and "bad" smells except in the case of invasive, toxic odors. In the *Kumulipo*, an ancient Hawaiian cosmogony and genealogy first published in print in 1889, smell is associated with birth in lines that move freely between "sacred scent" and "stench": "The sacred scent from the gourd stem proclaims [itself] / The stench breaks forth in the time of infancy."[70] Entangled with Indigenous spirituality and genealogies, both fragrant and pungent smells carry generative and connective potential. Trask's decolonial approach to smell distinguishes not between pleasant (commodified) and repulsive odors, but between autochthonous and toxic, Indigenous and foreign.

For Trask, smell is more than an element of environmental description or a metaphor for colonialism's "stench." Her framing of colonialism as a toxic atmosphere builds on the profound significance of air in Hawaiian religion and political theory. While many of her poems (discussed below) explicitly describe Hawaiian deities in terms of breath and scent, her accounts of air are also informed by the interconnected definitions of the term *ea* in Hawaiian language and culture. Among the definitions given in Pukui and Elbert's *Hawaiian Dictionary* are: "ea. 1. n. Sovereignty, rule, independence. . . . *Ho'iho'i ke ea o Hawai'i*, restore the sovereignty of Hawai'i. 2. n. Life, air, breath, respiration, vapor, gas; fumes, as of tobacco; breeze, spirit. . . . *Kaha ea*, to deprive of rights of livelihood. *Wai ea*, aerated waters. *Ho'opuka ea*, exhaust fumes. . . . 4. vi. To smell. Also 'ea . . . *ea pilau*, evil-smelling, rotten-smelling."[71] The complexity of *ea*—a simultaneously material and political concept that blends air, sovereignty, and vitality—informs the motto of Hawai'i, *Ua mau ke ea o ka 'āina I ka pono* ("the life of the land is perpetuated in righteousness").[72] Yet, *ea* can also refer to polluted atmospheres ("exhaust fumes") as well as the emitted odors that modulate the air and alert us to atmospheric threats ("to smell"). This provokes questions that would be unimaginable to Western thinkers who typically imagine sovereignty as inodorate: What is the smell of Hawaiian sovereignty? And how can that smell be recuperated from colonialism's differentially deodorized and polluted atmospheres? *Ea* invokes a cosmology in which sovereignty is not only present in political decision making but materially immanent in everyday atmospheric exposures.[73]

Trask's *Light in the Crevice Never Seen* (1994), "the first book of poems by a native Hawaiian to be published in North America,"[74] loses no time in framing colonization as an olfactory affront. The book opens with "A People Lost," an account of the atmospheric "dysplacement" visited upon the Kānaka Maoli:

> strange unscented trees
> from Asia and the Middle
> East, great gouges of
> Northern white

Nothing familiar in
The Arctic wind how
did this happen here?
my ill-clothed people
black hair freezing

in the American air
sores and frost on their tender
lungs, gasping for life
in our native Hawai'i[75]

Trask opens the book with a poem about atmospheric alienation—
the strangeness of "unscented" invasive vegetation and "freezing . . .
American air." Colonialism affects not only the land and bodies of the
colonized, but their debilitated lungs: "gasping for life" in such a cold
and unfamiliar atmosphere accounts for the gaps and silences surrounding Trask's brief and frequently enjambed lines.

The title of Trask's book refers to the Earth Mother, or
Papahānaumoku—"Papa who gives birth to islands," a central deity in
Hawaiian and Oceanic cosmology.[76] In Trask's account, colonization has
poisoned the creations of the life-giving Earth. Recalling Wendt's indictment of Oceania's tourist hotels as "air-conditioned coffins," a poem
titled "Missionary Graveyard" evokes the deadly atmospheric effects of
colonization's landscapes:

graveyard Hawai'i Nei:
coffin buildings, concrete parking
lots, maggot freeways

smell of death
smeared across the land

killing in the heart (*LC*, 13)[77]

The poem's graveyard, it turns out, refers not to the burial place of
dead missionaries but to all of "Hawai'i Nei" transformed by deodorized settler architectures and the pervasive "smell of death." Rather than

describe this smell, Trask goes on to detail its consequences for the body and breath:

> a disease of the heart
> out of breath at every street corner
> going home with swollen legs
> watery eyes, a slow burning
> in the chest.

"Missionary Graveyard" depicts the slow violence of differential deodorization: the outward construction of apparently hygienic, efficient structures juxtaposed with the debilitating effects of these spatial transformations. The resultant "killing in the heart" could be read as psychosomatic (an affective response to the land's transformation by automobiles, concrete, steel, asphalt, and glass), physiological (directly caused by traffic fumes, construction dust, pesticides, industrial and military pollutants), or both. The atmosphere's insidious, accretive physical effects on the eyes, legs, and lungs physically debilitate the people—particularly those who must walk the streets without relying on air-conditioned, carbon-burning cars. The "smell" of slow death thus transforms all of Hawai'i into a graveyard of the living constructed by missionaries and their settler descendants.

"Hawai'i," the longest poem in *Light in the Crevice*, begins with an idyllic sketch conveying the smells of a day at the beach:

> The smell of the sea
> at Hale'iwa, mixed with
> early smoke, a fire
> for fish and buttered clams
>
> in a rapturous morning. (*LC*, 34)

While these lines could be taken as an account of Hale'iwa's natural and sensory pleasures, Trask soon reveals that the poem's real subject is theft, shifting our attention to "that ruddy face / coming from cold breakers," and noting how "they take our pleasures / thoughtlessly" (*LC*, 34). The lines pivot on the double meaning of "rapturous"—being seized or carried off with pleasure, a word that shares its origin with "rape." Fragrant with cooking smoke and sea air, the idyll here belongs to settlers and tourists, not to the Kānaka Maoli.

From this scene of stolen sensory pleasures, the poem turns to the environmental and religious threats posed by the drilling of geothermal wells. In an endnote, Trask comments, "Geothermal energy development on Hawai'i Island threatens the sanctity of Pele, Hawaiian deity of the volcano, and her sister, Hi'iaka, deity of the forest" (*LC*, 40). In her informative analysis of the role of the *mo'olelo* ("hi/story") of Pele and Hi'iaka in Trask's writings, McDougall explains that, in addition to providing important figures of generation (where "Pele, as the volcano goddess, creates land" and "Hi'iakaikapoliopele . . . greens the earth after the lava has cooled"), these divinities have come to embody *mana wahine* ("feminine power") and "resistance to Christian and colonial ideology."[78] Trask's poem suggests that harnessing "Energy" from the earth desecrates these gods, along with the breath of Papahānaumoku—the Earth Mother worshipped as a progenitor of the Hawaiian people:

> Breath of Papa's life
> miraculously becomes
> Energy
> stink with
>
> sulfurous sores. Hi'iaka
> wilting in her wild home:
> black *lehua*, shriveled
> *Pukiawe*, unborn *'a'ali'i*. (*LC*, 37)

Trask's account—which associates the "miracle" of purportedly "green" energy with the "wilting," blackening, and shriveling of both the goddess Hi'iaka (Pele's sister, associated with Hawai'i, *hula*, and medicine) and several fragrant indigenous plants (as well as the Hawaiian language used to name them)[79]—echoes the concerns of protestors who opposed the drilling of geothermal wells in the Wao Kele O Puna rainforest. As Paul Faulstich reports, "One hundred and forty-one people, led by

Native Hawaiians, were arrested on 25 March 1990 as part of the largest demonstration yet against geothermal development in Hawaii."[80] Trask's account of "energy/stink" refers (among other things) to the hydrogen sulfide emitted by geothermal wells: "a toxic gas that, when mixed with air, becomes sulfuric acid (one of the main components of acid rain). . . . The levels of hydrogen sulfide that will be emitted by the wells can cause, among other things, headaches, lung irritations, nausea, and vomiting. The toxic gases emitted by a single geothermal well drilled nearby in the early 1980s become so bad that at one point the operation had be shut down and residents evacuated."[81] In the poem's following section, the "stink" of hydrogen sulfide is transmuted into acid rain:

> VII
> From the frozen heavens
> a dense vapor
> colored like the skin
>
> of burnt milk, descending
> onto our fields, and
> mountains and waters
>
> into the recesses
> of our poisoned
> na'au. (LC, 37)

Trask's stanzas track the movement of Papa's desecrated breath as its poison moves from geothermal wells to the sky, fields, and waters and finally into the people's bodies and ways of being. As she notes, "Na'au means, literally, intestines. But metaphorically, na'au also represents what the heart means to Westerners, that is, the home of emotions, of understanding. Na'au can also refer, in a figurative sense, to a child" (LC, 40). Air, soil, water, emotions, understanding, bodily organs, and future generations (underscored by the image of "burnt milk") are all suffused with poison as Trask traces the transmutations of energy's stink. The poem concludes by acknowledging that "these foreigners / these Americans" have given rise to "a foul stench / among our children" (LC, 38). "Hawai'i" thus traces a dystopian trajectory from the commodified, "rapturous" smell of the sea to anxieties about the changed (and changing) atmosphere in which "our children" exist.

Light in the Crevice juxtaposes these recurring toxic scents with positive instances of decolonial olfaction. "Dark Time," for example, shifts from a photograph of Hawaiian men at hard labor in the "Kāne'ohe wind scented / with sad gardenia torn / *ulu* branches" to a faraway "familiar smell / of aging earth // coursing back through clouded / bloodlines" (*LC*, 17–18). "Comin Home," composed in pidgin, describes the funereal ceremonies for Trask's twenty-six-year-old cousin, whose ashes are wrapped with *pua kenikeni* ("fragrant orange flower") as mourners throw ginger and "Lily of da Valley" (*LC*, 97). And, referring to the *kāla'au* or "Hawaiian dance with long sticks" (*LC*, 94) performed in the *Hula*, Trask describes a "fragrant clack clack / from the shadows" as the impact of the sticks striking one another releases their scent (*LC*, 75). These brief encounters with invigorating and dignifying scents look forward to the decolonial approach to olfaction developed in Trask's second book of poetry, *Night Is a Sharkskin Drum* (2002).

While the book's title evokes the sonic and tactile sensations of drumming, olfaction also plays a vital role in the book's multisensory approach to decolonization. *Sharkskin Drum* juxtaposes invocations of Hawaiian deities—most centrally the volcanic goddess Pele—with a middle section, titled "A Fragrance of Devouring," whose poems decry the desolation wrought by settler colonialism.[82] Here, Trask brings olfactory language to bear on the colonization of the landscape, the atmosphere, and the senses:

> A common horizon:
> smelly shores
> under spidery moons,
> pockmarked *maile* vines,
> rotting *'ulu* groves,
> the brittle *clack*
> of broken lava stones.
>
> OUT OF THE EAST
>   a damp stench of money
>   burning at the edges. (*SD*, 12–13)

The stench of polluted shores and money degrades the *'ulu* (breadfruit) and *maile*—defined in the book's glossary as "a native twining shrub with fragrant shiny leaves used for decoration and *lei*" (*SD*, 67). The broken lava stones allude to the generative volcanic force of the divinity Pele, whose sulfuric emanations have been supplanted here by "a damp stench of money." Colonization's "common horizon" takes the form of insidious and pervasive atmospheric transformations, which slowly erode the health of indigenous plants.

Other poems in this section extend Trask's olfactory critique of colonialism. "Smiling Corpses" contrasts the corruption of the settler colonial Democratic Party with an enigmatic scent:

> Below, from the banana spires,
>   rotten steam,
>
>   a fragrance
>   of devouring. (*SD*, 24)

The apparent incongruity of Trask's shift from the "stench" of money and imperialism to the "fragrance / of devouring" registers the ways in which olfactory judgments are culturally determined. How can this rotten steam be both fragrant and noxious? Settler colonialism dissimulates its "devouring"—as well as its atmospheric pollution—with projects of deodorization and artificial fragrance. On another level, Trask's steamy "fragrance / of devouring" alludes to the pungent volcanic power of Pele, who is invoked in an earlier poem: "Pele, Pele'aihonua / traveling the uplands, / *devouring* the foreigner" (*SD*, 8, emphasis added). As McDougall comments, "Trask's depiction of Pele'aihonua's angry consuming of the foreigner represents her own outrage at the foreigner's presence."[83] By calling forth these diametrically opposed readings, Trask's evocation of the "fragrance / of devouring" suggests that smell can be mobilized as either a tool of colonialism or a means of decolonization.

By ascribing stench to ostensibly deodorized objects, Trask rejects both the use of olfactory stigma to denigrate Indigenous bodies and colonial education's disqualification of olfactory knowledge. In a poem that decries the militarized centennial celebration of the overthrow of the

Kingdom of Hawai'i in 1893, Trask writes, "In 1993, poisoned islands /
the stench of treason" (*SD*, 27). Despite its professed commitment to
deodorization, colonization's military, infrastructural, and industrial
drives bring a stench that both materially and ideologically "poison[s]"
the people. Another poem condemns the hypocrisy of colonial funereal
ritual, addressing a Hawaiian corpse embalmed and laid out in a coffin.
Trask's critique of Western embalming practices offers a stark contrast to
the fragrant mourning practices described in her earlier poem, "Comin
Home": "as if / the gleam of your magnificent / time could be muted / by
the waxy smell / of missionary lies" (*SD*, 29). In "Dispossessions of Empire," Trask describes the new hierarchies of racialized settlers, tourists,
and Indigenous Hawaiians introduced by colonization:

> Slow-footed Hawaiians
>   amidst flaunting
> foreigners: rich
>   Americans, richer
>
> JAPANESE, SMELLING
>   of greasy perfume,
> tanning with the stench
>   of empire. (*SD*, 33)

Echoing her earlier invocation of the "stench of money," Trask associates perfume—a luxury scent product intended to mark its wearer's
social distinction—with grease and "stench." The poem's concluding
lines elaborate on "the stench / of empire" by shifting our attention to
noxious Indigenous landscapes masked by tourist hotels and designer
scents: "An orphaned smell / of ghettos in this tourist / archipelago:
shanties / on the beach, slums // in the valleys, corruption / and trash
everywhere" (*SD*, 36). Throughout "A Fragrance of Devouring," Trask
employs olfactory perceptions and metaphors to frame colonization as
a process of differential deodorization in which the production of toxic
atmospheres—primarily in Indigenous communities—is a constitutive
condition of perfumed bodies and pristine landscapes.

Trask's incisive accounts of colonialism's differentiated smellscapes
set the scene for the lyrical efforts to decolonize the senses presented in

Sharkskin Drum's third section—"Chants of Dawn." Encompassing all five senses, the poems in this section imaginatively clear the air of empire's stench. As Barbara Jane Reyes notes, the section is set "in a place or a time away from the ugly machine of tourism and empire, almost like an imagined, alternate/alternative place and time, in which she may honor her ancestors and her land, in which she may once again incant and pray."[84] "To Hear the Mornings" is structured by a series of sensuous sketches whose infinitive verbs—"To hear," "To watch," "To breathe," "To sense"—grammatically suspend these activities between the optative and imperative moods. In a striking invocation of breath, Trask writes,

> To breathe the Akua:
>   *lehua* and *makani,*
>   *pua* and *lāʻī,*
>   *maile* and *palai,* . . .
>   pungent *kino lau.*
>
> To sense the ancients,
>   *Ka wā mamua*—from time before
>   . . . within the bosom of Pele. (*SD,* 41)

Akua, according to the book's glossary, refers to "God; supernatural; divine" (*SD,* 63). The poem elaborates the idea of breathing divinity with a catalogue of scented forms: *lehua* (which Trask glosses as as "flower of the *ʻōhiʻa* tree"), *makani* ("wind, breeze"), *pua* ("flower"), *lāʻī* ("*ti* leaf"), *maile, palai* ("Native Hawaiian fern, important to Laka, goddess of the *hula*") (*SD,* 67, 68, 66). The pungent "*kino lau*" in the stanza's concluding line refers to the "many forms taken by a god, such as the *ti* leaf as a form of the *moʻo* (lizard) god" (*SD,* 66). Here, kinship is both genealogical and material: in accordance with Kanaka Maoli cosmogonies, all forms of life are descended from the gods,[85] and their breath sustains—and is sustained by—direct and ongoing connection to "the ancients." Underscoring the pungent scents of *kino lau,* Trask conceives of the divine not only in connection with a multitude of worldly forms, but as a trans-corporeal atmosphere that inhabits and transforms bodies through breath.

Other poems expand this project of olfactory decolonization, in which Indigenous smells are associated with forces of generation and regeneration for both individuals and the land. In "Returning," the image of "Slow-hipped Kāneʻohe, / wet-scented lover // chanting / us in" blends sexual pleasure with ecological attunement and the resurgence of Indigenous geographies: Trask notes that "Kāneʻohe" can refer to a "Land division on the windward side of Oʻahu" (the windward side being more wet, lush, and windy) as well as "the bamboo of the god Kāne; or, alternately, bamboo husband" (*SD*, 65). Another poem turns to the smell of rock slits as a natural, sensuous resource for a precarious fern: "where the fern / clings, lingering / above slit // rock, shadows / musky in hot perfume" (*SD*, 49). As McDougall notes, the erotic imagery in these poems rejects colonial legacies that stigmatize sexuality, instead drawing on "the erotic or sexual [as] a traditional Hawaiian metaphor" for "the life force and proliferous vitality behind any valuable endeavor."[86]

"From Kaʻaʻawa to Rarotonga"—a poem that associates the *ʻiwa* bird with the broader geography of Oceania (Rarotonga is the most populous of the Cook Islands, located almost three thousand miles south of Kaʻaʻawa)—deploys smell to convey the speaker's sensual connections with land and atmosphere. The poem opens with

> rainswept banana groves
> under a burdened sky
>
> REFRESHED BY SMELLS
> of seawind, blowing
>
> clouds to breadfruit islands,
> my tribal spirit
> dreaming flight,
> from Kaʻa ʻawa
> to Rarotonga (*SD*, 45)

As political scientist Noenoe Silva (Kanaka Maoli) notes in her study of Indigenous Hawaiian ontologies and epistemologies, "Winds are a part of the sensual nature of Hawaiian geography. . . . We feel them and smell the fragrances or odors they carry with them."[87] In the atmospheric exchange ("smells of seawind" and blown clouds) between Hawaiʻi and Rarotonga the extensive atmospheric resources made available by

Oceania's vast, interconnected "sea of islands" offer some respite from colonialism's "burdened sky."[88] Trask's lines—which echo the Kanaka Maoli songwriter Carlos Andrade's invocation of "the cold wind . . . carrying the cool, soft, sweet / fragrance of the tiare Maori" in "Ocean Road from Rarotonga to Hawai'i"[89]—recast decolonization as a project that extends far beyond Hawai'i: the resurgence of Indigenous sovereignty and its associated smells requires coordination across all the militarized, hyperexploited nations of Oceania. For Trask, the fate of the earth is immanent in these "smells of seawind" crossing the Pacific: as she explains, "The first world nations must still learn what Pacific Islanders have known for millennia: upon the survival of the Pacific depends the survival of the world."[90]

Trask's poetry decolonizes smell by attending to Indigenous scents suppressed by settler colonial atmospherics: sea winds, maile, Pele's smoke, rock musk—all the "pungent *kino lau*" or worldly forms assumed by the shapeshifting gods. Shifting from Oceania to the Indigenous lands occupied by the United States, and from literary forms to material practices of air conditioning (albeit mediated through literary nonfiction), the following section considers smudging and sweetgrass restoration in the work of Robin Wall Kimmerer (Potawatomi) as decolonial practices of air conditioning.

Decolonial Air Conditioning

Smudging—a spiritual healing ceremony practiced by numerous Indigenous nations—challenges us to rethink this book's earlier discussions of "air conditioning" and olfactory aesthetics. Despite the centrality of atmospheric engineering to the literature, culture, and spatial productions of Western modernity, it is important to keep in mind that both atmospheric engineering and olfactory aesthetic interventions have rich traditions in Indigenous and non-Western societies. A traditional ceremony with pre-Columbian origins, smudging indicates that Indigenous people recognized the power and health effects of atmospheric engineering long before the battlefield deployment of mustard gas (which Sloterdijk identifies as the originary moment of Western "air conditioning"). Smudging also challenges the genealogies of olfactory art discussed in chapter 3: if aesthetics, following Rancière, is characterized by "a certain recasting of the distribution of the sensible," then smudging can be understood, in part, as an instance of olfactory aesthetics that draws attention to the simultaneously spiritual and material dimensions of invisible olfactory experience. As an Indigenous practice of air conditioning, smudging decolonizes smell on two levels: first, by asserting the value of olfaction as a means of acquiring embodied, trans-corporeal knowledge; and second, by transforming settler smellscapes in ways supportive of place-based knowledge and Indigenous sovereignty.

As a settler scholar interested in understanding Indigenous olfactory knowledge, I ground my discussion by centering the work of Indigenous scholars who have described and analyzed smudging ceremonies and other olfactory practices. Although smudging includes sensory, material, and spiritual exchanges that far exceed the sense of smell, I focus on how it transforms both material and affective atmospheres through olfactory experience. In a remarkable assessment of representations of sweetgrass and sweetgrass smudging informed by new materialist scholarship, Métis artist, writer, and scholar Warren Cariou writes, "In the cultures I am most familiar with—Métis, Cree, and Anishinaabe—sweetgrass is used in ceremonies for the purposes of healing, purification, and clearing the mind. Its rich and aromatic scent, both when fresh and when it is burned, is regarded as an important part of its healing power. Indeed, one could say that the plant's scent is its most direct mode of physical communication with human beings, bringing them knowledge that has bodily, spiritual, and psychological effects and meanings."[91] Cariou singles out scent as the plant's "most direct mode of physical communication" with humans—a mode of communication that works on both a material and semiotic level (that is, it conveys both "effects and meanings"). A trans-corporeal message, the scent of sweetgrass hails and reintegrates breathers into a network of place-based kin relations that cross the lines of nations, species, and taxonomical kingdoms. What sweetgrass heals is not a discrete, individual human body but a reciprocal relationship between human, nonhuman, earthly, and atmospheric bodies: "The scent of wihkaskwa makes me feel good—alive, refreshed, calmed, rested, cleansed. It reminds me of my connection to the earth, which it holds and broadcasts in its very scent."[92] Like the Kanaka Maoli scents featured in Trask's poems, the scent of sweetgrass communicates modes of atmospheric knowledge and relation that have sustained Indigenous nations through the genocidal, ecocidal, and indeed postapocalyptic conditions of colonization: as Kyle Powys Whyte (Potawatomi) writes, "The value of these local stories and relationships derives from indigenous people's knowledge of what it means to survive and flourish in times our ancestors would have likely imagined to be dystopian."[93]

In her illuminating discussion of the relations between the smudging ceremony and multiculturalism's project of Indigenous assimilation, sociologist Vanessa Watts (Anishinaabe and Haudenosaunee) underscores the spiritual and place-based qualities of Anishinaabeg smudging:

> In the smudging ceremony[,] which involves the burning of sage as a purification cleansing ritual so as to cleanse the person's mind, spirit, body, and emotions of negative energy, we are asking the spirit world and the spirit of the sage itself to aid in our emotional, physical, spiritual, and mental cleansing. The sage that is burnt is materially cleansing these parts of ourselves. The spirit world is engaged in ceremony with us through the usage of sage, and correspondingly the spirit world can also affect us and other beings through dreams, signs, and ceremonies. This shared affectual relationship is both accommodated by place and embodied in place—the basis of which is reciprocity.[94]

Watts describes smudging as a practice oriented by reciprocal relations between human and nonhuman bodies, as well as between bodies and spirits: "a place-based . . . method of exchange between humans, nonhumans and the spirit world" ("ST," 163). Through the material and spiritual qualities of air, smudging both manifests and re-creates connections between Anishinaabeg people and their ancestral land. Watts describes it as a mode of "communication" that "affirms the embodied relation we have to place" ("ST," 152). Because colonial modes of knowledge and spirituality do not share these intimate connections with place, they threaten to disembody and displace Indigenous cosmologies: "In the presence of a reciprocal and interdependent relationship, when place is altered, is the spirit world altered as well?" ("ST," 155, 151).

Watts powerfully conveys both the cosmological significance of smudging and the ways in which displacement and ecological colonialism—as well as the settler appropriations and officially tolerated performances that she terms "boardroom smudging" ("ST," 163)—further settler colonialism's elimination of Indigenous ways of being. Recent settler prohibitions on smudging deploy legal rhetorics of nuisance and public safety to extend earlier bans on Indigenous spiritual practices enforced by Christian missionaries and residential boarding schools. For example, in many apartment buildings in Winnipeg (which is located on Anishinaabe land), building codes and the installation of smoke detectors have made smudging and sweat ceremonies impracticable at home, despite the importance of these practices in sustaining "Indigenous therapeutic spaces, intimately connected to the land."[95] Many colleges prohibit or heavily regulate smudging in dormitories, despite its religious significance. As Gene Thin Elk, Native American cultural adviser at the University of South Dakota, explains, "These plants' lives are not used as incense, but as a sacred rite in which the plants give their lives so that we can live a good life. In turn, one day we shall give our lives so that the plant nations may live."[96] In 2016, an Indigenous Xicana, Josie Valadez Fraire, was detained for praying with smoking sage at an anti-Trump rally in Denver.[97] These cases exemplify the tension between the settler state's interest in deodorization (framed in terms of health and security concerns) and Indigenous experiences of smudging as a therapeutic and spiritual ceremony.

This tension is only partially resolved when settler institutions make exceptions for smudging. For example, the incorporation of smudging at some museums as an Indigenous or "culturally sensitive" curatorial practice is an important but limited exception to the conservationist atmospherics analyzed in chapter 3. Curators at the National Museum of Natural History's Department of Anthropology provide a space in the storage facility for Native American visitors who wish to smudge sacred objects in the collection.[98] At the National Museum of the American Indian's storage facility, "the Human Remains Vault is smudged with a mixture of tobacco, sage, sweetgrass, and cedar every week."[99] Nancy Rosoff also notes that smudging may offer an alternative to conservation methods that isolate objects from surrounding air to protect them from insects: "Current standard museum treatments such as plastic bags, freezing, and low-oxygen atmospheres may be inappropriate for certain objects because they might 'suffocate' a living entity. Therefore, the staff have begun investigating traditional Native American fumigation techniques such as regular smudging and the use of certain aromatic botanical substances in sachets."[100] These curatorial concessions designate exceptional spaces where "certain objects" are treated as materially continuous with the atmosphere. While these incorporations of smudging offer important models for curating and interacting with Indigenous entities, they also point to a broader need to support smudging practices beyond exceptional, specially designated spaces. As Watts writes in her critique of "boardroom smudging," "The act of ceremony outside of traditional places (for example, in colonial spaces such as boardrooms), can still be meaningful, but could also be a measure of disembodiment (the corruption of the spiritual life of place). This disembodiment is further intensified when it is used for purposes counter to spiritual processes. When the state engages in Indigenous ceremonies with Indigenous peoples to gain further concessions from place (e.g., extracting resources), both place and ceremony become increasingly damaged" ("ST," 163). How can an Indigenous olfactory practice like smudging be supported and revitalized as a decolonial practice of atmospheric sovereignty rather than as an exceptional practice circumscribed—and at times appropriated—by settler institutions?[101] This question is the point of departure for my reading of Potawatomi environmental biologist Robin Wall Kimmerer's discussions of Indigenous smellscapes and their ecological underpinnings in *Braiding Sweetgrass: Indigenous Wisdom, Scientific Knowledge, and the Teachings of Plants* (2013).

Braiding Sweetgrass, which received the 2014 Sigurd F. Olson Nature Writing Award, is a series of essays reflecting on Indigenous botanical knowledge derived not from detached observations made in laboratories but from generations of reciprocal coexistence with plants and other forms of nonhuman life. Unlike Wendt's narrator, who mobilizes scientific discourses and diagrams in his project of deodorization, Kimmerer elucidates the scientific insights already inherent in Indigenous cosmologies and stewardship practices. The book's preface begins with a figurative gift of sweetgrass, laid in the reader's hand "loose and flowing, like newly washed hair." Kimmerer then juxtaposes the plant's taxonomical classification with its Potawatomi name and a description of its evocative scent: "Hold the bundle up to your nose. Find the fragrance of honeyed vanilla over the scent of river water and black earth and you understand its scientific name: *Hierochloe odorata*, meaning the fragrant, holy grass. In our language it is called *wiingasshk*, the sweet-smelling hair of Mother Earth. Breathe it in and you start to remember things you didn't know you'd forgotten."[102] In his commentary on this passage, Cariou explains that "the idea of sweetgrass triggering memories of 'things you didn't know you had forgotten' suggests that the plant itself embodies cultural teachings that have been preserved from the deep past—as if the land's own memory is speaking through the scent of the sweetgrass."[103] Embodying both the scent of "your mother's . . . hair" and the "sweet-smelling hair of Mother Earth," the smell of sweetgrass evokes both individual and collective memories: "What words can capture that smell? The fragrance of your mother's newly washed hair as she holds you close, the melancholy smell of summer slipping into fall, the smell of memory that makes you close your eyes for a moment, and then a moment longer" (*BrS*, 263). The central conceit of Kimmerer's book is the collaborative weaving of sweetgrass, held by the reader and braided by the author—"woven from three strands: indigenous ways of knowing, scientific knowledge, and the story of an Anishnabekwe scientist trying to bring them together in service to what matters most" (*BrS*, x). This extended metaphor frames the entire book in terms of interaction and haptic reciprocity suffused with the multilayered scent of "fragrant, holy" sweetgrass.

While references to sweetgrass appear throughout Kimmerer's book, the plant and its fragrance are most prominently featured in the essay titled "Putting Down Roots." "Roots" opens by presenting two contrasting scenes separated by a four-hundred-year span at Kanatsiohareke, a settlement on the banks of the Mohawk River: four centuries ago, a woman harvesting sweetgrass with rhythmic motions; in the present, Kimmerer's own rhythmic motions as she replants sweetgrass clumps along the shore. Like the book's preface, this chapter opens with an olfactory sensation: "The sunshine pours down around us, warming the grass and releasing its scent" (*BrS*, 254). The essay goes on to contextualize the dislocations that constitute this scene: What happened to the indigenous sweetgrass here, and why does it need to be replanted? What is a Potawatomi botanist doing on ancestral Mohawk land?

"Roots" explains that many of the Mohawks, driven from their ancestral lands at Kanatsiohareke in the 1700s, resettled in Akwesasne on land that straddles the US-Canadian border. Kanatsiohareke was recently resettled by a group of Mohawks led by Sakokwenionk, or Tom Porter. Tom and his friends left Akwesasne, in part, because power dams and heavy industry had recently made it "one of the most contaminated communities in the country" (*BrS*, 257). But they were also motivated by a vision of Kanatsiohareke as "Carlisle in reverse"—a center for the resurgence of Mohawk language, culture, and identity oriented by Tom's motto, "Heal the Indian, Save the Language" (*BrS*, 258). Mohawk children had been shipped to the notorious Carlisle Indian Industrial School, where they were subjected to a program of cultural genocide that aimed (among other things) to deodorize students' bodies and re-organize their senses: "The scent of sweetgrass was replaced by the soap smells of the barracks laundry" (*BrS*, 255).

Replanting sweetgrass makes a vital contribution to Tom's project of "Carlisle in reverse," restoring Mohawk ecologies and psyches dam-aged by generations of settler warfare, relocation, ecological colonialism, heavy industry, and cultural genocide. Kimmerer notes that because sweetgrass propagates more readily through rhizomes than through seeds, it is especially vulnerable to the paved roads, concrete build-ings, and invasive plant species characteristic of settler landscapes. At Kanatsiohareke, the plant's disappearance has world-shattering implica-tions: "When Skywoman first scattered the plants, sweetgrass flourished along this river, but today it is gone. Just as the Mohawk language was replaced by English and Italian and Polish, the sweetgrass was crowded out by immigrants. Losing a plant can threaten a culture in much the same way as losing a language. Without sweetgrass, the grandmothers don't bring the granddaughters to the meadows in July. Then what be-comes of their stories? Without sweetgrass, what happens to the baskets? To the ceremony that uses these baskets?" (*BrS*, 261). The loss of sweet-grass threatens the material basis for an activity that has been central to the sustenance of Indigenous social, ecological, spiritual, and economic relations. In a discussion of basket weaving that contextualizes the title of her book, Kimmerer writes, "Even an empty basket contains the smell of the land, weaving the link between people and place, language and identity" (*BrS*, 257). In this formulation, it is not the basket's contents but the scent of its braided sweetgrass that materially interweaves "peo-ple and place, language and identity." Noting that her own grandfather had been among the more than 10,500 Indigenous children shipped to Carlisle Indian Industrial School, Kimmerer frames her ecological restoration work as a project of self-restoration: "When I was young, I had no one to tell me that, like the Mohawks, Potawatomi people revere sweetgrass as one of the four sacred plants. No one to say that it was the first plant to grow on Mother Earth and so we braid it, as if it were our mother's hair, to show our loving care for her. The runners of the story could not find their way through a fragmented cultural landscape to me. The story was stolen at Carlisle" (*BrS*, 263). Thus, the essay circuitously yet ineluctably arrives at the cultural and biological death-world of Carlisle, a city whose numerous memorials to settler heroes and histories dissemble its pivotal historical role in the devastation of Indigenous lives and cultures.[104] While the damage wrought there is unaccountable and on many levels irreversible, Kimmerer suggests that sweetgrass may point the way—if not to literal restoration, then to ecologies, sensory experiences, and spiritual practices supportive of Indigenous futures. "What we contemplate here is more than ecological restoration; it is the restoration of relationship between plants and people" (*BrS*, 263).

When Kimmerer and other descendants of the Indian School's survivors were invited to Carlisle as part of the city's tricentennial celebration, many of them gathered for a ceremony at the school's cemetery. Here, at one of the epicenters of colonial biopolitics (epitomized by Richard Henry Pratt's motto "Kill the Indian, and save the man"), the smell of sweetgrass and sage purifies the air:

> The scent of burning sage and sweetgrass wrapped the small crowd in prayer. Sweetgrass is a healing medicine, a smudge that invokes kindness and compassion, coming as it does from our first Mother. The sacred words of healing rose up around us.
>
> Stolen children. Lost bonds. The burden of loss hangs in the air and mingles with the scent of sweetgrass. (*BrS*, 265)

"Wrap[ping]" the crowd in prayer, sweetgrass binds these descendants representing numerous Indigenous nations into a single group. It evokes compassion even at this site of immeasurable atrocities, as its scent simultaneously "mingles" with "the burden of loss" and the human and nonhuman exhalations already in the air. This fragrance does not heal bodies individually so much as it restores "lost bonds," drawing the senses back to reciprocal social and environmental relationships: "the small crowd" and "our first Mother." If the title of Kimmerer's essay, "Putting Down Roots," invokes the figure of rootedness frequently associated with concepts of racial and land-based identity, it also comes to encompass the importance of air as a medium for regenerating human and ecological rootedness. The restored sweetgrass at Kanatsiohareke produces a decolonized atmosphere supportive of Tom's project of undoing the decimation of Mohawk culture enacted by boarding schools and other settler institutions.

Kimmerer traces a reciprocal cycle of material exchanges between sweetgrass and its humans. For example, she describes its scent as "beckoning" in a passage that Cariou glosses as follows: "This subtle olfactory message is described in agential terms, with the grass 'beckoning' to the potential harvester who, if attracted to the meadow, will revitalize and strengthen the plant through the act of cutting and braiding the grass."[105] Sweetgrass has evolved symbiotically with the Mohawks: its scent is a "message" that not only purifies and heals but solicits humans to enter into relations of harvesting, weaving, and stewardship. Both the plant and its human weavers benefit from these activities: "Basket making also brings economic security," particularly for women; "The most vigorous stands [of sweetgrass] are the ones tended by basket makers. Reciprocity is a key to success" (BrS, 257, 262). Finally, the scent of sweetgrass mingles with human bodies themselves, through breath and skin, transforming the plant's breathers, harvesters, weavers, and planters into another medium of propagation: "And so we are here along the river, kneeling in the earth with the smell of sweetgrass on our hands" (BrS, 266).

Throughout this book, I have set aside the much-discussed topic of smell's mnemonic qualities in order to keep the focus on smell as a vehicle for communicating trans-corporeal risks. But Kimmerer's account of smudging challenges any distinction between evoking memories and sustaining health: the question of whose memories are supported by the smellscape turns out to be inextricably entangled with whose physical, mental, and spiritual well-being it sustains. As she writes of the aroma of sautéed wild leeks, "Just breathing it in is good medicine. The sharp pungency dissipates quickly and the fragrance that lingers is deep and savory, with a hint of leaf mold and rainwater" (BrS, 199). Here, "medicine" encompasses a web of material relations: between Kimmerer and the wild leeks she has respectfully harvested, between the leeks and the decaying leaves and rain that fed them, and between this occasion and the countless others—both past and present—when Kimmerer and others have inhaled this smell. As Kimmerer notes, there is a chemical explanation for the physiological benefits of inhaling familiar scents: "Breathing in the scent of Mother Earth stimulates the release of the hormone oxytocin, the same chemical that promotes bonding between mother and child, between lovers" (*BrS*, 236). Oxytocin does not just benefit the individual body by reducing stress and promoting the feeling of well-being—more fundamentally, it strengthens bonds in reciprocal relationships. *Braiding Sweetgrass* radically expands the concept of health—a concept frequently framed in accordance with liberal, capitalist values like self-reliance and the capacity to perform productive labor[106]—to encompass reciprocal relations between humans, nonhumans, and place. Where Western, settler colonial health experts tend to view deodorization (ironically, even when it is brought about with synthetic chemicals) as a means of defending individual bodies against trans-corporeal environmental influences, sweetgrass heals by affirming humans' connections with environment, atmosphere, and other breathers. For Kimmerer, the unit of health is not the individual but the world they inhabit and are inhabited by.

Like the scents of seawind, *maile, palai,* and other *kino lau* in Trask's *Sharkskin Drum,* the smell of sweetgrass helps constitute an atmosphere supportive of Indigenous human and nonhuman lives. Kimmerer's account of environmental reciprocity resonates with Whyte's framing of Indigenous ecology in terms of "collective continuance"—"an ecological system, of interacting humans, nonhuman beings (animals, plants, etc.), and entities (spiritual, inanimate, etc.), and landscapes (climate regions, boreal zones, etc.) that are conceptualized and operate purposefully to facilitate a collective's (such as an Indigenous people) adaptation to changes."[107] The atmospheric, trans-corporeal experiences of sweetgrass described by Kimmerer reframe concepts of identity, health, and sovereignty in terms of these reciprocal, place-based ecological relationships. Sweetgrass also embodies cosmological bonds in its twofold significance as a medicinal plant gifted by Skywoman and as "the sweet-smelling hair of Mother Earth." Despite its vital connections with place, the atmospheric "roots" sustained by sweetgrass may also exceed local and national delineations, as when it beckons Kimmerer to do restoration work on ancestral Mohawk land, or when the smudging ceremony at Carlisle enwraps a group of Indigenous people from different nations. *Braiding Sweetgrass* attests to the multiple modes of engagement—from personal healing to cultural and political resurgence—solicited by the smell of Indigenous plants. As decolonial practices of air conditioning, the acts of smudging and sweetgrass restoration narrated by Kimmerer do more than resist settler atmospherics: they revivify Indigenous cosmologies whose stories, sensations, and material contexts have been eroded by settler colonialism.

* * *

Whether it takes the form of air-conditioned architecture, cultural deodorization, industrial agriculture, military weapons testing, or Skunk Water, smell plays a vital and often unnoticed role in reproducing colonial relations. As I have shown in this chapter, colonialism and neocolonialism have leveraged smell by imposing a deodorized (and inherently racializing) hierarchy of the senses, by producing and maintaining differentially deodorized spaces, by decimating Indigenous smellscapes, and by intoxicating Indigenous bodies. Even the critical instances of olfactory aesthetics discussed in chapters 2, 3, and 4—intended to expose environmental toxicity or to stage atmospheric intimacies with racialized immigrants—are oriented toward making settler air conditioning more equitable and inclusive, not abolishing it. Wendt, Trask, and Kimmerer's writings convey both the need and some possible techniques for undoing colonialism's atmospheric manipulations. Their texts indicate how, in addition to exposing psychological, cultural, and environmental violence, destigmatizing smell and learning to think in olfactory terms can provide a sensory basis for decolonial practices of air conditioning and the revivification of atmospheres supportive of Indigenous sovereignty.

Epilogue

Reshaping Olfactory Ecologies

This book has interrogated the geographically differentiated and trans-corporeally embodied qualities of olfaction across a range of aesthetic forms and historical contexts. It has traced the dynamics of deodorization and atmospheric intoxication across genres preoccupied with smell, such as detective stories, naturalist novels, illness narratives by people with multiple chemical sensitivity, and environmental justice narratives (chapters 1 and 2). It has elaborated the ocularcentric framings of body, environment, and air that underpin Western art museums and galleries as well as the porous body and molecular circuits of chemosensation staged by olfactory artworks (chapter 3). And it has considered how Asian diasporic and Indigenous authors, artists, and ecologists leverage olfaction to imagine social relations that transgress the racial atmospheres and olfactory stigmas diffused by capitalism's patterns of production, extraction, and conquest (chapters 4 and 5). In the literary and mixed-media works I have considered, smell is not only an element of setting that contributes to effects of authenticity or place specificity but also, more vitally, a biochemical medium that suffuses geographies, populations, and affective atmospheres. As such, its effects range from (both semiotically and biochemically) communicating environmental toxicity to producing affective atmospheres that manifest shared vulnerabilities, molecular intimacies, and practices of ecological reciprocity.

How do the literary and mixed-media works analyzed in this book change the way we think about actual, material olfactory practices? Beyond the confines of the literary text and the art gallery, how might olfactory aesthetics intervene in our entanglements with everyday atmospheres and spaces? This book's argument about the simultaneously differentiating and trans-corporeal force of smell clarifies the stakes of olfactory projects ranging from advocacy for "fragrance-free" spaces to the deployment of stink bombs (or malodorous candles) and Indigenous smudging ceremonies and the utilization of scents in conjure and folk medicine. Insofar as they underscore and materially intervene in racial capitalism's inequitable and violent distribution of odors, these practices enact modes of *air conditioning from below*—a concept that pushes back against Sloterdijk's framing of "air conditioning" entirely as a mechanism of crowd control imposed from above (what Amy Patton and Steve Corcoran translate as "terror from the air").[1]

In framing odor as a vehicle of biochemical risk that transforms ideas of embodiment, collectivity, and environmental relation, the writers and artists discussed in this book implicitly challenge the fragrance-free movement that has become perhaps the most influential discourse on everyday olfactory ethics in the United States. The movement for fragrance-free spaces of work and association has provided much-needed critical perspective on synthetic scents. Although fragrance-free advocates may appear aligned with the drive toward deodorization (for example, the movement echoes Kant's critical assessment of the perfumed handkerchief discussed in the introduction), they reverse conventional valuations of odor by focusing not on the undesirability of organic odors but on the potential toxicity of synthetic scents that are frequently added to cleaning products and cosmetics, and in many cases left unspecified in ingredient lists.

Despite this critical attention to synthetic fragrances and chemical risk factors, fragrance-free advocacy is too often restricted to middle-class concerns such as inodorate office spaces and the disclosure of fragrance ingredients in consumer products. The movement has certainly helped diminish the ambient synthetic chemicals present in some spaces (not only certain workplaces but also schools, public buildings, and places of worship—as well as in the home, cafes, and libraries where this monograph was written). However, the notion of being free from fragrance becomes untenable in the face of widespread scenarios of unavoidable atmospheric slow violence: schools situated near toxic dumps or freeways, coal mines and incinerators where workplace odors have little to do with scented cosmetic products. The issue is not only that some smells are perceived as toxic, but that certain populations are consigned to toxic atmospheres and denied the freedom to choose under what circumstances they encounter and inhale toxic materials. At the same time, fragrance free—despite the movement's focus on synthetic fragrances—has a tendency to reinscribe modernity's valorization of in-odorate bodies and spaces, foreclosing the possibility that smells (even synthetic smells, under certain circumstances) might be productive ma-terials for thought, feeling, and politics—a possibility explored in the foregoing discussions of Anicka Yi, Haunani-Kay Trask, and Robin Wall Kimmerer (chapters 4 and 5).

The patterns of differential deodorization underscored in this book challenge us to rethink olfactory politics on a larger scale. If differen-tial deodorization works by producing and sustaining a multiplicity of fragmented, hierarchized atmospheres across all scales, then olfactory activism cannot be constrained to a single, local scene. Let us recall Val Plumwood's injunction: "We must smell a bit of wrecked Ogoniland in the exhaust fumes from the air-conditioner, the ultimate remoteness, put-it-somewhere-else-machine."[2] Following Plumwood's theorization of "shadow places," we might consider the multifarious, geographically uneven distribution of "shadow smells" whose ongoing emission—a process of chemical "off-gassing" that frequently crosses boundaries of class, race, and nation—enables the deodorized (or synthetically reo-dorized) everyday atmospheres that characterize Western middle-class interiors. But how is it possible to simultaneously be immersed in air conditioning and smell its exhaust, along with the fumes of oil spills in Ogoniland? If the very definition of "shadow smells" specifies that they exist elsewhere in the shadow places whose exploitation and devastation are disregarded by conventional regimes of representation, then under what circumstances would it be possible for those who benefit most from racial capitalism to perceive them?

Olfactory artworks such as De Cupere's *Smell of a Stranger* and Yi's *Life Is Cheap* have staged shadow smells within the contexts of con-temporary art exhibitions.[3] But if the power of olfaction lies in its vis-ceral and biochemical effects on breathers, then perhaps the project of transforming deliberations about acceptable risk requires introducing shadow smells into the deodorized spaces of corporate privilege. Here, it is worth recalling that Yi concluded an interview about her artistic practice by announcing that she was on her way to set off a stink bomb at Abercrombie & Fitch: the very qualities of passive and involuntary reception that made olfaction seem of little value to Enlightenment philosophers make it a powerful tool for reaching out to—and reaching into—disinterested audiences. Olfactory aesthetic interventions—along with their biochemical transformations of bodies, minds, and moods— can be literally unavoidable.

Toward the end of Indra Sinha's fictionalized rendering of the long aftermath of the Bhopal chemical catastrophe, *Animal's People* (2007), a stink bomb dramatically displaces shadow smells back onto their corporate American perpetrators. After nearly two decades of organized protest, a boycott, and a hunger strike on the part of the hundreds of thousands of survivors whose health has been affected by poison gas released from a local pesticide factory, corrupt government officials arrange a meeting with lawyers representing the US chemical Kampani in an effort to reach an out-of-court settlement that would sidestep the community's demands for justice. The negotiation begins in a meeting room of a luxury hotel, but it is interrupted by a noxious gas:

> They had begun their arguing and haggling when without warning their eyes began to sting. An evil burning sensation began in their noses and throats, a little like the smoke of burning chillies, it caught nastily in the throat, it seared the lungs, they were coughing, but coughing made it ten times worse. Something was in the room, something uninvited, an invisible fire, by the time they had realised this it was already too late. These big shot politicians and lawyers, they got up in a panic, they reeled around, retching, everything they did just made the pain and burning worse. Tears streamed from their eyes, hardly could they see. One of the lawyers was trying to vomit, the rest of them ran in panic. . . . These Kampani heroes, these politicians, they were shitting themselves, they thought they were dying, they thought they'd been attacked with the same gas that leaked on that night, and every man there knew exactly how horrible were the deaths of those who breathed the Kampani's poisons.[4]

Although this scene evokes something like the terror of the Bhopal catastrophe, the gaseous agent is much less toxic: the novel indicates that a doctor aligned with the activists "emptied a bottle of stink bomb juice into the air conditioner."[5] The stink bomb momentarily reverses racial capitalism's typical trajectories of "air conditioning," in which toxic atmospheres are redirected from wealthy spaces and white bodies to vulnerable racialized communities. In doing so, it withholds from these politicians and corporate lawyers the atmospheric conditions of political deliberation and economic calculation; at the same time, the terror it evokes exposes something of the everyday terror experienced by those living in conditions of slow violence produced by multinational corporations. Whereas much of Sinha's novel details modes of political protest that either require or exacerbate the debilitation of chemical victims—for example, boycotting a health clinic, staging a hunger strike, or occupying (and burning down again) the poisoned site of the chemical factory—making a stink affects the privileged bodies of those who benefit from minimizing accountability for the preventable chemical catastrophe. Sinha presents the noxious gas as a deus ex machina that leads to a provisional victory in the community's long struggles against the Kampani. In doing so, he suggests that the immediacy of olfaction may make it a powerful weapon of environmental protest—particularly when that protest is directed against the dynamics of atmospheric violence. If the fantasy of chemical products that are either risk-free or without risk to white Westerners is essential to the brand image of corporations such as Union Carbide and Dow Chemical (the companies most immediately responsible for the Bhopal catastrophe), the stink bomb belies this fantasy by temporarily exposing the air-conditioned meeting room and its US corporate lawyers to an odor that makes them fall to pieces.

Also in 2007, the Yes Men—a culture-jamming duo known for impersonating representatives of the World Trade Organization, Dow Chemical (on the twentieth anniversary of the Bhopal catastrophe), and the US Department of Housing and Urban Development (in the wake of Hurricane Katrina)—enacted a similar intervention at GO-EXPO, Canada's largest oil industry conference. Posing as an ExxonMobil and National Petroleum Council representative named Shepard Wolff, Jacques Servin delivered a keynote speech in which he announced a renewable biofuel called Vivoleum. Noting that "U.S. and Canadian energy policies (notably the massive, carbon-intensive exploitation of Alberta's oil sands, and the development of liquid coal) are increasing the chances of huge global calamities," Wolff explained plans to capitalize on human fatalities through a process that would render human flesh into a fuel: "In the worst case scenario, the oil industry could 'keep fuel flowing' by transforming the billions of people who die into oil."[6] As he spoke to a packed room of oil and gas executives, an animated video depicted the production process, and volunteers passed out over two hundred candles in the effigy of a Black man. As these pungent candles were lit, Wolff presented a tribute video featuring a deceased Exxon janitor named Reggie Watts (played by the comedian Reggie Watts) who, after learning that he was terminally ill (possibly a result of working in "toxic spill cleanup"), had volunteered to be transformed into Vivoleum candles: "I think I'd like to be a candle." Watts's announcement in the video associates the candles burning on each of the banquet tables with the smell of burning flesh; at this point, conference attendees appeared either bewildered or offended, and security guards rushed on stage to stop the video.

At one level, the Vivoleum hoax enacted a scenario of olfactory blowback similar to Sinha's stink bomb: candles consisting of wax and human hair dispersed an unfamiliar noxious odor associated with oil emissions and geographically and racially uneven distributions of precarity and death that are predicted (and have already been proliferating) as climate change ramps up. The Vivoleum candles compress time and space in the service of exposing environmental slow violence: they evoke the odor of future climate fatalities disproportionately concentrated throughout the Global South in a room filled with oil and gas executives. At the same time, the idea that Watts had worked in "toxic spill cleanup" suggests that fumes emitted by his rendered flesh are not only unpleasant but toxic. The Yes Men endeavor to leverage olfaction's tendency to collapse any distance between perceiver and perceived while also extending far beyond olfaction's conventional features of presence, immediacy, and spatial boundedness: the scent of human hair on fire manifests as a "shadow smell" referencing climate consequences that are temporally and geographically far removed from this conference room in Alberta. To invoke a term coined by geographer Neil Smith, Vivoleum is a "scale-jumping" smell that connects this air-conditioned room to the Athabasca oil sands as well as global geographies of present and future climate precarity.[7]

However, Vivoleum's olfactory politics cannot be disentangled from the Black body used to represent its source both in the tribute video and in the noxious candles—each of which was molded into an effigy of the Yes Men's collaborator, Reggie Watts. In distributing and igniting

mass-produced images of a Black man, the Yes Men attempt to implicate their audience (as well as themselves) in both the commodification
of the Black body and the ongoing legacies of lynching. The smell of a
Black body burned in effigy evokes the "overwhelming odor" of lynching.[8] As Erica Fretwell writes in her analysis of James Weldon Johnson's
account of witnessing a lynching in *The Autobiography of an Ex-Colored
Man*, "Smell . . . reveals the impossibility of distance for the witness—
once the body is in the nose, and in the body, the witness has become an
active participant."[9] If the candles evoke the future by anticipating the
innumerable fatalities that will result from climate change, they simultaneously extend backward into the past by referencing long-standing
patterns of racial desire and antiblack violence. The candles are an olfactory instance of what Kyla Wazana Tompkins characterizes as the persistent fantasy of the "consumable black body."[10] In Tompkins's account,
the white desire to ingest, absorb, and so obliterate the Black subject
frequently gives rise to "racial indigestion"—to "moments when the in-
gestion and figuration of blackness . . . *chokes*—in other words when
blackness pushes back at its devouring racial other and thus not only
rejects white desire but also complicates the mythology of whiteness itself."[11] The odor of singed hair—which the tribute video associates with
the putatively dead, processed flesh of Reggie Watts—similarly refuses to
go down easy: instead, it connects the energy regime of racial capitalism
with historical and ongoing structures of antiblackness, distilled into a
troubling, undeniable scent.

Although the Vivoleum intervention's allusion to lynching is deeply
problematic insofar as it was orchestrated by two white men, and although the Yes Men have not indicated whether the lynching allusion
was intentional, it nevertheless stages the constitutive historical connections between antiblack violence and climate change. Entangling the
odor of lynching with the anticipatory stench of future climate fatalities,
the Vivoleum candle resonates with geographer Kathryn Yusoff's discussion of Black Anthropocenes, wherein an intimacy between Black and
brown bodies (marked as inhuman) and the earth (similarly marked as
inhuman) positions Blackness as a buffer that enables diverse forms of
environmental violence. As Yusoff writes, this intimacy "is predicated on
the presumed absorbent qualities of black and brown bodies to take up
the body burdens of exposure to toxicities and to buffer the violence of

the earth. Literally stretching black and brown bodies across the seismic fault lines of the earth, Black Anthropocenes subtend White Geology as a material stratum."[12] The ritual dehumanization of lynching—which materially reduces the Black body to fuel, ash, earth, and smoke— positions petrochemical executives as practitioners of a White Geology premised on the exploitation of racialized bodies, earth, and air.

It is worth noting that the olfactory interventions in *Animal's People* and the Vivoleum hoax are staged by white activists endeavoring to act in the interest of populations targeted by environmental racism. If this effort to act in the interest of the global and disproportionately racialized victims of chemical emissions and climate change involves a problematic tendency toward racial impersonation (a white woman in a burqa, white men orchestrating a performance that involves a Black actor and candles molded in his image), it also channels white privilege and mobility into the project of rescaling olfactory perception. These activists—an American doctor running a free clinic in India and two tenured professors collaborating with a Black actor—leverage their race and class privilege to redirect shadow smells into the air-conditioned meeting spaces of the corporate elite. Instead of ventriloquizing the citizens of Khaufpur or Black and brown victims of environmental violence, they present disconcerting odors associated with these groups. "Making a stink" in material (rather than merely discursive) terms, these interventions go beyond the Yes Men's conception of their practice as "culture jamming": they jam the atmosphere itself, undermining the respiratory conditions that enable the appearance of disinterested political and economic deliberation.

As an intervention that exposes atmospheric disparities (both by rendering them as media spectacles and by exposing atmospherically privileged breathers to shadow smells that are typically redistributed to more vulnerable populations), making a stink offers a provocative alternative to fragrance-free advocacy. Insisting on a sense of atmospheric interconnectedness that includes sites of production, disposal, and emissions as well as consumer choices, Sinha and the Yes Men radically expand the scale of olfactory politics. Their stagings of the shadow smells that underpin the petrochemical industry insistently connect the transnational scale that frequently characterizes atmospheric slow violence with the molecular scale of trans-corporeal inhalation. In doing so, they extend the fragrance-free movement's consciousness raising concerning chemical risks across local and transnational geographies of differential deodorization. Whereas fragrance-free advocates model an ethics of transparency and responsibility concerning toxic chemicals, Sinha's stink bomb and the Yes Men's Vivoleum candles leverage the power of olfaction to underscore patterns of chemical exposure that are not subject to individual cosmetic choices. In doing so, they reframe odor not as a nuisance to be eradicated but as a vital tool for reshaping perception. Like the olfactory narratives and artworks considered throughout this book, these stink bombs enact a redistribution of the sensible, making shadow smells—normally obscured by their dispersal across vast spatial and temporal scales—a matter of immediate, unavoidable concern.

In addition to critically staging the atmospheric disparities that frequently manifest as "shadow smells," olfactory interventions can transform existing atmospheres into more physically, mentally, and affectively supportive environments. The accounts of Indigenous smudging ceremonies and sweetgrass reseeding discussed in chapter 5 demonstrate that olfactory politics can extend beyond making a stink to restoring connections between human breathers, nonhumans, spirit, and place. Similarly, the smells of Black diasporic conjure roots and *curanderismo*-inspired self-medication with garlic alluded to in texts like "John Archer's Nose" and *Under the Feet of Jesus* produce atmospheres intended to sustain both physical health and cultural identity. Olfactory practices such as these exemplify powerful modes of spiritual practice, cross-species communication, and folk medicine that have been suppressed by biomedicine, Christianity, and related institutions of deodorization.

Stink bombs and olfactory practices such as smudging and conjure exemplify the critical and reparative potential of air conditioning from below. They call for a radically expanded conception of olfactory aesthetics—one that would encompass not only the literary and mixed-media engagements with olfaction discussed in this book but also experiments with scent in everyday spaces. These interventions critique and enact alternatives to conventional processes of differential deodorization: their smells are intended to transform how breathers experience olfactory ecologies, either by expanding the scale of atmospheric relations or by offering smells that materialize cultural memories, spiritual connections, and health practices eroded by colonialism and racial domination. These enactments of olfactory aesthetics in everyday atmospheres offer an important rejoinder to fragrance-free advocacy: rather than focusing on the elimination of toxic odors from some spaces, these interventions materially enjoin breathers to experience smell as a catalyst for thinking, perceiving, and feeling differently. In addition to advocating for spaces that are free from noxious, synthetic fragrances, we must also make space for olfactory encounters that disclose new or suppressed modes of social and ecological intimacy. Such encounters demand a broader framing of olfactory justice—one that would ensure equal access to olfactory modes of knowledge and ecological relation, while supporting projects of air conditioning enacted by those who have historically suffered most from atmospheric disparities.

ACKNOWLEDGMENTS

This book could not have been written without generous support from colleagues, family, friends, students, artists, and funding institutions. For research funds and writing time, I'm grateful to the American Council of Learned Societies, the UC Humanities Research Institute, the Obama Institute for Transnational American Studies, the UC Davis Humanities Institute, and the Creative Capital / Andy Warhol Foundation Arts Writers Grant Program.

While all mistakes are my own, my interdisciplinary thinking about olfaction has been oriented and challenged by conversations with colleagues and artists. At UC Davis, Kathleen Frederickson, Mike Ziser, Tobias Menely, Mark Jerng, Desirée Martín, Margaret Ronda, Elizabeth Miller, Louis Warren, Parama Roy, Elizabeth Freeman, Susette Min, Julie Sze, and Timothy Choy have been deeply appreciated interlocutors and colleagues; I'm also grateful to Omri Moses, Stephen Ross, Jonathan Sachs, Manish Sharma, Jessica Bardill, Nathan Brown, Jesse Arsenault, Nicola Nixon, Mary Esteve, Jill Didur, Nalini Mohabir, David Howes, Richard Jean So, Masha Salazkina, Luca Caminati, Rachel Berger, Theresa Ventura, and Yumna Siddiqi for warmly welcoming me to collegial communities at Concordia University and in Montreal. For formal and informal feedback on the ideas in this book, I'm especially grateful to Jean-Thomas Tremblay, Mike Ziser, Sarah Jaquette Ray, Henry Wonham, Sharada Balachandran Orihuela, Edlie Wong, Robert Levine, Jeffrey Moro, Rachel Lee, Shu-Mei Shih, Jina Kim, Erica Fretwell, Andrew Kettler, Hans Rindisbacher, Alfred Hornung, Hans Bergthaller, Shu-ching Chen, Yanoula Athanassakis, Jill Gatlin, Rebecca Hogue, David Howes, and Paul Lyons, who is greatly missed. For conceptually and sensorially informative studio tours, workshops, and conversations about olfactory art, I am indebted to Dorothée King, Caro Verbeek, Boris Raux, Peter de Cupere, Miles Regis, Anicka Yi, Beatrice Glow, Brian Goeltzenleuchter, Gwen-Aël Lynn, Frank Bloehm, Aleesa Cohene, and Saskia Wilson-

Brown. I have been fortunate to work and learn with brilliant graduate students including Cara Shipe, Molly Ball, Sophia Bamert, Rebecca Hogue, Ryan Wander, Bryan Yazell, Kristin George Bagdanov, and William Elliott. Thanks to the students who shared their enthusiasm and insight in my seminars on Geographies of Risk, Aesthetics of Air, Aesthetics of the Chemical Senses, and Naturalism and the Environment. As always, I am grateful to my mentors—Samuel Otter, Caren Kaplan, Colleen Lye, William Handley—and to other scholars such as Priscilla Wald, Shelley Fisher Fishkin, Lawrence Buell, and Wai-Chee Dimock who have inspired and supported my work over the years.

I presented research from this project at the University of Texas at Austin, Johannes Gutenberg University, Dickinson College, the City University of Hong Kong, the University of Maryland, National Chung-Hsing University, National Chengchi University, Bielefeld University, the University of Regensburg, Worcester Polytechnic Institute, New York University, the University of Mexico, UC Davis, the Association for the Study of Literature and the Environment, the American Studies Association, the Modern Language Association, the Association for Asian American Studies, and the Association for the Study of the Arts of the Present. I am grateful for these opportunities to share my work and, especially, for the invaluable comments and criticisms offered on these occasions.

At NYU Press, Eric Zinner encouraged this book from its early stages, and perceptive, rigorous, and supportive comments offered by the two readers greatly improved the final draft. I am also thankful for Dolma Ombadykow's expert guidance through the production process, for Joseph Dahm's keen copyediting, and for Louis Pigeon-Owen and Ali Pinkney's expert assistance with preparing the final MS.

Earlier versions of chapters 2 and 3 were previously published in the journals *American Literature* 88, no. 4 (December 2016) and *Resilience: A Journal of the Environmental Humanities* 4, no. 1 (Winter 2016); brief excerpts from chapters 1, 3, and 4 appeared in "Smelling Setting," *modernism/modernity* online Print+ cluster on "Modernist Setting," ed. Dora Zhang and Hannah Freed-Thall (March 2018); Hsuan L. Hsu and Edlie Wong, "Uncollected: Remapping Edith Maude Eaton / Sui Sin Far," in *Asian American Literature in Transition, Vol. 1*, ed. Josephine Lee and Julia Lee (Cambridge: Cambridge University Press, forthcoming);

and "Boris Raux and the Smell of Narcissus," *Senses & Society* 14, no. 1 (March 2019): 15–30.

This book was written in dark times, through which I have been sustained by deeply appreciated friends, and especially by my family: Kang, Hsiang-Lin, Kang Jr., Christina, Kyle, Kalissa, Lin, Jason, Myron, Ellie, and Lucy. Zayn arrived just in time to teach me life lessons in love and olfaction. I'm always filled with gratitude to Beenash for a partnership that sustains my mind and soul.

NOTES

INTRODUCTION

1 Richard Powers, *Gain* (New York: Picador, 1998), 60. Further citations are given parenthetically as *G*.

2 Shepard Krech III, *The Ecological Indian: Myth and History* (New York: Norton, 1999); Mark Smith, *How Race Is Made: Slavery, Segregation, and the Senses* (Chapel Hill: University of North Carolina Press, 2006), 14.

3 Ulrich Beck, *Risk Society: Towards a New Modernity*, trans. Mark Ritter (London: SAGE, 1992), 23.

4 G. Neil Martin, *The Neuropsychology of Smell and Taste* (Sussex: Psychology Press, 2013), 3.

5 "Although this lower limit of greater than 1 trillion is several orders of magnitude more than distinguishable colors or tones, it is presumably dramatically lower than the actual number of discriminable olfactory stimuli." C. Bushdid et al., "Humans Can Discriminate More Than 1 Trillion Olfactory Stimuli," *Science* 343, no. 6177 (March 21, 2014): https://science.sciencemag.org.

6 See Aprajita Mohanty and Jay Gottfried, "Examining Emotion Perception and Elicitation via Olfaction," in *The Cambridge Handbook of Human Affective Neuroscience*, ed. Jorge Armony and Patrik Vuilleumier (Cambridge: Cambridge University Press, 2013), 241–64; J. Gottfried et al., "Remembrance of Odors Past: Human Olfactory Cortex in Cross-Modal Recognition Memory," *Neuron* 42, no. 4 (May 27, 2004): 687–95.

7 Joy Parr, *Sensing Changes: Technologies, Environments, and the Everyday, 1953–2003* (Vancouver: UBC Press, 2010), 141.

8 Ibid., 138.

9 Lois Gibbs, *Love Canal and the Birth of the Environmental Health Movement* (Washington, DC: Island Press, 2011), 32.

10 Timothy Choy, "Distribution," *Field Sights*, January 21, 2016, https://culanth.org; see also Timothy Choy and Jerry Zee, "Condition—Suspension," *Cultural Anthropology* 30, no. 2 (May 2015): 210–23.

11 In *Upper Dublin Township v. Gung Tao Li, d/b/a/ Wok's Chinese Restaurant, et al.*, 136 *Montgomery County Law Reporter* II (1999): 301–4, for example, grease smells from a Chinese restaurant were deemed "noxious" in comparison with the "odor of wood burning" from a nearby pizza restaurant (304).

12 Immanuel Kant, *Critique of Judgment*, trans. James Meredith (1790; Oxford: Oxford University Press, 2007), 121–22.

13 Peter Sloterdijk, *Foams: Spheres III*, trans. Wieland Hoban (Los Angeles: Semiotext(e), 2016), 95.

14 Ibid., 173.

15 Peter Adey, "Air's Affinities: Geopolitics, Chemical Affect and the Force of the Elemental," *Dialogues in Human Geography* 5, no. 1 (2015): 55.

16 Jane Bennett, *Vibrant Matter: A Political Ecology of Things* (Durham, NC: Duke University Press, 2010).

17 See M. H. Abrams and Geoffrey Harpham, *A Glossary of Literary Terms* (Boston: Cengage Learning, 2015), 20; and Hans Ulrich Gumbrecht, *Atmosphere, Mood, Stimmung: On a Hidden Potential of Literature* (Palo Alto, CA: Stanford University Press, 2012).

18 Peter Adey, *Air: Nature and Culture* (London: Reaktion, 2014); Kate McLean, "Communicating and Mediating Smellscapes: The Design and Exposition of Olfactory Mappings," in *Designing with Smell: Practices, Techniques, and Challenges*, ed. Victoria Henshaw et al. (New York: Routledge, 2018), 67–78; Victoria Henshaw, *Urban Smellscapes: Understanding and Designing City Smell Environments* (New York: Routledge, 2014); Marjin Nieuwenhuis, "Atmospheric Governance: Gassing as Law for the Protection and Killing of Life," *Environment and Planning D* 36, no. 1 (2018): 78–95; and Derek McCormack, *Atmospheric Things: On the Allure of Elemental Envelopment* (Durham, NC: Duke University Press, 2018).

19 Ben Anderson, "Affective Atmospheres," *Emotion, Space, and Society* 2 (2009): 78; Juhani Pallasmaa, "Space, Place and Atmosphere: Emotion and Peripherical Perception in Architectural Experience," *Lebenswelt* 4 (2014): 230–45; Kathleen Stewart, "Atmospheric Attunements," *Environment and Planning D* 29, no. 3 (2011): 445–53; Timothy Choy, "Air's Substantiations," in *Lively Capital: Biotechnologies, Ethics, and Governance in Global Markets*, ed. Kaushik Sunder Rajan (Durham, NC: Duke University Press, 2012), 121–54; Teresa Brennan, *The Transmission of Affect* (Ithaca, NY: Cornell University Press, 2004).

20 McCormack, *Atmospheric Things*; Tim Ingold, "The Atmosphere," *Chiasmi International* 14 (2012): 75–87; Jesse Oak Taylor, *The Sky of Our Manufacture: The London Fog in British Fiction from Dickens to Woolf* (Charlottesville: University of Virginia Press, 2016).

21 Andreas Philippopoulos-Mihalopoulos, *Spatial Justice: Body, Lawscape, Atmosphere* (London: Routledge, 2014), 108.

22 Ibid., 136.

23 Renisa Mawani, "Atmospheric Pressures: On Race and Affect" (unpublished paper, n.d.); Kristen Simmons, "Settler Atmospherics," *Cultural Anthropology Fieldsights*, November 20, 2017, https://culanth.org; Neel Ahuja, "Intimate Atmospheres: Queer Theory in a Time of Extinctions," *GLQ* 21, nos. 2–3 (2015): 365–85; Christina Sharpe, *In the Wake: On Blackness and Being* (Durham, NC: Duke University Press, 2016), 102–34. Sharpe comments on toxics more directly in Christina Sharpe, "Antiblack Weather vs. Black Microclimates," *Funambulist* 14 (November–December 2017): 48–53.

24 See Donna Haraway, "Anthropocene, Capitalocene, Plantationocene, Chthulu-
cene," *Environmental Humanities* 6, no. 1 (2015): 159–65, and Jason Moore, ed.,
Anthropocene or Capitalocene? Nature, History, and the Crisis of Capitalism (Oak-
land: PM Press, 2016).

25 See Françoise Vergès, "Racial Capitalocene," in *Futures of Black Radicalism*, ed.
Gaye Theresa Johnson and Alex Lubin (London: Verso, 2017), 72–82; Kathryn
Yusoff, *A Billion Black Anthropocenes or None* (Minneapolis: University of Minne-
sota Press, 2019); Kyle Powys Whyte, "Our Ancestors' Dystopia Now: Indigenous
Conservation and the Anthropocene," in *The Routledge Companion to the Envi-
ronmental Humanities*, ed. Ursula Heise, Jon Christensen, and Michelle Niemann
(London: Routledge, 2017), 206–15.

26 Val Plumwood, "Shadow Places and the Politics of Dwelling," *Australian Humanities Review* 44 (March 2008), http://australianhumanitiesreview.org.

27 McCormack, *Atmospheric Things*, 9.

28 Qtd. in Sloterdijk, *Foams*, 173.

29 Stacy Alaimo, *Bodily Natures: Science, Environment, and the Material Self* (Bloomington: Indiana University Press, 2010), 2. Alaimo's materialist approach to the
environment's human consequences offers an important counterpoint to Jameson,
who views smell primarily as a figurative rather than a trans-corporeal "vehicle"
for affect: "the usefulness of smells as a vehicle for different types of affect derives
at least in part from its marginalized status, its underdevelopment, so to speak, as
a symbolic element." Fredric Jameson, *The Antinomies of Realism* (London: Verso,
2013), 35.

30 Ingold, "Atmosphere," 77.

31 Ashon Crawley, *Blackpentecostal Breath: The Aesthetics of Possibility* (New York:
Fordham University Press, 2017), 38.

32 Tim J. Van Hartevelt and Morten L. Kringelbach, "The Olfactory System," in *The
Human Nervous System*, ed. Jürgen Mai and George Paxinos, 3rd ed. (London:
Academic Press, 2012), 1221.

33 Timothy Morton, *Hyperobjects: Philosophy and Ecology after the End of the World*
(Minneapolis: University of Minnesota Press, 2013), 1.

34 Lindsey Dillon and Julie Sze, "Police Power and Particulate Matters: Environmental Justice and the Spatialities of In/Securities in U.S. Cities," *ELN* 54, no. 2 (Fall/
Winter 2016): 14.

35 Patrick Süskind, *Perfume: The Story of a Murderer*, trans. John Woods (New York:
Vintage, 1986), 155.

36 World Health Organization, "Air Pollution" (2020), www.who.int.

37 See, e.g., Harriet Washington, *A Terrible Thing to Waste: Environmental Racism
and Its Assault on the American Mind* (New York: Little, Brown Spark, 2019);
David Marcotte, "Something in the Air? Air Quality and Children's Educational
Outcomes," *Economics of Education Review* 56 (February 2017): 141–51; J. Rotton,
"Affective and Cognitive Consequences of Malodorous Pollution," *Basic and
Applied Social Psychology* 4 (1983): 171–91; Guo-Zhen Lin et al., "The Impact of

Ambient Air Pollution on Suicide Mortality: A Case-Crossover Study in Guangzhou, China," *Environmental Health* 15 (2016).

38 See Julie Sze, "Gender, Asthma Politics, and Urban Environmental Justice Activism," in *New Perspectives on Environmental Justice: Gender, Sexuality, and Activism*, ed. Rachel Stein (New Brunswick, NJ: Rutgers University Press, 2004), 177–90.

39 Jasbir Puar, *The Right to Maim: Debility, Capacity, Disability* (Durham, NC: Duke University Press, 2017), xviii.

40 Nirmala Erevelles, "Becoming Disabled/Becoming Black: Crippin' Critical Ethnic Studies from the Periphery," in *Critical Ethnic Studies: A Reader*, ed. Critical Ethnic Studies Editorial Collective (Durham, NC: Duke University Press, 2016), 231–51. See also Puar, *Right to Maim*; Clare Barker and Stuart Murray, "Disabling Postcolonialism: Global Disability Cultures and Democratic Criticism," *Journal of Literary and Cultural Disability Studies* 4, no. 3 (2010); Jina Kim, "Cripping East Los Angeles: Enabling Environmental Justice in Helena María Viramontes's *Their Dogs Came with Them*," in *Disability Studies and the Environmental Humanities: Toward an Eco-Crip Theory*, ed. Sarah Jaquette Ray and Jay Sibara (Reno: University of Nebraska Press, 2017), 502–30.

41 Kim, "Cripping," 516.

42 On race and asthma, see Gregg Mitman, *Breathing Space: How Allergies Shape Our Lives and Landscapes* (New Haven, CT: Yale University Press, 2007), 130–66. See Dillon and Julie Sze, "Police Power and Particulate Matters."

43 Rob Nixon, *Slow Violence and the Environmentalism of the Poor* (Cambridge, MA: Harvard University Press, 2011), 2.

44 Ivan Penn, "'We Cannot Breathe': A Poor Alabama Town Has Lived with the Rotten Egg Stench of Gas for 8 Years," *Los Angeles Times*, October 15, 2016, www.latimes.com.

45 Ibid.

46 See Smith, *How Race Is Made*.

47 Mark Jenner, "Civilization and Deodorization? Smell in Early Modern English Culture," in *Civil Histories: Essays Presented to Sir Keith Thomas*, ed. Peter Burke, Brian Harrison, and Paul Slack (Oxford: Oxford University Press, 2000), 127–44; Jenner, "Follow Your Nose? Smell, Smelling, and Their Histories," *American Historical Review* 116, no. 2 (April 2011): 335–51.

48 Select Committee on Metropolitan Sewage Manure, "Report no. 474" (1846), 109.

49 Caroline Jones, *Eyesight Alone: Clement Greenberg's Modernism and the Bureaucratization of the Senses* (Chicago: University of Chicago Press, 2006), 395.

50 Sarah Jaquette Ray, *The Ecological Other: Environmental Exclusion in American Culture* (Tucson: University of Arizona Press, 2013), 5–6.

51 Kant, *Critique of Judgment*, 158.

52 Immanuel Kant, "Lecture of the Winter Semester 1775–1776 Based on the Transcriptions *Friedländer 3.3 (Ms 400), Friedländer 2 (Ms399)* and *Prieger*," trans. G.

Felicitas Munzel, in *Lectures on Anthropology*, ed. Allen Wood and Robert Louden (Cambridge: Cambridge University Press, 2012), 67.

53 Constance Classen, David Howes, and Anthony Synnott, *Aroma: The Cultural History of Smell* (New York: Routledge, 1994), 3–4.

54 Jones, *Eyesight Alone*, 391. See also Howes on Western thought's "denial of nasality" (David Howes, *Sensual Relations: Engaging the Senses in Culture and Social Theory* [Ann Arbor: University of Michigan Press, 2003], 193) and Larry Shiner and Yulia Kriskovets, "The Aesthetics of Smelly Art," *Journal of Aesthetics and Art Criticism* 65, no. 3 (Summer 2007): 275–79. For an argument against tastes and smells as aesthetic media, see A. T. Winterbourne, "Is Oral and Olfactory Art Possible?," *Journal of Aesthetic Education* 15 (April 1981): 95–102.

55 Max Nordau, *Degeneration* (New York: Appleton, 1895), 503; Sigmund Freud, *Civilization and Its Discontents*, trans. James Strachey (1929; New York: Norton, 1962), 46–47n1; Theodor Adorno and Max Horkheimer, *Dialectic of Enlightenment*, trans. John Cumming (1944; London: Verso, 1997), 184.

56 Caroline Jones, "The Mediated Sensorium," in *Sensorium: Embodied Experience, Technology, and Contemporary Art*, ed. Caroline Jones (Cambridge, MA: MIT Press, 2006), 15.

57 Philippopoulos-Mihalopoulos, *Spatial Justice*, 145.

58 Laurence Minsky, Colleen Fahey, and Caroline Fabrigas, "Inside the Invisible but Influential World of Scent Branding," *Harvard Business Review*, April 11, 2018, https://hbr.org.

59 Sarah E. Tracy, "Delicious Molecules: Big Food Science, the Chemosenses, and Umami," *Senses and Society* 13, no. 1 (2018): 89–107, 98.

60 Brennan, *Transmission of Affect*, 9.

61 Ibid., 10.

62 Silvan Tomkins, "The Varieties of Shame and Its Magnification," in *Exploring Affect: The Selected Writings of Silvan S. Tomkins*, ed. E. Virginia Demos (Cambridge, MA: Harvard University Press, 1995), 399.

63 J. Douglas Porteous, "Smellscape," *Progress in Physical Geography* 9, no. 3 (September 1985): 356–78.

64 Bruno Latour, "How to Talk about the Body? The Normative Dimension of Science Studies," *Body & Society* 10, nos. 2–3 (2004): 205–29, 207.

65 Qtd. in Catherine Maxwell, *Scents and Sensibility: Perfume in Victorian Literary Culture* (Oxford: Oxford University Press, 2017), 7.

66 Erica Fretwell, *Sensory Experiments: Psychophysics and the Aesthetics of Feeling in Nineteenth-Century America* (Durham, NC: Duke University Press, forthcoming).

67 Hans Rindisbacher, *The Smell of Books: A Cultural-Historical Study of Olfactory Perception in Literature* (Ann Arbor: University of Michigan Press, 1992); Janice Carlisle, *Common Scents: Comparative Encounters in High-Victorian Fiction* (New York: Oxford University Press, 2004); Emily Friedman, *Reading Smell in Eighteenth-Century Fiction* (Lewisburg, PA: Bucknell University Press, 2016).

68 Christopher Looby, "'The Roots of the Orchis, the Iuli of Chesnuts': The Odor of Male Solitude," in *Solitary Pleasures: The Historical, Literary, and Artistic Discourses of Autoeroticism*, ed. Paula Bennett and Vernon Rosario II (New York: Routledge, 1995), 163–88; Stephen Casmier, "The Funky Novels of John Edgar Wideman: Odor and Ideology in *Reuben, Philadelphia Fire*, and *The Cattle Killing*," in *Critical Essays on John Edgar Wideman*, ed. Bonnie TuSmith and Keith Byerman (Knoxville: University of Tennessee Press, 2006), 191–204; Daniela Babilon, *The Power of Smell in American Literature: Odor, Affect, and Social Inequality* (Frankfurt: Peter Lang, 2017); Fretwell, *Sensory Experiments*.

69 See, e.g., Jones, *Eyesight Alone*; Jim Drobnick, "Toposmia: Art, Scent, and Interrogations of Spatiality," *Angelaki* 7, no. 1 (2002): 31–47; Jim Drobnick, ed., *The Smell Culture Reader* (New York: Berg, 2006).

70 Alain Corbin, *The Foul and the Fragrant: Odor and the French Social Imagination* (1982; Cambridge, MA: Harvard University Press, 1986).

71 Melanie Kiechle, *Smell Detectives: An Olfactory History of Nineteenth-Century Urban America* (Seattle: University of Washington Press, 2017).

72 See Smith, *How Race Is Made*; Andrew Kettler, *The Smell of Slavery: Olfactory Racism and the Atlantic World* (Cambridge: Cambridge University Press, 2020); Connie Chiang, "Monterey-by-the-Smell: Odors and Social Conflict on the California Coastline," *Pacific Historical Review* 73, no. 2 (May 2004): 183–214; Joel Lee, "Odor and Order: How Caste Is Inscribed in Space and Sensoria," *Comparative Studies of South Asia, Africa, and the Middle East* 37, no. 3 (December 2017): 470–90; Martin F. Manalansan IV, "Immigrant Lives and the Politics of Olfaction in the Global City," in Drobnick, *Smell Culture Reader*, 41–52; and Deborah Jackson, "Scents of Place: The Dysplacement of a First Nations Community in Canada," *American Anthropologist* 113, no. 4 (November 2011): 606–18.

73 Jacques Rancière, *The Politics of Aesthetics*, trans. Gabriel Rockhill (London: Continuum, 2004), 12.

74 "The aesthetical Judgment rather than the intellectual may bear the name of a communal sense" (Kant, *Critique of Judgment*, 103).

75 Rancière, *Politics of Aesthetics*, 59.

76 See Alaimo, *Bodily Natures*; Nixon, *Slow Violence*; Mel Chen, *Animacies: Biopolitics, Racial Mattering, and Queer Affect* (Durham, NC: Duke University Press, 2012), 159–222; and Serenella Iovino and Serpil Oppermann, eds., *Material Ecocriticism* (Bloomington: Indiana University Press, 2014).

77 See also Iovino and Oppermann, *Material Ecocriticism*.

78 Karen Barad, *Meeting the Universe Halfway: Quantum Physics and the Entanglement of Matter and Meaning* (Durham, NC: Duke University Press, 2007), 33.

79 Cécile Roudeau, "*How the Earth Feels*: A Conversation with Dana Luciano," *Transatlantica*, August 2015, https://journals.openedition.org.

80 Taylor, *Sky of Our Manufacture*, 15.

81 Edward T. Hall, *The Hidden Dimension* (New York: Doubleday, 1966), 45.

82 See, e.g., Leslie Haynsworth, "Sensational Adventures: Sherlock Holmes and His Generic Past," *English Literature in Transition, 1880–1920* 44, no. 4 (2001): 459–85, and Donald Pizer, "Late Nineteenth-Century American Literary Naturalism: A Re-introduction," *American Literary Realism* 38, no. 3 (Spring 2006): 12.

83 See, for example, Caroline Levine, *Forms: Whole, Rhythm, Hierarchy, Network* (Princeton: Princeton University Press, 2015), and Paula M. L. Moya, *The Social Imperative: Race, Close Reading, and Contemporary Literary Criticism* (Palo Alto, CA: Stanford University Press, 2015).

CHAPTER 1. "EVERY CRIME HAS ITS PECULIAR ODOR"

1 Spider Robinson, "By Any Other Name," *Analog* 96, no. 11 (November 1976): 14–67, 29. Further citations are given parenthetically as "BA." Robinson subsequently expanded this novella into the full-length novel *Telempath* (New York: Putnam, 1976).

2 Robinson's "muskies"—gaseous entities that feed on anthropogenic air pollution—reference Senator Muskie's comparatively robust approach to regulating air pollution, which focused on severely polluted working-class communities.

3 Mark Neocleous, "The Smell of Power: A Contribution to the Critique of the Sniffer Dog," *Radical Philosophy* 167 (May–June 2011), www.radicalphilosophyarchive .com. For a broad discussion of the ongoing recruitment of nonhuman animals as agents of olfactory surveillance, see Amber Marks, *Headspace: On the Trail of Sniffer Dogs, Wasp Wardens and Other Dumb Friends in the Surveillance industry* (London: Virgin Books, 2008).

4 Edgar Allan Poe, "Murders in the Rue Morgue" (1841) and "The Purloined Letter" (1844), in *Collected Works of Edgar Allan Poe*, ed. Thomas Ollive Mabbott, 3 vols. (Cambridge, MA: Harvard University Press, 1969–78), 2:545; 3:990.

5 Poe, "Murders," 2:553.

6 Thomas Pynchon, *Bleeding Edge* (New York: Penguin, 2013).

7 For a fascinating refiguration of the hyperosmic detective in a fantasy world influenced by African cosmologies (rather than by deodorizing public health initiatives), see Marlon James, *Black Leopard, Red Wolf* (New York: Riverhead, 2019).

8 Poe, "Purloined," 3:974.

9 Arthur Conan Doyle, *The Original Illustrated "Strand" Sherlock Holmes: The Complete Facsimile Edition* (Chatham: Wordsworth Editions, 1998), 711. Further citations are given parenthetically as *OI*.

10 Sarah Marusek, "Reasonable or Offensive? Smell, Jurisdiction, and Public Right," in *Non Liquet: Law and the Senses Series, Smell*, April 2015, 41, https://nonliquetlaw .files.wordpress.com.

11 Jesse Oak Taylor, *The Sky of Our Manufacture: The London Fog in British Fiction from Dickens to Woolf* (Charlottesville: University of Virginia Press, 2016), 162.

12 Ibid., 153.

13 On US detective fiction's central concern with racial heterogeneity, see Jinny Huh, *The Arresting Eye: Race and the Anxiety of Detection* (Charlottesville: University of

Virginia Press, 2015) and Michelle Robinson, *Dreams for Dead Bodies: Blackness, Labor, and the Corpus of American Detective Fiction* (Ann Arbor: University of Michigan Press, 2016).

14 Walter Benjamin, *The Arcades Project*, trans. Howard Eiland and Kevin McLaughlin (Cambridge, MA: Harvard University Press, 1999), 439.

15 Mark Twain, "A Double-Barreled Detective Story," in *The Writings of Mark Twain. Vol. 23. The Man That Corrupted Hadleyburg and Other Essays and Stories* (1902; New York: Harper and Brothers, 1906), 298.

16 John Dollard, qtd. in Mark Smith, *How Race Is Made: Slavery, Segregation, and the Senses* (Chapel Hill: University of North Carolina Press, 2006), 83.

17 Dan Hinkel and Joe Mahr, "Tribune Analysis: Drug-Sniffing Dogs in Traffic Stops Often Wrong," *Chicago Tribune*, January 6, 2011, www.chicagotribune.com.

18 Caroline Jones, "The Mediated Sensorium," in *Sensorium: Embodied Experience, Technology, and Contemporary Art*, ed. Caroline Jones (Cambridge, MA: MIT Press, 2006), 13.

19 For material feminist accounts of interactionism, see Karen Barad, *Meeting the Universe Halfway: Quantum Physics and the Entanglement of Matter and Meaning* (Durham, NC: Duke University Press, 2007); Nancy Tuana, "Viscous Porosity: Witnessing Katrina," in *Materia Feminisms*, ed. Stacy Alaimo and Susan Hekman (Indianapolis: Indiana University Press, 2008), 188–213; and Stacy Alaimo, *Bodily Natures: Science, Environment, and the Material Self* (Bloomington: Indiana University Press, 2010).

20 Rudolph Fisher, "John Archer's Nose," in *City of Refuge: The Collected Stories of Rudolph Fisher*, ed. John McCluskey Jr. (Columbia: University of Missouri Press, 2008), 187. Further citations are given parenthetically as "JA."

21 Robert Crafton, *The African American Experience in Crime Fiction: A Critical Study* (Jefferson, NC: McFarland, 2015), 73. Fisher died at the age of thirty-seven from abdominal cancer, probably as a result of his experimental research with X-rays.

22 Carolyn Morrow Long, *Spiritual Merchants: Religion, Magic, and Commerce* (Knoxville: University of Tennessee Press, 2001), 99–126.

23 Jeffrey Anderson, *Conjure in African American Society* (Baton Rouge: Louisiana State University Press, 2005), 84. Anderson cites a WPA interview from 1937 in which John Barker reported that a powder derived from horned toads "was to be applied to the bottoms of shoes in order to throw dogs off the trail of escaped slaves" (84).

24 David Levering Lewis, "Reading the Harlem Renaissance," in *The Harlem Renaissance*, ed. Harold Bloom (Philadelphia: Chelsea House, 2004), 144.

25 Rudolph Fisher, "City of Refuge," in McCluskey, *City of Refuge*, 38.

26 Rudolph Fisher, "High Yaller," 111, and Fisher, "Fire by Night," 142, both in McCluskey, *City of Refuge*.

27 Rudolph Fisher, "Blades of Steel," in McCluskey, *City of Refuge*, 159.

28 Bruce Robbins, "The Smell of Infrastructure: Notes toward an Archive," *boundary* 2 34, no. 1 (2007): 26.

29 Sean McCann, *Gumshoe America: Hard-Boiled Crime Fiction and the Rise and Fall of New Deal Liberalism* (Durham, NC: Duke University Press, 2000), 3.

30 See Leonard Cassuto, "The American Novel of Mystery, Crime, and Detection," in *A Companion to the American Novel*, ed. Alfred Bendixen (Oxford: Blackwell, 2012), 296.

31 The editors of the *Annotated Big Sleep* note a significant atmospheric disjunction between the novel's dust jacket synopsis and its actual content: "The dust jacket synopsis of the first hardcover edition assured readers that the detective 'clears the atmosphere and leaves the reader content that justice, though of an unexpected sort, will be done.' Our hero seems to think otherwise" (Owen Hill, Pamela Jackson, and Anthony Rizzuto, eds., *The Annotated Big Sleep* [New York: Vintage, 2018], 455n17).

32 Dashiell Hammett, "Dead Yellow Women" (1927), in *The Dashiell Hammett Story Omnibus*, ed. Lillian Hellman (London: Cassell, 1966), 172; Raymond Chandler, qtd. in Peter Wolfe, *Something More Than Night: The Case of Raymond Chandler* (Bowling Green, OH: Popular Press, 1985), 16. For a discussion of olfactory discourses targeting the Asian diaspora, see chapter 4.

33 Raymond Chandler, "The Simple Art of Murder," *Atlantic Monthly* 174 (December 1944): 59.

34 Raymond Chandler, *The Big Sleep* (1939; New York: Vintage, 1992), 185.

35 Ibid., 187.

36 Renisa Mawani, "Atmospheric Pressures: On Race and Affect" (unpublished paper, n.d.).

37 Chester Himes, *The Heat's On* (1961; Chatham, NJ: The Chatham Bookseller, 1966), 30. Further citations are given parenthetically as *HO*.

38 Robbins, "Smell of Infrastructure."

39 Chester Himes, *Plan B* (Jackson: University of Mississippi Press, 1993), 51. Further citations are given parenthetically as *PB*.

40 See Chester Himes, *The Real Cool Killers* (New York: Vintage, 1988).

41 David Naguib Pellow, *Garbage Wars: The Struggle for EJ in Chicago* (Cambridge, MA: MIT Press, 2002), 68; see Natalie Moore, *South Side: A Portrait of Chicago and American Segregation* (New York: Picador, 2016).

42 Qtd. in Pellow, *Garbage Wars*, 68.

43 Sara Paretsky, *Blood Shot: A V. I. Warshawski Novel* (New York: Random House, 1988), 1. Further citations are given parenthetically as *BS*.

44 *The Sniffer* (Netflix, 2017).

45 On struggles for medical recognition of emergent illnesses such as chronic fatigue syndrome and multiple chemical sensitivity (MCS), see Joseph Dumit, "Illnesses You Have to Fight to Get: Facts as Forces in Uncertain, Emergent Illnesses," *Social Science & Medicine* 62, no. 3 (2006): 577–90.

46 Steve Kroll-Smith and H. Hugh Floyd, *Bodies in Protest: Environmental Illness and the Struggle over Medical Knowledge* (New York: New York University Press, 1997), xii, xiii.

47 Alaimo, *Bodily Natures*, 131.

48 Ibid., 132.

49 Mel Chen, *Animacies: Biopolitics, Racial Mattering, and Queer Affect* (Durham, NC: Duke University Press, 2012), 198–99.

50 Sophia Jaworski, "Tracing Chemical Intimacies," *Engagement*, November 1, 2017, https://aesengagement.wordpress.com.

51 Canetti, qtd. in Peter Sloterdijk, *Foams: Spheres III*, trans. Wieland Hoban (Los Angeles: Semiotext(e), 2016), 173.

52 Bonnye Matthews, *Chemical Sensitivity: A Guide to Coping with Hypersensitivity Syndrome, Sick Building Syndrome and Other Environmental Illnesses* (Jefferson, NC: McFarland, 2008), 49.

53 Gail McCormick, *Living with Multiple Chemical Sensitivity: Narratives of Coping* (Jefferson, NC: McFarland, 2001), 83.

54 Ibid., 7.

55 Hermitra Elan*tra Vedenetra, *Silicone Injury: Memoir of a Life and of a Spiritual Journey* (Bloomington, IN: AuthorHouse, 2013), 36.

56 Matthews, *Chemical Sensitivity*, 49.

57 Donald L. Dudley, "MCS: Trial by Science," in *Defining Multiple Chemical Sensitivity*, ed. Bonnye Matthews (Jefferson, NC: McFarland, 1998), 9–26, 9.

58 Ibid., 22.

59 Ibid., 22, 21.

60 Iris Bell, Claudia Miller, and Gary Schwartz, "An Olfactory-Limbic Model of Multiple Chemical Sensitivity Syndrome: Possible Relationships to Kindling and Affective Spectrum Disorders," *Biological Psychiatry* 32, no. 3 (August 1992): 218–42.

61 Ibid., 221.

62 Ibid., 221.

63 Ibid., 221.

64 Alaimo, *Bodily Natures*, 134.

65 Jacob Berkson, *A Canary's Tale: The Final Battle; Politics, Poisons, and Pollution vs. the Environment and the Public Health*, vols. 1–2 (Hagerstown, MD: Jacob Berkson, 1996), 4.

66 Ibid., 1.

67 Bonnye Matthews, "My Experience with Chemical Sensitivity," in Matthews, *Defining Multiple Chemical Sensitivity*, 136.

68 Ibid., 136.

69 Qtd. in Kroll-Smith and Floyd, *Bodies in Protest*, 75.

70 See Ed Cohen, *A Body Worth Defending: Immunity, Biopolitics, and the Apotheosis of the Modern Body* (Durham, NC: Duke University Press, 2009).

71 Kroll-Smith and Floyd, *Bodies in Protest*, 11.

72 Alaimo, *Bodily Natures*, 130.

73 Lynn Lawson, "Notes from a Human Canary," in *Illness and the Environment: A Reader in Contested Medicine*, ed. Steve Kroll-Smith, Phil Brown, and Valerie Gunter (New York: New York University Press, 2000), 338.

74 On olfactory training as a process of "learning to be affected," see Bruno Latour, "How to Talk about the Body? The Normative Dimension of Science Studies," *Body & Society* 10, nos. 2–3 (2004): 205–29, 206.

75 Alan Bell, *Poisoned: How a Crime-Busting Prosecutor Turned His Medical Mystery into a Crusade for Environmental Victims* (New York: Skyhorse, 2017), 154. Further citations are given parenthetically as *P.*

76 See A. C. Steinemann et al., "Fragranced Consumer Products: Chemicals Emitted, Ingredients Unlisted," *Environmental Impact Assessment Review* 31 (2011): 328–33.

77 Matthews, *Chemical Sensitivity*, 6.

78 Gregg Mitman, *Breathing Space: How Allergies Shape Our Lives and Landscapes* (New Haven, CT: Yale University Press, 2007), 89–129.

79 Alison Johnson, *Amputated Lives: Coping with Chemical Sensitivity* (Brunswick, ME: Cumberland Press, 2008).

80 "Moises," in *Casualties of Progress: Personal Histories from the Chemically Sensitive*, ed. Alison Johnson (Brunswick, ME: MCS Information Exchange, 2000), 134.

81 Terri Crawford Hansen, testimonial in McCormick, *Living with Multiple Chemical Sensitivity*, 203. Further citations are given parenthetically as TCH.

82 For an extensive discussion of sweetgrass and smudging, see chapter 5.

CHAPTER 2. NATURALIST SMELLSCAPES AND ENVIRONMENTAL JUSTICE

1 Frank Norris, *Vandover and the Brute*, ed. Russ Castronovo (1914; Peterborough, ON: Broadview, 2015), 82. Further citations are given parenthetically as *V.*

2 As early as in 1713, Bernardino Ramazzini noted the chemical effects of paint on artisans: "Nearly all the painters whom I know . . . are sickly. . . . For their liability to disease, there is a more immediate cause. I mean the materials of the colors they handle and smell constantly such as red lead, cinnabar, white lead, varnish, nut oil and linseed oil which they use for mixing colors; and the numerous pigments made of mineral substances" (Bernardino Ramazzini, *Diseases of Workers*, trans. Wilmer Wright [London: Hafner, 1964], 275). "Only in 1984, in California, did American artists first win their right to know what was in the materials they were using that could kill them" (John Merryman, Albert Elsen, and Stephen Ulrice, *Law, Ethics, and the Visual Arts* [Alphen aan den Rijn: Kluwer, 2007], 838).

3 See Ulrich Beck, *Risk Society: Towards a New Modernity*, trans. Mark Ritter (London: SAGE, 1992), 21.

4 Lawrence Buell, *Writing for an Endangered World: Literature, Culture, and Environment in the U.S. and Beyond* (Cambridge, MA: Harvard University Press, 2001), 129–69.

5 See Gina Rossetti, *Imagining the Primitive in Naturalist and Modern Literature* (Columbia: University of Missouri Press, 2006), 26–65; Michael Lundblad, *The Birth of a Jungle: Animality in Progressive-Era U.S. Literature and Culture* (New York: Oxford University Press, 2013); and Mark Seltzer, *Bodies and Machines* (London: Routledge, 1992).

6 Jennifer Fleissner, *Women, Compulsion, Modernity: The Moment of American Naturalism* (Chicago: University of Chicago Press, 2004), 7.

7 Timothy Choy, "Air's Substantiations," in *Lively Capital: Biotechnologies, Ethics, and Governance in Global Markets*, ed. Kaushik Sunder Rajan (Durham, NC: Duke University Press, 2012), 128.

8 Ibid., 125.

9 In addition to physiology, Zola—who had a strong influence on Norris's writing—cites the field of chemistry as an important model for the naturalist "experimental novel" (Émile Zola, "The Experimental Novel," in *The Experimental Novel and Other Essays*, trans. Belle Sherman [New York: Casselle, 1893], 2, 6, 23).

10 Georg Lukács, "Narrate or Describe?," in *Writer and Critic and Other Essays*, ed. and trans. Arthur Kahn (London: Merlin Press, 1978), 110–48, 139.

11 Kevin Trumpeter, "The Language of the Stones: Literary Naturalism and the New Materialism," *American Literature* 87, no. 2 (June 2015): 225–52, 237.

12 See Jasbir Puar, *The Right to Maim: Debility, Capacity, Disability* (Durham, NC: Duke University Press, 2017); Clare Barker and Stuart Murray, "Disabling Postcolonialism: Global Disability Cultures and Democratic Criticism," *Journal of Literary and Cultural Disability Studies* 4, no. 3 (2010); Nirmala Erevelles, "Becoming Disabled/Becoming Black: Crippin' Critical Ethnic Studies from the Periphery," in *Critical Ethnic Studies: A Reader*, ed. Critical Ethnic Studies Editorial Collective (Durham, NC: Duke University Press, 2016), 231–51.

13 For other studies of twentieth-century neo-naturalist genres, see Donald Pizer, *Twentieth-Century American Literary Naturalism: An Interpretation* (Carbondale: Southern Illinois University Press, 1982); Paul Civello, *American Literary Naturalism and Its Twentieth-Century Transformations: Frank Norris, Ernest Hemingway, Don DeLillo* (Athens: University of Georgia Press, 1994); Jeff Jaeckle, "American Literary Naturalism and Film Noir," and Gary Scharnhorst, "Naturalism and Crime," both in *The Oxford Handbook of American Literary Naturalism*, ed. Keith Newlin (New York: Oxford, 2011); Fleissner, *Women, Compulsion, Modernity*, 275–80; and special issues of *Studies of American Naturalism* on naturalism and African American culture, ed. John Dudley (7, no. 1 [Summer 2012]), and on naturalism and science fiction, ed. Eric Carl Link (8, no. 1 [Summer 2013]).

14 J. Douglas Porteous, "Smellscape," *Progress in Physical Geography* 9, no. 3 (September 1985): 356–78. For a detailed account of the emergence of public health in rapidly growing nineteenth-century cities, see Julie Sze, *Noxious New York: The Racial Politics of Urban Health and Environmental Justice* (Cambridge, MA: MIT Press, 2006), 31–37.

15 Peter Sloterdijk, *Foams: Spheres III*, trans. Wieland Hoban (Los Angeles: Semiotext(e), 2016), 173. Sloterdijk suggests that the experiences of alienation narrated in twentieth-century novels are expressions of this atmospheric splintering (172).

16 Jim Drobnick, "Toposmia: Art, Scent, and Interrogations of Spatiality," *Angelaki* 7, no. 1 (2002): 31–47, 33.

17 Ibid., 42.

18 Peter Adey, "Air/Atmospheres of the Megacity," *Theory, Culture, & Society* 30, nos. 7/8 (2013): 293. For other important studies of atmosphere and affect by cultural geographers, see Ben Anderson, "Affective Atmospheres," *Emotion, Space, and Society* 2 (2009): 78, and Andreas Philippopoulos-Mihalopoulos, "Withdrawing from Atmosphere: An Ontology of Air Partitioning and Affective Engineering," *Environment and Planning D: Society and Space* 34 (2015): 150–67.

19 Select Committee on Metropolitan Sewage Manure, "Report no. 474" (1846), 109.

20 Alain Corbin, *The Foul and the Fragrant: Odor and the French Social Imagination* (1982; Cambridge, MA: Harvard University Press, 1986), 7.

21 John Waldman, *Heartbeats in the Muck: The History, Sea Life, and Environment of New York Harbor* (New York: Fordham University Press, 1999), 107.

22 JoAnne Brown, "Crime, Commerce, and Contagionism: The Political Languages of Public Health and the Popularization of Germ Theory in the United States, 1870–1950," in *Scientific Authority and Twentieth-Century America*, ed. Ronald G. Walters (Baltimore: Johns Hopkins University Press, 1997), 78, 57.

23 For an informative analysis of olfactory references in realism, naturalism, and regionalism, see Daniela Babilon, *The Power of Smell in American Literature: Odor, Affect, and Social Inequality* (Frankfurt: Peter Lang, 2017), 113–49.

24 On the atmosphere of Davis's novella, see Jill Gatlin, "Disturbing Aesthetics: Industrial Pollution, Moral Discourse, and Narrative Form in Rebecca Harding Davis's 'Life in the Iron Mills,'" *Nineteenth-Century Literature* 68, no. 2 (2013): 201–33; Hsuan L. Hsu, "Smelling Setting," essay cluster on "Modernist Setting," ed. Dora Zhang and Hannah Freed-Thall, *Modernism/Modernity Print+*, March 2018, https://modernismmodernity.org; Babilon, *Power of Smell*, 123–29; and Lauren Peterson, "Miasmatic Ghosts in Rebecca Harding Davis's 'Life in the Iron Mills,'" *Literary Geographies* 5, no. 1 (2019), www.literarygeographies.net.

25 Although arsenic was most frequently found in green wallpaper pigment, "arsenic pigments were still being used (at least in the United States) to dye [wall]papers colors other than green, where the consumer might not suspect the use of arsenic, as [*sic*] least well into the 1880s)" (John Parascandola, *King of Poisons: A History of Arsenic* [Dulles, VA: Potomac Books, 2012], 121).

26 Stephen Crane, *Maggie, a Girl of the Streets and Other New York Writings* (New York: Random House, 2001), 156, 159.

27 Stephen Crane, "In the Depths of a Coal Mine," *McClure's Magazine* 3, no. 3 (August 1894): 200.

28 Rose Ellen Lessy, "'This Mysterious Miasma': Environmental Risk, Edith Wharton, and the Literature of Bad Air" (PhD diss., Cornell University, 2008).

29 Referencing "A Harp in the Wind" in the title of *Sister Carrie*'s final chapter, Dreiser suggests the need to rethink the Aeolian harp—the classical figure for a detached poetics that passively records what's in the wind—in the face of modernity's toxic air flows (Theodore Dreiser, *Sister Carrie* [1900; New York: Bantam, 1958], 386, 397.

30 Upton Sinclair, *The Jungle* (1906; New York: Signet, 1960), 29–30, 129–30. In her discussion of Sinclair's olfactory references, Babilon writes, "Smell is . . . used by Sinclair as *the* symbol of capitalist corruption" (*Power of Smell*, 137).

31 Ernest Marchand, *Frank Norris: A Study* (Palo Alto, CA: Stanford University Press, 1942), 93.

32 See Timothy Morton, *Ecology without Nature: Rethinking Environmental Aesthetics* (Cambridge, MA: Harvard University Press, 2007).

33 "The more we descend in the vertebrates the greater is the olfactory, and the smaller the frontal, lobe. . . . The olfactory perceptions only furnish a minimum contribution to the concepts which are formed out of ideational elements" (Max Nordau, *Degeneration* [New York: Appleton, 1895], 503).

34 Nordau, *Degeneration*, 13. Jameson offers a more appreciative analysis of Zola's description of pungent cheeses, in which embodied affect is expressed through "virtually an autonomous unfolding of sense data." Fredric Jameson, *The Antinomies of Realism* (London: Verso, 2013), 59.

35 Corbin, *Foul and the Fragrant*, 206.

36 Bill Brown, *A Sense of Things: The Object Matter of American Literature* (Chicago: University of Chicago Press, 2003); Trumpeter, "Language of the Stones."

37 Mel Chen, *Animacies: Biopolitics, Racial Mattering, and Queer Affect* (Durham, NC: Duke University Press, 2012).

38 Jack London, *The People of the Abyss* (1903; London: Macmillan, 1904), 303, 258.

39 See Norris, *Vandover*, 217n1.

40 Russ Castronovo, "Introduction," in Norris, *Vandover*, 14.

41 Most reviewers in 1914 framed *Vandover* primarily as evidence of Norris's considerable—but not yet fully developed—abilities as a young writer; see the reviews collected in Joseph McElrath Jr. and Katherine Knight, eds., *Frank Norris: The Critical Reception* (New York: Burt Franklin, 1981), 335–64.

42 Immanuel Kant, *Anthropology from a Pragmatic Point of View*, trans. Robert Louden (New York: Cambridge University Press, 2006), 49.

43 Ibid., 49.

44 Drobnick, "Toposmia," 32.

45 See Sherwood Williams, "The Rise of a New Generation: Decadence and Atavism in *Vandover and the Brute*," *ELH* 57 (Fall 1990): 709–36 and Dana Seitler, "Down on All Fours: Atavistic Perversions and the Science of Desire from Frank Norris to Djuna Barnes," *American Literature* 73 (September 2001): 525–62.

46 Nordau, *Degeneration*, 503.

47 Jim Drobnick, "The Museum as Smellscape," in *The Multisensory Museum: Cross-Disciplinary Perspectives on Touch, Sound, Smell, Memory, and Space*, ed. Nina Levent and Alvaro Pascual-Leone (Lanham, MD: Rowman & Littlefield, 2014), 177–96, 191.

48 Michelle Murphy, *Sick Building Syndrome and the Problem of Uncertainty: Environmental Politics, Technoscience, and Women Workers* (Durham, NC: Duke University Press, 2006).

49 On "brain fog" as a figure for environmental debilitation, see Mel Chen, "Brain Fog: The Race for Cripistemology," *Journal of Literary and Cultural Disability Studies* 8, no. 2 (2014): 171–84.

50 Fleissner, *Women, Compulsion, Modernity*, 43.

51 Beck, *Risk Society*, 49.

52 Molly Ball, "Writing Out of Time: Temporal Vulnerability in Nineteenth-Century U.S. Literatures" (PhD diss., University of California, Davis, 2016). On race and remasculinization in naturalist texts, see Colleen Lye, *America's Asia: Racial Form and American Literature, 1893–1945* (Princeton: Princeton University Press, 2004); John Dudley, *A Man's Game: Masculinity and the Anti-aesthetics of American Literary Naturalism* (Tuscaloosa: University of Alabama Press, 2004); John Eperjesi, *The Imperialist Imaginary: Visions of Asia and the Pacific in American Culture* (Hanover, NH: Dartmouth College Press, 2005), 58–85; Mita Banerjee, *Color Me White: Naturalism/Naturalization in American Literature* (Heidelberg: Universitätsverlag, 2013). For an influential critique of literary historians' excessive emphasis on naturalism's antimodern narratives of male decline, however, see Fleissner, *Women, Compulsion, Modernity*, 13–18.

53 Sze, *Noxious New York*, 32.

54 On the ties between American eugenics, imperialism, and the wilderness ideal, see Sarah Jaquette Ray, *The Ecological Other: Environmental Exclusion in American Culture* (Tucson: University of Arizona Press, 2013), 11–16; on "nature-cultures," see Bruno Latour, *We Have Never Been Modern*, trans. Catherine Porter (Cambridge, MA: Harvard University Press, 1993).

55 Buell, *Writing for an Endangered World*, 129–69.

56 Sloterdijk, *Foams*, 173.

57 Ibid., 102.

58 Ibid., 95.

59 Scott Christianson, *The Last Gasp: The Rise and Fall of the American Gas Chamber* (Berkeley: University of California Press, 2011), 1.

60 On racial mustard gas experiments (which sought to discern racial disparities in chemical sensitivity), see Susan L. Smith, *Toxic Exposures: Mustard Gas and the Health Consequences of World War II in the United States* (New Brunswick, NJ: Rutgers University Press, 2017), 42–70.

61 For a detailed history of Gee Jon's execution, see Christianson, *Last Gasp*, 69–89; Christianson notes that the Mexican American youth Thomas Russell and Gee Jon's Chinese accomplice Hughie Sing were also sentenced to the gas chamber

around this time: although these two men were spared, the sentences bear witness to the state's apparent interest in testing this new technology on nonwhite subjects (79).

62 Ibid., 113.

63 Noting its intersections with Wright's style and subject matter, Jay Garcia reports that "critics described *The Street* as an example of naturalism in the vein of Wright's *Native Son*" (Garcia, *Psychology Comes to Harlem: Rethinking the Race Question in Twentieth-Century Harlem* [Baltimore: Johns Hopkins University Press, 2012], 101). See also Don Dingledine, "'It Could Have Been Any Street': Ann Petry, Stephen Crane, and the Fate of Naturalism," *Studies in American Fiction* 34, no. 1 (Spring 2006): 87–106. For a comparison of Viramontes's and Steinbeck's approaches to social realism and migrant laborers, see Paula Moya, *Learning from Experience: Identities, Multicultural* (Berkeley: University of California Press, 2002), 190–91.

64 For an influential discussion of "social reproduction"—or the means by which people reproduce themselves across time and generations—see Cindi Katz, "Vagabond Capitalism and the Necessity of Social Reproduction," *Antipode: A Radical Journal of Geography* 33, no. 4 (September 2001): 709–28. Katz discusses the environment as a material basis for social reproduction, along with children's vulnerability to environmental pollutants (713–14).

65 Ann Petry, *The Street* (1946; Boston: Mariner Books, 1998), 2. Further citations are given parenthetically as *S*.

66 For an extensive discussion of racial health disparities in Petry's novel, see Jay Sibara, "Disability and Dissent in Ann Petry's *The Street*," *Literature and Medicine* 36, no. 1 (Spring 2018): 1–26.

67 Mark Smith, *How Race Is Made: Slavery, Segregation, and the Senses* (Chapel Hill: University of North Carolina Press, 2006), 132.

68 Ray, *Ecological Other*.

69 Helena María Viramontes, "Feminism, Ethnicity, and Identity," interview with Jose Jesus Romero, April 4, 2010, www.calstatela.edu.

70 Ibid.

71 David Vázquez, Sarah Wald, Paula Moya, and Helena María Viramontes, "'We Carry Our Environments within Ourselves': A Conversation with Helena María Viramontes," in *Latinx Environmentalisms: Place, Justice, and the Decolonial*, ed. Sarah D. Wald, David J. Vázquez, Priscilla Solis Ybarra, and Sarah Jaquette Ray (Philadelphia: Temple University Press, 2019), 169.

72 Helena María Viramontes, *Under the Feet of Jesus* (New York: Plume, 1995), 9. Further citations are given parenthetically as *UF*.

73 Linda Nash, *Inescapable Ecologies: A History of Environment, Disease, and Knowledge* (Berkeley: University of California Press, 2006).

74 Jill Harrison, *Pesticide Drift and the Pursuit of Environmental Justice* (Boston: MIT Press, 2011), 2. Nash notes that in the decades following World War II, "crews

of workers were frequently sprayed directly by overflying planes, leaving them drenched in chemicals" (Nash, *Inescapable Ecologies*, 150).

75 Harrison, *Pesticide Drift*, 29.

76 Curtis Marez, *Farm Worker Futurism: Speculative Technologies of Resistance* (Minneapolis: University of Minnesota Press, 2016), 24.

77 Rob Nixon, *Slow Violence and the Environmentalism of the Poor* (Cambridge, MA: Harvard University Press, 2011), 210.

78 Vázquez et al., "'We Carry Our Environments,'" 168.

79 For an incisive analysis of the theme of unknowability in this novel, see Mitchum Huehls, "Ostension, Simile, Catachresis: Misusing Helena Viramontes's *Under the Feet of Jesus* to Rethink the Globalization-Environmentalism Relation," *Discourse* 29, no. 2 (2007): 346–66.

80 For a related discussion of this novel's "dystopian atmosphere," see Edén Torres, "A Chicana Dystopian Novel and the Economic Realities of *Their Dogs Came with Them*," in *Dialectical Imaginaries: Materialist Approaches to U.S. Latino/A Literature*, ed. Marcial Gonzalez and Carlos Gallego (Ann Arbor: University of Michigan Press, 2018), 263–86.

81 Robert Bullard and Glenn Johnson, *Just Transportation: Dismantling Race and Class Barriers to Mobility* (Gabriola Island: New Society, 1997), 18. On the contested process of freeway construction in Los Angeles, see Eric Avila, *The Folklore of the Freeway: Race and Revolt in the Modernist City* (Minneapolis: University of Minnesota Press, 2014); Gilbert Estrada, "If You Build it, They Will Move: The Los Angeles Freeway System and the Displacement of Mexican East Los Angeles, 1944–1972," *Southern California Quarterly* 87, no. 3 (2005): 287–315; Norman Klein, *The History of Forgetting: Los Angeles and the Erasure of Memory* (London: Verso, 1997), 38–50. For an analysis of an earlier story ("Neighbors") in which Viramontes dramatizes the dissolution of community and place-based collective memory brought about by freeways in East Los Angeles, see Raúl Homero Villa, *Barrio-Logos: Space and Place in Urban Chicano Literature and Culture* (Austin: University of Texas Press, 2000), 115–34.

82 Eric Avila, "East Side Stories: Freeways and Their Portraits in Chicano Los Angeles," *Landscape Journal* 26, no. 1 (2007): 83.

83 Daniel Olivas, "Interview with Helena María Viramontes," *La Bloga*, April 2, 2007, https://labloga.blogspot.com.

84 In their work on transportation racism, Robert Bullard and Glenn Johnson write, "African-Americans and Latinos live in these Los Angeles communities with the dirtiest air; the South Coast Air Quality Management District estimates 71 percent of African-Americans and 50 percent of Latinos live in areas with the most polluted air, compared to 34 percent of white people" (Bullard and Johnson, *Just Transportation*, 18).

85 Karl Marx and Friedrich Engels, *The Communist Manifesto* (New York: Verso, 2012), 38.

86 Helena María Viramontes, *Their Dogs Came with Them* (New York: Washington Square Press, 2007), 5. Further citations are given parenthetically as *TD*. Viramontes's attention to the various phases of dust and soot resonates with Choy and Zee's interest in atmospheric suspension as particulates are dispersed into and eventually settle out of air (see Timothy Choy and Jerry Zee, "Condition—Suspension," *Cultural Anthropology* 30, no. 2 [May 2015]: 210–23).

87 Jina Kim, "Cripping East Los Angeles: Enabling Environmental Justice in Helena María Viramontes's *Their Dogs Came with Them*," in *Disability Studies and the Environmental Humanities: Toward an Eco-Crip Theory*, ed. Sarah Jaquette Ray and Jay Sibara (Reno: University of Nebraska Press, 2017), 511.

88 Frantz Fanon, *A Dying Colonialism*, trans. Haakon Chevalier (1959; New York: Grove, 1965), 65. For influential discussions of Fanon's reflections on atmosphere, see Renisa Mawani, "Atmospheric Pressures: On Race and Affect" (unpublished paper, n.d.) and Christina Sharpe, *In the Wake: On Blackness and Being* (Durham, NC: Duke University Press, 2016).

89 Jean-Thomas Tremblay, "Breath: Image and Sound, an Introduction," *New Review of Film and Television Studies* 16, no. 2 (2018): 94.

90 Dean Franco, "Metaphors Happen: Miracle and Metaphor in Helena María Viramontes's *Their Dogs Came with Them*," *Novel* 48, no. 3 (2015): 345.

91 Paula M. L. Moya, "'Against the Sorrowful and Infinite Solitude': Environmental Consciousness and Streetwalker Theorizing in Helena María Viramontes's *Their Dogs Came with Them*," in Wald et al., *Latinx Environmentalisms*, 255; Kim, "Cripping," 517.

92 Canetti, qtd. in Sloterdijk, *Foams*, 173.

93 On smell walking and olfactory mapping, see Victoria Henshaw, *Urban Smellscapes: Understanding and Designing City Smell Environments* (New York: Routledge, 2014), 42–58, and Kate McLean, "Smellmap: Amsterdam—Olfactory Art and Smell Visualisation," *Leonardo* 50 (2017): 92–93; on olfactory art, see chapter 3.

94 On naturalism's interests in evolution and degeneration, see Seitler, "Down on All Fours"; Rossetti, *Imagining the Primitive*; and Rick Armstrong, "'First Principles of Morals': Evolutionary Morality and American Naturalism," in Newlin, *Oxford Handbook of American Literary Naturalism*, 139–53.

95 "[Estrella] establishes . . . a practice of responsibility and care for her community on this shifting ground" (Janet Fiskio, "Unsettling Ecocriticism: Rethinking Agrarianism, Place, and Citizenship," *American Literature* 84, no. 2 [June 2012]: 313). See also Carol Henderson, "The 'Walking Wounded': Rethinking Black Women's Identity in Ann Petry's *The Street*," *Modern Fiction Studies* 46, no. 4 (2000): 853–59.

96 Nagahara Shōshon, *Lament in the Night*, trans. Andrew Leong (Los Angeles: Kaya, 2011), 75. Andrew Leong, introduction to "Excerpt: Lament in the Night," in *Asian American Writers' Workshop: The Margins*, December 6, 2012, https://aaww.org.

97 John Steinbeck, *The Grapes of Wrath* (New York: Penguin, 2006), 27.

98 Civello, *American Literary Naturalism*; Frank Lentricchia, "Tales of the Electronic Tribe," in *New Essays on White Noise*, ed. Frank Lentricchia (Cambridge: Cambridge University Press, 1991), 99. For an influential analysis of DeLillo's treatment of everyday toxic riskscapes, see Ursula Heise, *Sense of Place, Sense of Planet: The Environmental Imagination of the Global* (New York: Oxford University Press, 2008), 160–77.

99 Cormac McCarthy, *The Road* (New York: Knopf, 2006), 156.

CHAPTER 3. OLFACTORY ART AND MUSEUM ECOLOGIES

1 Tate Modern, "The Unilever Series: Ai Weiwei: Sunflower Seeds," www.tate.org.uk.

2 Ulrich Beck, *Risk Society: Towards a New Modernity*, trans. Mark Ritter (London: SAGE, 1992), 72.

3 Stacy Alaimo, *Bodily Natures: Science, Environment, and the Material Self* (Bloomington: Indiana University Press, 2010), 2.

4 On Western ocularcentrism and its detractors, see David Michael Levin, ed., *Modernity and the Hegemony of Vision* (Berkeley: University of California Press, 1993) and Martin Jay, *Downcast Eyes: The Denigration of Vision in Twentieth-Century French Thought* (Berkeley: University of California Press, 1993).

5 Official—though frequently contested—acceptable levels for chemical exposures are determined and published by the Occupational Safety and Health Administration (OSHA).

6 Nia McAllister, "The Case for Arts Institutions as Sites of Refuge from Environmental Injustice," *moadsf*, December 5, 2018, www.moadsf.org.

7 See Steve Lerner, *Sacrifice Zones: The Front Lines of Toxic Chemical Exposure in the United States* (Cambridge, MA: MIT Press, 2010); on Bayview and Hunters Point, see Lindsey Dillon, "The Breathers of Bayview Hill: Redevelopment and Environmental Justice in Southeast San Francisco," *Hastings Environmental Law Journal* 227 (2018): 227–36.

8 Peter Sloterdijk, *Foams: Spheres III*, trans. Wieland Hoban (Los Angeles: Semiotext(e), 2016), 181, 66.

9 Ibid., 182.

10 Fernando Domínguez Rubio, "Preserving the Unpreservable: Docile and Unruly Objects at MoMA," *Theory and Society* 43, no. 6 (November 2014): 617.

11 Ibid., 620.

12 For a critique of the standardized "white cube" space of twentieth-century art galleries, see Brian O'Doherty, *Inside the White Cube: The Ideology of the Gallery Space* (Berkeley: University of California Press, 1986).

13 Stephen Rees-Jones and Derek Linstrum, "Series Editors' Preface," in Garry Thomson, *The Museum Environment*, 2nd ed. (1978; London: Butterworth, 1986), n.p.

14 Carol Kino, "Keeping Art, and Climate, Controlled," *New York Times*, April 3, 2009, www.nytimes.com. According to Kino, climate control standards were first

laid out in Harold Plenderleith, *The Conservation of Antiquities and Works of Art: Treatment, Repair, and Restoration* (Oxford: Oxford University Press, 1956) and subsequently expanded in Thomson, *Museum Environment.*

15 Rubio, "Preserving the Unpreservable," 625.

16 Hanwell, "Museum Dust Monitoring for Internal Dust Accumulation," www .the-imcgroup.com.

17 Caroline Jones, *Eyesight Alone: Clement Greenberg's Modernism and the Bureaucratization of the Senses* (Chicago: University of Chicago Press, 2006), 394.

18 Sloterdijk, 314.

19 Jim Drobnick, "Volatile Effects: Olfactory Dimensions of Art and Architecture," in *Empire of the Senses: The Sensual Culture Reader,* ed. David Howes (London: Bloomsbury, 2005), 267.

20 Thomson, *Museum Environment,* 130, 148.

21 For important critiques of "wilderness" ideology, see William Cronon, "The Trouble With Wilderness; or, Getting Back to the Wrong Nature," in *Uncommon Ground: Rethinking the Human Place in Nature,* ed. William Cronon (New York: Norton, 1996), 69–90, and Bruce Braun, "'On the Raggedy Edge of Risk': Articulations of Race and Nature After Biology," in *Race, Nature, and the Politics of Difference,* ed. Donald Moore, Jake Kosek, and Anand Pandian (Durham, NC: Duke University Press, 2003), 175–203.

22 Donna Haraway, "Teddy Bear Patriarchy: Taxidermy in the Garden of Eden, New York City, 1908–1936," *Social Text* 11 (Winter 1984–85): 25.

23 Bruno Latour, "Sensitizing," in *Experience: Culture, Cognition, and the Common Sense,* ed. Caroline A. Jones, David Mather, and Rebecca Uchill (Cambridge, MA: MIT Press, 2016), 316.

24 Ramachandra Guha, "Radical American Environmentalism and Wilderness Preservation: A Third World Critique," *Environmental Ethics* 11 (Spring 1989): 75. For a more recent discussion of the production of "conservation refugees" in post-apartheid South Africa, see Rob Nixon, *Slow Violence and the Environmentalism of the Poor* (Cambridge, MA: Harvard University Press, 2011), 175–98.

25 Sarah Jaquette Ray, *The Ecological Other: Environmental Exclusion in American Culture* (Tucson: University of Arizona Press, 2013), 6.

26 See Alaimo, *Bodily Natures*; Bruno Latour, *We Have Never Been Modern,* trans. Catherine Porter (Cambridge, MA: Harvard University Press, 1993), 11; Beck, *Risk Society.*

27 Nixon, *Slow Violence,* 13, 15.

28 For neuroscience perspectives on the aesthetics of scent, see Richard Stevenson, "The Forgotten Sense: Using Olfaction in a Museum Context: A Neuroscience Perspective," 151–66, and Andreas Keller, "The Scented Museum," 167–76, both in *The Multisensory Museum: Cross-Disciplinary Perspectives on Touch, Sound, Smell, Memory, and Space,* ed. Nina Levent and Alvaro Pascual-Leone (Lanham, MD: Rowman & Littlefield, 2014).

29 Mark Graham, "Queer Smells: Fragrances of Late Capitalism or Scents of Subversion?," in *The Smell Culture Reader*, ed. Jim Drobnick (Oxford: Berg, 2006), 305.

30 Chandler Burr, the perfume critic and curator of the Museum of Art and Design's groundbreaking exhibition "The Art of the Scent (1889–2012)," uses "olfactory art" to frame perfumes as artworks that appeal almost exclusively to the sense of smell (see Jimmy Stamp, "The First Major Museum Show to Focus on Smell," *Smithsonian*, January 16, 2013, www.smithsonianmag.com).

31 Peter De Cupere, "Olfactism: Olfactionism—Olfactorism—Olfactourism," in *Peter de Cupere: Scent in Context* (Antwerp: Stockmans, 2016), 101. Caro Verbeek offers a similar definition: "The intentional addition of an olfactory layer to a work of art and the intentional use of smell inherent to the used material, without which the work of art in question would lose its effect, function, or meaning, and/or the presentation of scent(s) with no other sensory exponents as an autonomous work of art" (Verbeek, "Inhaling History of Art: A Smelly Business?," in *Es Liegt Was in der Luft!* [Burgrieden, Germany: Museum Villa Rot, 2015], 8–23, 11).

32 De Cupere, "Olfactism," 102–3.

33 Ibid., 103.

34 Brian Goltzenleuchter, "Scenting the Antiseptic Institution," in *Designing with Smell: Practices, Techniques, and Challenges*, ed. Victoria Henshaw et al. (New York: Routledge, 2018), 248.

35 Ashraf Osman, "Olfactory Art" (seminar paper, Postgraduate Programme in Curating, Zürcher Hochschule der Künste, June 14, 2013), 6–12. Jim Drobnick provides a similar timeline in "Towards an Olfactory Art History: The Mingled, Fatal, and Rejuvenating Perfumes of Paul Gauguin," *Senses & Society* 7, no. 2 (2012): 197.

36 On food and olfactory art, see Jim Drobnick, "Eating Nothing: Cooking Aromas in Art and Culture," in Drobnick, *Smell Culture Reader*, 342–56.

37 For an analysis of Chicago's piece, see Jim Drobnick, "Toposmia: Art, Scent, and Interrogations of Spatiality," *Angelaki* 7, no. 1 (2002): 31–47, 42–43.

38 Ibid., 32.

39 Hirst has produced numerous works incorporating an olfactory element, including *Black Sun*, *A Thousand Years*, and a series of ashtray sculptures (1995–97).

40 For another account of artists who have used these devices, see Larry Shiner and Yulia Kriskovets, "The Aesthetics of Smelly Art," *Journal of Aesthetics and Art Criticism* 65, no. 3 (Summer 2007): 278–79.

41 Cf. ibid., 274: "Creating olfactory artwork may require chemical training to enable the artists to work with aromatic substances."

42 Ibid., 274.

43 Developed in the 1980s, Headspace uses a vacuum to capture odors emanated by an environment or object. Susie Rushton, "The Sweat Hog," *New York Times*, August 27 2006, www.nytimes.com.

44 International Flavors and Fragrances, "IFF Fragrances: Fine Fragrances" (2020), www.iff.com.

45 Sissel Tolaas, "The City from the Perspective of the Nose," in *Ecological Urbanism*, ed. Mohsen Mostafavi and Gareth Doherty (Baden: Lars Müller, 2010), 146–55, 146, 150. On Tolaas's exhibition based on "smellwalking" and scent sampling in Detroit, see Chris Ip, "On the Nose," *Engadget*, October 26, 2018, www.engadget.com.

46 Saskia Wilson-Brown, "Founding Statement" (Los Angeles: Institute of Art and Olfaction, 2012), http://artandolfaction.com.

47 See http://air-variable.org.

48 In collaboration with Ravat's Berlin-based Smell Lab, IAO initiated an annual international Experimental Scent Summit (the first such event blending talks and workshops for olfactory makers) in 2017.

49 Boris Raux, *The Swimming Pool* (*La Piscine*), 2005.

50 Stéphane Verlet-Bottéro, "Fragrant Misdemeanors," in *La Douche Froide: Une Exposition des Oeuvres de Boris Raux/Cold Shower: An Exhibition of the Works of Boris Raux 5 December 2014–30 March 2015*, press folder (Grasse: International Perfume Museum, 2014), 12–17, 12.

51 Qtd. in Jane Draycott, "Smelling Trees, Flowers and Herbs in the Ancient World," in *Smell and the Ancient Senses*, ed. Mark Bradley (New York: Routledge, 2014), 69.

52 Boris Raux, email exchange with the author, November 13, 2018.

53 Jones, *Eyesight Alone*, 397.

54 Jacques Lacan, "The Mirror Stage as Formative of the I Function, as Revealed in Psychoanalytic Experience," in *Écrits: A Selection*, trans. Bruce Fink (1966; New York: Norton, 2004), 5, 6.

55 Drobnick, "Toposmia," 33.

56 Ibid., 33.

57 Jim Drobnick, "The Museum as Smellscape," in Levent and Pascual-Leone, *Multisensory Museum*, 177–96, 190.

58 "I like this term, *breathers*, which I borrow from environmental economics; it refers to those who accrue the unaccounted-for costs that attend the production and consumption of goods and services, such as the injuries, medical expenses, and changes in climate and ecosystems" (Timothy Choy, "Air's Substantiations," in *Lively Capital: Biotechnologies, Ethics, and Governance in Global Markets*, ed. Kaushik Sunder Rajan [Durham, NC: Duke University Press, 2012], 128).

59 On "miasmas," see Alain Corbin, *The Foul and the Fragrant: Odor and the French Social Imagination* (1982; Cambridge, MA: Harvard University Press, 1986), 1–34, and Melanie Kiechle, *Smell Detectives: An Olfactory History of Nineteenth-Century Urban America* (Seattle: University of Washington Press, 2017). In their textbook *The New Public Health*, Tulchinsky and Varavikova suggest that in spite of the biomedical advances brought about by germ theory, "environmental factors of the physical, social, economic, and cultural environment have emerged as important modern applications of the miasma theory"

(Theodore Tulchinsky and Elena Varavikova, *The New Public Health: An Intro-duction for the 21st Century*, 3rd ed. [London: Elsevier, 2014], 237).

60 Jessica Silverman Gallery, "Sean Raspet/Residuals" (n.d.), http://jessicasilvermangallery.com.

61 Drobnick, "Museum as Smellscape," 183.

62 Jessica Silverman Gallery, "Sean Raspet/Residuals."

63 See Kino, "Keeping Art" and Vanessa Thorpe, "Tate Director Sir Nicholas Serote Urges Art Galleries to Turn down the Heating," *Guardian*, November 12, 2011, www.theguardian.com.

64 Anicka Yi, quoted in Wendy Vogel, "What's That Smell in the Kitchen? Art's Olfactory Turn," *Art in America*, April 8, 2015, www.artinamericamagazine.com; Lauren O'Neill-Butler, "Anicka Yi," *Artforum* (2015), www.artforum.com.

65 Vogel, "What's That Smell in the Kitchen?"

66 Social Mail, "The Kitchen Presents Anicka Yi: You Can Call Me F," www.socialmail.com.

67 Drobnick, "Toposmia," 42.

68 Social Mail, "Kitchen Presents."

69 Ibid.

70 Caroline A. Jones, "Biofiction and the *Umwelt*: Anicka Yi," in *The Hugo Boss Prize: 20 Years* (New York: Guggenheim Museum, 2016), 93.

71 Priscilla Wald, *Contagious: Cultures, Carriers, and the Outbreak Narrative* (Durham, NC: Duke University Press, 2008), 2.

72 On Anicka Yi and miasma theory, see Jane Yong Kim, "Feminist Fumes: Anicka Yi's Miasmatic Art," *Paris Review*, April 6, 2015, www.theparisreview.org.

73 Social Mail, "Kitchen Presents."

74 Mel Chen, *Animacies: Biopolitics, Racial Mattering, and Queer Affect* (Durham, NC: Duke University Press, 2012), 196.

75 Deboleena Roy, *Molecular Feminisms: Biology, Becomings, and Life in the Lab* (Seattle: University of Washington Press, 2018), 91.

76 Shiner and Kriskovets, "Aesthetics of Smelly Art," 274.

77 Prior to being exhibited in Havana, *Smoke Cloud* was first shown in De Cupere's solo exhibition *The Art of Smelling, an Olfactory Art Research* (2014) in the Netherlands. The artist has noted, however, that the smell of air pollution in Havana inspired this piece (see note 78 below).

78 Sam Steverlynck, "A Major Exhibition of Belgian Art Opens in Havana," *Havana Live*, February 23, 2015, www.havana-live.com.

79 Peter De Cupere, personal communication with the author, March 20, 2016.

80 For an account of De Cupere's original intentions to include "the scents of sperm, sweat, dead bodies, money, gun powder, air pollution, a hamburger, and Belgian fries," see Katherine Brooks, "Artist 'Scent Engineers' Plants to Smell Like Dead Bodies, Sperm, and Air Pollution," *Huffington Post*, May 13, 2015, www.huffingtonpost.com; information about the omitted scents provided by Peter De Cupere, personal communication.

81 Qtd. in Brooks, "Artist 'Scent Engineers' Plants."
82 See, e.g., Martin F. Manalansan IV, "Immigrant Lives and the Politics of Olfaction in the Global City," 41–52, Gale Largey and Rod Watson, "The Sociology of Odors," 29–40, and Alan Hyde, "Offensive Bodies," 53–58, all in Drobnick, *Smell Culture Reader*.
83 Sara Alonso Gómez, "Exhibition 'The Smell of a Stranger' by Peter de Cupere," *Facebook*, May 23, 2015, www.facebook.com.
84 De Cupere explains that Belgian fries refer to his own complicity as a Belgian and European, so as "not to blame or focus only on the American eating culture" (De Cupere, personal communication).
85 Lauren Berlant, "Slow Death (Sovereignty, Obesity, Lateral Agency)," *Critical Inquiry* 33 (Summer 2007): 754–80.
86 The smell of gunpowder here echoes several pieces that juxtaposed bullets and army helmets with the scents of dead bodies and blood that De Cupere included in his curated exhibition *The Smell of War* earlier in 2015.
87 Nixon, *Slow Violence*, 3.
88 Beck, *Risk Society*, 65.

CHAPTER 4. ATMO-ORIENTALISM

 1 Martin F. Manalansan IV, "Immigrant Lives and the Politics of Olfaction in the Global City," in Drobnick, *Smell Culture Reader*, 41–52, 45.
 2 Martin F. Manalansan IV, "The Messy Itineraries of Queerness," *Cultural Anthropology*, July 21, 2015, https://legacy.culanth.org.
 3 Suzana Sawyer and Arun Agrawal, "Environmental Orientalisms," *Cultural Critique* 45 (Spring 2000): 71–108, 73; Gisli Pálsson, "Human-Environmental Relations: Orientalism, Paternalism and Communalism," in *Nature and Society: Anthropological Perspectives*, ed. Philippe Descola and Gisli Pálsson (London: Routledge, 2003), 73–91; Diana K. Davis, "Imperialism, Orientalism, and Environment in the Middle East: History, Policy, Power, and Practice," in *Environmental Imaginaries of the Middle East and North Africa*, ed. Diana K. Davis and Edmund Burke III (Athens: Ohio University Press, 2011), 1–22, 4.
 4 Sarah Jaquette Ray, *The Ecological Other: Environmental Exclusion in American Culture* (Tucson: University of Arizona Press, 2013), 1.
 5 See Mark Smith, *How Race Is Made: Slavery, Segregation, and the Senses* (Chapel Hill: University of North Carolina Press, 2006), 80–83.
 6 See Henri Lefebvre, *The Production of Space*, trans. Donald Nicholson-Smith (Oxford: Blackwell, 1991).
 7 Alain Corbin, *The Foul and the Fragrant: Odor and the French Social Imagination* (1982; Cambridge, MA: Harvard University Press, 1986), 5.
 8 Renisa Mawani, "Atmospheric Pressures: On Race and Affect" (unpublished paper, n.d.).
 9 Kyla Wazana Tompkins, *Racial Indigestion: Eating Bodies in the 19th Century* (New York: New York University Press, 2012), 3.

10 See Smith, *How Race Is Made*; Connie Chiang, "Monterey-by-the-Smell," *Pacific Historical Review* 73, no. 2 (May 2004): 183–214; Kelvin Low, *Scent and Scentsibilities: Smell and Everyday Life Experiences* (Cambridge: Cambridge Scholars Press, 2008), 84–121.

11 Constance Classen, *Worlds of Sense: Exploring the Senses in History and across Cultures* (London: Routledge, 1993), 80.

12 Andrew Kettler, *The Smell of Slavery: Olfactory Racism and the Atlantic World* (Cambridge: Cambridge University Press, 2020), 15.

13 Iyko Day, *Alien Capital: Asian Racialization and the Logic of Settler Colonial Capitalism* (Durham, NC: Duke University Press, 2016), 6; Colleen Lye, *America's Asia: Racial Form and American Literature, 1893–1945* (Princeton: Princeton University Press, 2004), 130.

14 Day, *Alien Capital*, 15.

15 Walt Whitman, "Song of Myself," in *The Complete Poems*, ed. Francis Murphy (New York: Penguin, 2004), 64.

16 Mark Jerng, *Racial Worldmaking: The Power of Popular Fiction* (New York: Fordham University Press, 2017), 66; see also Jerng's discussion of "Blackness as Atmosphere," 117–23.

17 See Ann Laura Stoler, "Tense and Tender Ties: The Politics of Comparison in North American History and (Post) Colonial Studies," in *Haunted by Empire: Geographies of Intimacy in North American History*, ed. Ann Laura Stoler (Durham, NC: Duke University Press, 2006), 23.

18 Melanie Kiechle, *Smell Detectives: An Olfactory History of Nineteenth-Century Urban America* (Seattle: University of Washington Press, 2017), 27.

19 "Need I say that I allude to the horrible tale, often quoted, of the Black Hole of Calcutta, and to the fearful mortality on board Coolie ships?" (F. Oppert, *Hospitals, Infirmaries, and Dispensaries: Their Construction, Interior Arrangement, and Management* [London: J. & A. Churchill, 1883], 27). "No Black Hole of Calcutta, no Atlantic steamship steerage hold, could be more densely packed," writes J. D. Edgar of the "Chinese thieves' quarter" in San Francisco's Chinatown (J. D. Edgar, "Celestial America," *Canadian Monthly and National Review* 6, no. 5 [November 1874]: 394–95).

20 Qtd. in Nayan Shah, *Contagious Divides: Epidemics and Race in San Francisco's Chinatown* (Berkeley: University of California Press, 2001), 1.

21 Charles McClain, *In Search of Equality: The Chinese Struggle Against Discrimination in Nineteenth-Century America* (Berkeley: University of California Press, 1994), 45.

22 Ibid., 45; Roger Daniels, *Asian America: Chinese and Japanese in the United States since 1850* (Seattle: University of Washington Press, 2011), 39; Paul Spickard, *Almost All Aliens: Immigration, Race, and Colonialism in American History* (New York: Routledge, 2009), 162.

23 *Report of the Joint Special Committee to Investigate Chinese Immigration* (Washington, DC: Government Printing Office, 1877), 655.

24 Ellen Pader, "Restructuring Immigrant Workers' Housing: When Does Policy or Design Become Discriminatory?," in *Sub-urbanisms: Casino Urbanization, Chinatowns, and the Contested American Landscape*, ed. Stephen Fan (New London, CT: Lyman Allyn Art Museum, 2014), 186–215, 187.

25 Spickard, *Almost All Aliens*, 162.

26 Jean Pfaelzer, *Driven Out: The Forgotten War Against Chinese Americans* (Berkeley: University of California Press, 2008), 75.

27 Chiang, "Monterey-by-the-Smell," 190.

28 Ibid., 185.

29 San Francisco Board of Supervisors, "Report of the Special Committee of the Board of Supervisors on the Condition of the Chinese Quarter," in *San Francisco Municipal Reports for the Fiscal Year 1884–85* (San Francisco: W. M. Hinton, 1885), 162–231, 175.

30 Ibid., 180, emphasis added.

31 Ibid., 180.

32 Otis Gibson, *The Chinese in America* (Cincinnati: Hitchcock & Walden, 1877), 63–64.

33 Ibid., 64.

34 Workingmen's Committee of California, "Chinatown Declared a Nuisance!" (San Francisco: Workingmen's Committee of California, 1880), 5.

35 Alfred Trumble, *The "Heathen Chinee" at Home and Abroad* (New York: R. K. Fox, 1882), 25.

36 On the mythic character of the "outbreak narrative" of disease emergence, see Priscilla Wald, *Contagious: Cultures, Carriers, and the Outbreak Narrative* (Durham, NC: Duke University Press, 2008).

37 Woods Hutchinson, "The Plague Situation in San Francisco and the Problem of Chinatown," *Medical Sentinel* 11, no. 6 (June 1903): 338.

38 See Pfaelzer, *Driven Out*.

39 Hutchinson, "Plague Situation," 337.

40 Ibid., 337.

41 See James Mohr, *Plague and Fire: Battling Black Death and the 1900 Burning of Honolulu's Chinatown* (Oxford: Oxford University Press, 2005).

42 Matthew Klingle, "Frontier Ghosts along the Urban Pacific Shore," in *Frontier Cities: Encounters at the Crossroads of Empire*, ed. Jay Gitlin, Barbara Berglund, and Adam Arenson (Philadelphia: University of Pennsylvania Press, 2013), 135.

43 Unsigned, "It Is Up to Us," *Riverside Enterprise*, May 29, 1906, 4. See "The Chinese Question," *Morning Oregonian*, March 24, 1890, 6, for an interesting argument against racially targeted smelling committees.

44 Kyla Schuller, *The Biopolitics of Feeling: Race, Sex, and Science in the Nineteenth Century* (Durham, NC: Duke University Press, 2017), 55.

45 Arthur Henderson Smith, *Chinese Characteristics* (New York: Revell, 1894), 142.

46 Lye, *America's Asia*, 89–93.

47 Frank Norris, *Moran of the Lady Letty* (New York: Doubleday & McClure, 1898), 33.

48 Susan Lanser, "Feminist Criticism, 'The Yellow Wallpaper,' and the Politics of Color in America," *Feminist Studies* 15, no. 3 (Autumn 1989): 415–41; Erica Fretwell, "Senses of Belonging: The Synaesthetics of Citizenship in American Literature, 1862–1903" (PhD diss., Duke University, 2011), 9–12. See also Sabine Doran, *The Culture of Yellow: or, The Visual Politics of Late Modernity* (London: Bloomsbury, 2013), 69–96.

49 Lanser, "Feminist Criticism," 427.

50 Jack London, "Chun Ah Chun" (1910), in *The House of Pride, and Other Tales of Hawai'i* (New York: Macmillan, 1919), 173–74.

51 Ibid., 175.

52 Qtd. in Lisa-Lone Marker, *David Belasco: Naturalism in the American Theatre* (Princeton: Princeton University Press, 1975), 64.

53 Sax Rohmer, *The Insidious Dr. Fu-Manchu*, in *The Book of Fu-Manchu* (New York: Robert M. McBride, 1929), 156–57. Further citations are given parenthetically as *FM*.

54 See, e.g., Sax Rohmer, *Bride of Fu Manchu* (1933; Cornwall: House of Stratus, 2009), 88; Rohmer, *The Trail of Fu Manchu* (1934; New York: Pyramid Books, 1964), 80.

55 Peter Sloterdijk, *Foams: Spheres III*, trans. Wieland Hoban (Los Angeles: Semiotext(e), 2016), 119.

56 Victor Halperin, dir., *Revenge of the Zombies* (Academy Pictures, 1936).

57 David Barnett, "Ios Book Review: Boneshaker, by Cherie Priest," *Independent*, November 25, 2012, www.independent.co.uk.

58 See Jerng, *Racial Worldmaking*.

59 Cherie Priest, *Boneshaker* (New York: Tom Doherty, 2009), 115. Further citations are given parenthetically as *B*.

60 Ulrich Beck, *Risk Society: Towards a New Modernity*, trans. Mark Ritter (London: SAGE, 1992).

61 Mel Chen, *Animacies: Biopolitics, Racial Mattering, and Queer Affect* (Durham, NC: Duke University Press, 2012), 164.

62 Ibid., 165.

63 Michael Ziser and Julie Sze, "Climate Change, Environmental Aesthetics, and Global Environmental Justice Cultural Studies," *Discourse* 29, nos. 2–3 (2007): 384–410, 394. As Sze notes elsewhere, "The growth of China's industrial economy must be understood in inverse relation to Germany's, which has seen its carbon emissions decline by 19 percent since 1990 as a significant percentage of its industrial production has moved offshore to China. Similarly, calculations of British carbon emissions leap if output within China for British factories is counted as U.K. rather than Chinese emissions" (Julie Sze, *Fantasy Islands: Chinese Dreams and Ecological Fears in an Age of Climate Crisis* [Berkeley: University of California Press, 2015], 32).

64 Alex Salkever, "Toxic Chinese Drywall Turns U.S. Homes into Smelly Cancer Traps," *Aol.com*, September 9, 2009, www.aol.com.

65 See, e.g., *Upper Dublin Township v. Gung Tao Li, d/b/a/ Wok's Chinese Restaurant, et al.*, 136 *Montgomery County Law Reporter* II (1999): 301–4, in which a Pennsylvania equity court decided that the threat that allegedly "noxious" odors emanating from a Chinese restaurant could deprive residents of "full enjoyment of their property," sicken them, and continually bother them "can not be outweighed by the situation faced by the appellant in closing down its business" (301).

66 Anita Mannur and Martin Manalansan IV, "Dude, What's That Smell? The Sriracha Shutdown and Immigrant Excess," *From the Square: NYU Press Blog*, January 16, 2014, www.fromthesquare.org.

67 See Judith Fetterley and Marjorie Pryse, eds., *Writing Out of Place: Regionalism, Women, and American Literary Culture* (Urbana: University of Illinois Press, 2003). There is no mention of Eaton, for example, in the important essay collection *Asian American Literature and the Environment* (Lorna Fitzsimmons, Youngsuk Chae, and Bella Adams, eds., *Asian American Literature and the Environment* [New York: Routledge, 2014]).

68 Martha Patterson, *Beyond the Gibson Girl: Reimagining the American New Woman, 1895–1915* (Urbana: University of Illinois Press, 2010), 111. See also Chapman, "Introduction," xiii.

69 Kiechle, *Smell Detectives*, 83.

70 Ibid., 83, 84.

71 Classen, *Worlds of Sense* 30.

72 Kiechle, *Smell Detectives*, 193.

73 Ibid., 195.

74 See p. XXX.

75 Several of the following paragraphs are adapted from paragraphs I drafted in collaboration with Edlie Wong, which appeared in Hsuan L. Hsu and Edlie Wong, "Uncollected: Remapping Edith Maude Eaton/Sui Sin Far," in *Asian American Literature in Transition*, vol. 1, ed. Josephine Lee and Julia Lee (Cambridge: Cambridge University Press, forthcoming).

76 See Sean X. Goudie, "Toward a Definition of Caribbean American Regionalism: Contesting Anglo-America's Caribbean Designs in Mary Seacole and Sui Sin Far," *American Literature* 80, no. 2 (June 2008): 293–322.

77 See David Livingstone, "Race, Space, and Moral Climatology: Notes toward a Genealogy," *Journal of Historical Geography* 28, no. 2 (2002): 159–80, and James Duncan, *In the Shadows of the Tropics: Climate, Race and Biopower in Nineteenth-Century Ceylon* (New York: Routledge, 2016).

78 Edith Maude Eaton (Sui Sin Far), "Away Down in Jamaica," in *Becoming Sui Sin Far: Early Fiction, Journalism, and Travel Writing by Edith Maude Eaton*, ed. Mary Chapman (1898; Montreal: McGill-Queen's University Press, 2016), 174, 177.

79 On accounts of Obeah's toxic odors, see Kettler, *Smell of Slavery*, 155–94.

80 Eaton, "Spring Impressions: A Medley of Poetry and Prose," in *Mrs. Spring Fragrance and Other Writings*, ed. Amy Ling and Annette White-Parks (1890; Urbana: University of Illinois Press, 1995), 184.

81 Eaton, "Leaves from the Mental Portfolio of an Eurasian," in Ling and White Parks, *Mrs. Spring Fragrance*, 218–30, 226. Eaton perhaps draws on this experience in "Sweet Sin" (1898), where she writes, "California sunshine and the balmy freshness of Pacific breezes had helped to make her a bewitching woman" (in Chapman, *Becoming Sui Sin Far*, 168).

82 Eaton, "'Its Wavering Image,'" in Ling and White Parks, *Mrs. Spring Fragrance*, 61–66, 61.

83 Shah, *Contagious Divides*, 50.

84 Eaton, "Tian Shan's Kindred Spirit" (1912), in Ling and White Parks, *Mrs. Spring Fragrance*, 119–25, 120. Further citations are given parenthetically as "TS."

85 Cf. "The Smuggling of Tie Co," in which Eaton describes how Chinese could be "[proven] to be an American citizen with the right to breathe United States air" (in Ling and White Parks, *Mrs. Spring Fragrance*, 104–9, 105).

86 J. B. Sibara argues that "Sui Sin Far's writings counter this characterization [of Chinese as public health threat] by demonstrating that racial inequality rendered the Chinese in North America vulnerable to illness and disability. Her writing thus reconfigures illness and disability as signs of imperialist violence rather than as symptoms of racial contamination" (J. B. Sibara, "Disease, Disability, and the Alien Body in the Literature of Sui Sin Far," *MELUS* 39, no. 1 [Spring 2014]: 56).

87 On the nearly two hundred documented purges of Chinese from settlements in California and other western states, see Pfaelzer, *Driven Out*; on states' alien land laws targeting Asian farmers, see Huping Ling, *Surviving on the Gold Mountain: A History of Chinese American Women and their Lives* (Albany: State University of New York Press, 1998), 75.

88 Eaton, "The Chinese in America, Part III" (1909), in Ling and White Parks, *Mrs. Spring Fragrance*, 233–58, 245.

89 Day, *Alien Capital*, 15. See William Cronon, "The Trouble With Wilderness; or, Getting Back to the Wrong Nature," in *Uncommon Ground: Rethinking the Human Place in Nature*, ed. William Cronon (New York: Norton, 1996), 69–90.

90 Eaton, "Wing Sing of Los Angeles on His Travels" (1904), in Chapman, *Becoming Sui Sin Far*, 201–36, 220. Further citations are given parenthetically as "WS."

91 On nineteenth-century anti-Chinese alien land laws that preceded the anti-Japanese Alien Land Law of 1913, see Mark Lazarus, "An Historical Analysis of Alien Land Law: Washington Territory and State: 1853–1889," *University of Puget Sound Law Review* 12, no. 1 (1987): 197–246. For a more detailed discussion of settler colonial investments in "Wing Sing," see Hsu and Wong, "Uncollected." On Asian American complicities with settler colonialism in another context, see Candace Fujikane and Jonathan Okamura, eds., *Asian Settler Colonialism: From*

Local Governance to the Habits of Everyday Life in Hawai'i (Honolulu: University of Hawai'i Press, 2008).

92 Willard Squire III, "The 24th Infantry Regiment and the Racial Debate in the U.S. Army" (MMAS thesis, Fort Leavenworth, KS, 1997), 71.

93 Bruce Braun, "'On the Raggedy Edge of Risk': Articulations of Race and Nature after Biology," in *Race, Nature and the Politics of Difference*, ed. Donald Moore, Jake Kosek, and Anand Pandian (Durham, NC: Duke University Press, 2003), 197.

94 Neel Ahuja, "Intimate Atmospheres: Queer Theory in a Time of Extinctions," *GLQ* 21, nos. 2–3 (2015): 371.

95 Mawani, "Atmospheric Pressures."

96 Ahuja, "Intimate Atmospheres," 377.

97 Anicka Yi, "How I Solved It: Transforming Ideas into Smells," *New Yorker*, May 9, 2017, www.newyorker.com.

98 Anicka Yi and Caroline Jones, "Quasi/Verbatim: An Exchange between Caroline A. Jones and Anicka Yi," in *Anicka Yi: 6,070,430K of Digital Spit*, ed. Alise Upitis (Cambridge, MA: MIT List Visual Arts Center/Mousse, 2016), 9–16, 9–10.

99 Johanna Burton, "Assault on the Senses," in Upitis, *Anicka Yi*, 19–24, 24.

100 Amanda Arnold, "Remembering Fierce, the Iconic, Inescapable Abercrombie & Fitch Cologne," *Broadly*, August 16, 2017, https://broadly.vice.com.

101 Burton, "Assault on the Senses," 24.

102 Tyler Green and Anicka Yi, *Modern Art Notes Podcast* 309 (October 2017).

103 Yi and Jones, "Quasi/Verbatim," 15. See Donna Haraway, *The Companion Species Manifesto: Dogs, People, and Significant Otherness* (Chicago: Prickly Paradigm Press, 2003).

104 Rachel Lee, "Metabolic Aesthetics: On the Feminist Scentscapes of Anicka Yi," *Food, Culture, and Society* 22, no. 5 (2019): 692–712, 697.

105 Ibid., 705.

106 Yi, "How I Solved It."

107 Ibid.

108 Ibid.

109 Jim Drobnick, "Volatile Effects: Olfactory Dimensions of Art and Architecture," in *Empire of the Senses: The Sensual Culture Reader*, ed. David Howes (London: Bloomsbury, 2005), 266.

110 Burton, "Assault on the Senses," 23.

111 Ibid., 19.

112 Caroline A. Jones, "Biofiction and the *Umwelt*: Anicka Yi," in *The Hugo Boss Prize: 20 Years* (New York: Guggenheim Museum, 2016), 93.

113 Katherine Brinson and Susan Thompson, Exhibition Description for Anicka Yi, *Life Is Cheap* (Guggenheim Museum, New York, 2017).

114 Ibid.

115 Katherine Brinson, qtd. in Lisa Wong Macabasco, "Artist Anicka Yi's Scents and Sensibilities," *Vogue*, May 5, 2017, www.vogue.com; Donna Haraway, "Teddy Bear

Patriarchy: Taxidermy in the Garden of Eden, New York City, 1908–1936," *Social Text* 11 (Winter 1984–85): 25.

116 Brinson and Thompson, Exhibition Description.

117 Jonathan Law, ed., *A Dictionary of Law*, 8th ed. (Oxford: Oxford University Press, 2015), 267.

118 Lee, "Metabolic Aesthetics," 705.

119 Ahuja, "Intimate Atmospheres," 368.

120 Yi, "How I Solved It."

121 Ibid.

122 Brinson and Thompson, Exhibition Description.

123 Lye, *America's Asia*, 90.

124 See Célestin Banza et al., "Sustainability of Artisanal Mining of Cobalt in DR Congo," *Nature Sustainability* 1 (2018): 495–504; Michael Kan, "Odor from Apple Supplier Factory in China Unbearable, Residents Say," *PCWorld*, October 18, 2011, www.pcworld.com; David Barboza, "Workers Sickened at Apple Supplier in China," *New York Times*, February 22, 2011, www.nytimes.com; Janice Lobo Sapigao, *Microchips for Millions* (San Francisco: Pawa, 2016).

125 Ahuja, "Intimate Atmospheres," 372.

126 "Yi uses unconventional materials to examine what she calls a 'biopolitics of the senses,' or how assumptions and anxieties related to gender, race, and class shape physical perception" (Brinson and Thompson, Exhibition Description).

127 Michel Foucault, *"Society Must Be Defended": Lectures at the Collège de France, 1975–1976*, trans. David Macey (New York: Picador, 2003), 254.

128 Cf. Springray on the "sensational pedagogy" enacted by the Toronto-based artist Diane Borsato's relational artwork "The Chinatown Foray": "Sensational pedagogies offer the potential to re-think the ideologies of domination that are materialized and preserved through smells" (Stephanie Springray, "'The Chinatown Foray' as Sensational Pedagogy," *Curriculum Inquiry* 41, no. 5 [2011]: 640).

129 Jasbir Puar, "Prognosis Time: Towards a Geopolitics of Affect, Debility and Capacity," *Women & Performance* 19, no. 2 (2009): 168–69.

130 Teresa Brennan, *The Transmission of Affect* (Ithaca, NY: Cornell University Press, 2004). On "racial smells as modes of attachment that produce a kind of social closeness or public intimacy," see Christine Kim, "The Smell of Communities to Come: Jeremy Lin and Post-racial Desire," *Journal of Intercultural Studies* 35, no. 3 (2014): 322.

131 Michelle Legro, "A Trip to Japan in Sixteen Minutes," *Believer* 98 (May 1, 2013), https://believermag.com.

132 Larissa Lai, *Salt Fish Girl* (Toronto: Thomas Allen, 2002). See Paul Lai, "Stinky Bodies: Mythological Futures and the Olfactory Sense in Larissa Lai's Salt Fish Girl," *MELUS* 33, no. 4 (2008): 167–87.

133 Beatrice Glow, "Circulating Undercurrents," *Cultural Politics* 13, no. 2 (2017): 194–201.

134 Bul later displayed the fish in plastic bags filled with potassium permanganate to neutralize the smell, but the chemical deodorant spontaneously combusted in storage at London's Hayward Gallery in 2018. See Andrea Gyorody, "Artist's Chemical Experiment with Rotting Fish Challenges the Museum," *Hyperallergic*, June 8, 2018, https://hyperallergic.com.

135 On "atmospheric thinking" and "atmospheric reading," see Jesse Oak Taylor, *The Sky of Our Manufacture: The London Fog in British Fiction from Dickens to Woolf* (Charlottesville: University of Virginia Press, 2016), 7.

136 Patrick Wolfe, "Settler Colonialism and the Elimination of the Native," *Journal of Genocide Research* 8, no. 4 (2006): 387–409.

CHAPTER 5. DECOLONIZING SMELL

1 Walter Mignolo and Rolando Vazquez, "Decolonial AestheSis: Colonial Wounds, Decolonial Healings," *Social Text Periscope*, July 15, 2013, https://socialtextjournal .org.

2 Jarrett Martineau and Eric Ritskes, "Fugitive Indigeneity: Reclaiming the Terrain of Decolonial Struggle through Indigenous Art," *Decolonization: Indigeneity, Education & Society* 3, no. 1 (2014): i–ii.

3 Macarena Gómez-Barris, *The Extractive Zone: Social Ecologies and Decolonial Perspectives* (Durham, NC: Duke University Press, 2017), 3.

4 For decolonial approaches to visual and sonic aesthetics, see Juan Ramos, *Sensing Decolonial Aesthetics in Latin American Arts* (Gainesville: University Press of Florida, 2018); Kency Cornejo, "Indigeneity and Decolonial Seeing in Contemporary Art of Guatemala," *FUSE Magazine* 36, no. 4 (2013): 24–31; Gabriel Levine, "Remixing Return: A Tribe Called Red's Decolonial Bounce," *Topia: Canadian Journal of Cultural Studies* 35 (2016): 27–46; and Gómez-Barris, *The Extractive Zone*.

5 Eve Tuck and K. Wayne Yang, "Decolonization Is Not a Metaphor," *Decolonization: Indigeneity, Education & Society* 1, no. 1 (2012).

6 Cajetan Iheka, *Naturalizing Africa: Ecological Violence, Agency, and Postcolonial Resistance in African Literature* (Cambridge: Cambridge University Press, 2018), 22.

7 On the sensory orchestration of racial difference and empire, see Andrew Rotter, "Empires of the Senses: How Seeing, Hearing, Smelling, Tasting, and Touching Shaped Imperial Encounters," *Diplomatic History* 35, no. 1 (January 2011): 3–19.

8 Norbert Elias, *The Civilizing Process: The History of Manners*, trans. Edmund Jephcott (New York: Urizen, 1978).

9 John Steele, "*Perfumeros* and the Sacred Use of Fragrance in Amazonian Shamanism," in in *The Smell Culture Reader*, ed. Jim Drobnick (Oxford: Berg, 2006), 228–34.

10 Andrew Kettler, "'Delightful a Fragrance': Native American Olfactory Aesthetics within the Eighteenth-Century Anglo-American Botanical Community," in *Em-*

pire of the Senses: Sensory Practices of Colonialism in Early America, ed. Daniela Hacke and Paul Musselwhite (Leiden: Brill, 2018), 223–54.

11 "Some examples include the ability to identify certain islands by the fragrance or stench of their predominant fruits. Polowatese navigators have claimed the ability to identify Nama because of its papayas. The pungent scent of ripened breadfruit is another traditional clue to the presence of land. As these examples reveal, scent is especially important in locating atolls in particular because of the absence of mountains, cliff lines, or hills" (Vicente M. Diaz, "Sniffing Oceania's Behind," *Contemporary Pacific* 24, no. 2 [2012]: 333).

12 Constance Classen, *Worlds of Sense: Exploring the Senses in History and across Cultures* (London: Routledge, 1993), 127.

13 Elizabeth Povinelli, *Geontologies: A Requiem to Late Liberalism* (Durham, NC: Duke University Press, 2016), 118–43.

14 Diaz, "Sniffing Oceania's Behind," 336.

15 Brandy Nālani McDougall, *Finding Meaning: Kaona and Contemporary Hawaiian Literature* (Tucson: University of Arizona Press, 2018), 46.

16 Diaz, "Sniffing Oceania's Behind."

17 Ibid., 326. See also Vicente M. Diaz, "Stepping in It: How to Smell the Fullness of Indigenous Histories," in *Sources and Methods of Indigenous Studies*, ed. Chris Andersen and Jean O'Brien (New York: Routledge, 2016), 86–92.

18 I have adapted this phrase from Zoe Todd's (Métis) critique of Western scholars' tendency to imagine climate "as a blank commons to be populated by very Euro-Western theories of resilience, the Anthropocene, Actor Network Theory" (Zoe Todd, "An Indigenous Feminist's Take on the Ontological Turn: 'Ontology' Is Just Another Word for Colonialism," *Journal of Historical Sociology* 29, no. 1 [March 2016]: 8).

19 On settler colonialism as a mode of "ecological domination," see Kyle Powys Whyte, "Settler Colonialism, Ecology, and Environmental Justice," *Environment and Society: Advances in Research* 9 (2018): 125. See also Alfred Crosby, *Ecological Imperialism: The Biological Expansion of Europe, 900–1900*, 2nd ed. (Cambridge: Cambridge University Press, 2015). One example of a colonial invasive species introduced for its scent is the thorny *Acacia farnesiana*, which settlers cultivated in Hawai'i as a perfuming ingredient.

20 See J. Gottfried et al., "Remembrance of Odors Past: Human Olfactory Cortex in Cross-Modal Recognition Memory," *Neuron* 42, no. 4 (May 27, 2004): 687–95; and J. Douglas Porteous, "Smellscape," *Progress in Physical Geography* 9, no. 3 (September 1985): 356–78.

21 Patrick Wolfe, "Settler Colonialism and the Elimination of the Native," *Journal of Genocide Research* 8, no. 4 (2006): 387–409; see also Whyte, "Settler Colonialism."

22 Michelle Murphy, "Alterlife and Decolonial Chemical Relations," *Cultural Anthropology* 32, no. 4 (2017): 494–503, 497.

23 Zitkala-Ša (Gertrude Bonnin), "Impressions of an Indian Childhood," *Atlantic Monthly* 85 (1900): 37–47, 40; Zitkala-Ša, "The School Days of an Indian Girl," *Atlantic Monthly* 85 (1900): 185–94, 188.

24 Zitkala-Ša, "School Days," 189.

25 John Dominis Holt, *On Being Hawaiian* (Honolulu: Star-Bulletin, 1964), 19–20.

26 Ibid., 20.

27 See Otto Heim, "Breath as Metaphor of Sovereignty and Connectedness in Pacific Island Poetry," *New Literatures Review* 47–48 (2011): 177.

28 Deborah Jackson, "Scents of Place: The Dysplacement of a First Nations Community in Canada," *American Anthropologist* 113, no. 4 (November 2011): 606–18, 606, 607. Jackson frames "dysplacement" as a concept that blends Glenn Albrecht's oft-cited characterization of *solastalgia* ("a form of homesickness one gets when one is still at home") with an attentiveness to sensory experience (615).

29 Ibid., 608.

30 Ibid., 613.

31 Kristen Simmons, "Settler Atmospherics," *Cultural Anthropology Fieldsights*, November 20, 2017, https://culanth.org.

32 Ibid.

33 Ibid.

34 Jasbir Puar, *The Right to Maim: Debility, Capacity, Disability* (Durham, NC: Duke University Press, 2017), 73.

35 Ulrich Beck, *Risk Society: Towards a New Modernity*, trans. Mark Ritter (London: SAGE, 1992), 54, emphasis original.

36 Unsigned, "The Product" (Odortec Ltd., n.d.), www.skunk-skunk.com.

37 Marijn Nieuwenhuis, "Skunk Water: Stench as a Weapon of War," *Open Democracy*, December 17, 2015, www.opendemocracy.net.

38 Ibid.; Chaya Eisenberg, "Shoko Drone Ready to Douse Rioters in Skunk Water," *Jerusalem Post*, May 16, 2018, www.jpost.com.

39 Nieuwenhuis, "Skunk Water."

40 Ibid.

41 Nadera Shalhoub-Kevorkian, "Jerusalem Live: What Does Settler Colonialism Look Like?," *Jerusalem Quarterly* 65 (2016): 5–8.

42 Simmons, "Settler Atmospherics."

43 Julia Feuer-Cotter, "Smellscape Narratives: Designing Olfactory Spaces as Infrastructure for Embodied Storytelling," in *Designing with Smell: Practices, Techniques, and Challenges*, ed. Victoria Henshaw et al. (New York: Routledge, 2018), 61.

44 Ibid., 61.

45 Ibid., 62.

46 Warren Cariou, "Tarhands: A Messy Manifesto," *Imaginations* 17, nos. 3–2 (2012): 17–34, 20. Further citations are given parenthetically as "T."

47 Gómez-Barris, *Extractive Zone.*

48 See Tuck and Yang, "Decolonization Is Not a Metaphor," 19.

49 Sarah D. Wald, David J. Vázquez, Priscilla Solis Ybarra, and Sarah Jaquette Ray, "Introduction: Why Latinx Environmentalisms?," in *Latinx Environmentalisms: Place, Justice, and the Decolonial*, ed. Sarah D. Wald, David J. Vázquez, Priscilla Solis Ybarra, and Sarah Jaquette Ray (Philadelphia: Temple University Press, 2019), 10. For another formative example of this decolonial recovery model, see Priscilla Solis Ybarra, *Writing the Goodlife: Mexican American Literature and the Environment* (Tucson: University of Arizona Press, 2016).

50 Albert Wendt, "I Will Be Our Saviour from the Bad Smell" (1984), in *The Birth and Death of the Miracle Man and Other Stories* (Honolulu: University of Hawai'i Press, 1986), 99. Further citations are given parenthetically as "BS."

51 See Melanie Kiechle, *Smell Detectives: An Olfactory History of Nineteenth-Century Urban America* (Seattle: University of Washington Press, 2017), 138–69.

52 Paul Sharrad, *Albert Wendt and Pacific Literature: Circling the Void* (Manchester: Manchester University Press, 2003), 167.

53 Ibid., 167.

54 Qtd. in Albert Wendt, "Towards a New Oceania," *MANA Review* 1, no. 1 (1976): 49–60, 50. Further citations are given parenthetically as "TNO."

55 Richard Sennett, *Flesh and Stone: The Body and the City in Western Civilization* (New York: Norton, 1994), 16.

56 Wendt's rot resonates with Derek Walcott's accounts of postcolonial "stench" and "rot" in "Ruins of a Great House." As Stoler comments, "[Walcott's] cadence joins the acidic stench of 'rotting lime' with an 'ulcerous crime,' a sensory regime embodied, gouged deep in sensibilities of the present" (Ann Laura Stoler, "'The Rot Remains': From Ruins to Ruination," in *Imperial Debris: On Ruins and Ruination*, ed. Stoler [Durham, NC: Duke University Press, 2013], 2–35, 2).

57 Albert Wendt, "A Sermon on National Development, Education, and the Rot in the South Pacific," in *Education in Melanesia: Papers Delivered at the Eighth Waigani Seminar Sponsored Jointly by the University of Papua New Guinea, the Australian National University, and the Council on New Guinea Affairs, Held at Port Moresby 5 to 10 May 1974*, ed. J. Brammall and Ronald J. May (Canberra: University of Papua New Guinea, 1975), 373–80, 375. Further citations are given parenthetically as "S."

58 Sharrad, *Albert Wendt and Pacific Literature*, 167.

59 Ybarra, *Writing the Goodlife*, 12.

60 Haunani-Kay Trask, "Writing in Captivity: Poetry in a Time of De-Colonization," *Wasafiri* 12, no. 25 (1997): 43. For critical commentaries on Trask's decolonial poetry, see Juiana Spahr, "Connected Disconnection and Localized Globalism in Pacific Multilingual Literature," *boundary 2* 31, no. 3 (Fall 2004): 77 and McDougall, *Finding Meaning*, 130–46.

61 Haunani-Kay Trask, "The Color of Violence," *Social Justice* 31, no. 4 (2004): 12.

62 Haunani-Kay Trask, *From a Native Daughter: Colonialism and Sovereignty in Hawai'i*, rev. ed. (1993; Honolulu: University of Hawai'i Press, 1999), 19, emphasis added.

63 William Bryan, *Natural History of Hawaii: Being an Account of the Hawaiian People, the Geology and Geography of the Islands, and the Native and Introduced Plants and Animals of the Group* (Honolulu: Hawaiian Gazette, 1915), 275. For a historical account of the sandalwood trade, see Noel Kent, *Hawaii: Islands under the Influence* (Honolulu: University of Hawai'i Press, 1993), 17–21.

64 Mark Twain, *Mark Twain's Letters from Hawaii*, ed. A. Grove Day (Honolulu: University of Hawai'i Press, 1966), 59.

65 Bryan, *Natural History*, 216.

66 Jim Drobnick, "Towards an Olfactory Art History: The Mingled, Fatal, and Rejuvenating Perfumes of Paul Gauguin," *Senses & Society* 7, no. 2 (2012): 196–208.

67 Haunani-Kay Trask, "'Lovely Hula Hands': Corporate Tourism and the Prostitution of Hawaiian Culture," in *From a Native Daughter*, 136–47, 136.

68 Martha Beckwith, *Hawaiian Mythology* (Honolulu: University of Hawai'i Press, 1976), 531.

69 Ty P. Kāwika Tengan and Lamakū Mikahala Roy, "'I Search for the Channel Made Fragrant by the Maile': Genealogies of Discontent and Hope," *Oceania* 84, no. 3 (2014): 318.

70 Martha Beckwith, ed. and trans., *The Kumulipo* (Honolulu: University of Hawai'i Press, 1972), 64.

71 Mary Kawena Pukui and Samuel H. Elbert, *Hawaiian Dictionary: Hawaiian-English, English-Hawaiian*, rev. ed. (Honolulu: University of Hawai'i Press, 1986), 36.

72 Ibid., 36.

73 See Noelani Goodyear-Ka'ōpua's discussion of *ea* in "Introduction," in *A Nation Rising: Hawaiian Movements for Life, Land, and Sovereignty*, ed. Noelani Goodyear-Ka'ōpua, Ikaika Hussey, and Erin Kahunawaika'ala Wright (Durham, NC: Duke University Press, 2014), 4–8.

74 Eleanor Wilner, "Introduction," in Haunani-Kay Trask, *Light in the Crevice Never Seen* (Corvallis, OR: CALYX, 1994), XVII.

75 Trask, *Light in the Crevice Never Seen*, 3. Further citations are given parenthetically as *LC*.

76 Noenoe K. Silva, *Aloha Betrayed: Native Hawaiian Resistance to American Colonialism* (Durham, NC: Duke University Press, 2004), 11.

77 The image of Hawai'i's landscape as a missionary necropolis invokes struggles over the exhumation of Hawaiian graves by developers—a topic that Trask addresses elsewhere in her poetry and essays (see, e.g., Trask, "Hawai'i," in *LC*).

78 McDougall, *Finding Meaning*, 123, 125, 127. McDougall presents an extensive analysis of "Hawai'i" that centers the *mo'olelo* of Pele and Hi'iaka (132–34).

79 As Spahr notes, "In [Trask's] work, italics mark not a foreignness but an emphasis on the history of how the Hawaiian language was outlawed in Hawai'i from 1896 to 1970" ("Connected Disconnection," 77). According to E. S. Handy, E. G. Handy, and Mary Kawena Pukui, "*Pukiawe* . . . had a particular use. Smoke from its burning wood was said to free a chief from sanctity so that he could mingle with commoners without harm to himself or them" (E. S. Handy, E. G. Handy, and Mary Kawena Pukui, *Native Planters in Old Hawaii: Their Life, Lore and Environment* [Honolulu: Bishop Museum Press, 1991], 241).

80 Paul Faulstich, "Hawaii's Rainforest Crunch: Land, People, and Geothermal Development," *Cultural Survival Quarterly Magazine*, December 1990, www .culturalsurvival.org.

81 Ibid.

82 Haunani-Kay Trask, *Night Is a Sharkskin Drum* (Honolulu: University of Hawai'i Press, 2002), 9. Further citations are given parenthetically as *SD*.

83 McDougall, *Finding Meaning*, 144.

84 Barbara Jane Reyes, review of *Night Is a Sharkskin Drum* (Chicago: Poetry Foundation, August 26, 2009), www.poetryfoundation.org.

85 See Beckwith, *The Kumulipo*.

86 McDougall, *Finding Meaning*, 139.

87 Noenoe K. Silva, *The Power of the Steel-Tip Pen: Reconstructing Native Hawaiian Intellectual History* (Durham, NC: Duke University Press, 2017), 91.

88 Epeli Hau'ofa, "Our Sea of Islands," in *We Are the Ocean: Selected Works* (Honolulu: University of Hawai'i Press, 2008), 27–40.

89 Quoted in Haunani-Kay Trask, "Decolonizing Hawaiian Literature," in *Inside Out: Literature, Culture, Politics, and Identity in the New Pacific*, ed. Vilsoni Hereniko and Rob Wilson (Lanham, MD: Rowman & Littlefield, 1999), 172. Trask devotes two pages to a discussion of Andrade's *mo'olelo*.

90 Haunani-Kay Trask, "Politics in the Pacific Islands: Imperialism and Native Self-Determination," *Amerasia* 16, no. 1 (1990): 1–19, 14.

91 Warren Cariou, "Sweetgrass Stories: Listening for Animate Land," *Cambridge Journal of Postcolonial Literary Inquiry* 5, no. 3 (September 2018): 342.

92 Ibid., 342.

93 Kyle Powys Whyte, "Our Ancestors' Dystopia Now: Indigenous Conservation and the Anthropocene," in *The Routledge Companion to the Environmental Humanities*, ed. Ursula Heise, Jon Christensen, and Michelle Niemann (London: Routledge, 2017), 213. On the postapocalyptic condition of Native American worlds, see Lawrence Gross, "The Comic Vision of Anishinaabe Culture and Religion," *American Indian Quarterly* 26, no. 3 (Summer 2002): 436–59.

94 Vanessa Watts, "Smudge This: Assimilation, State-Favoured Communities and the Denial of Indigenous Spiritual Lives," *International Journal of Child, Youth and Family Studies* 7, no. 1 (2016): 148–70, 151. Further citations are given parenthetically as "ST."

95 Dominic Alaazi et al., "Therapeutic Landscapes of Home: Exploring Indigenous Peoples' Experiences of a Housing First Intervention in Winnipeg," *Social Science & Medicine* 147 (2015): 35.

96 DaShanne Stokes, "Sage, Sweetgrass, and the First Amendment," *Chronicle of Higher Education*, May 18, 2001, www.chronicle.com.

97 Iris Rodriguez, "Sage Against the Machine: Josie Speaks," *Xica Nation*, July 5, 2016, https://xicanation.com.

98 Gillian Flynn and Deborah Hull-Walski, "Merging Traditional Indigenous Curation Methods with Modern Museum Standards of Care," *Museum Anthropology* 25, no. 1 (2001): 31–40, 36.

99 Nancy Rosoff, "Integrating Native Views into Museum Procedures: Hope and Practice at the National Museum of the American Indian," in *Museums and Source Communities: A Routledge Reader*, ed. Alison Brown and Laura Peers (New York: Routledge, 2005), 75.

100 Ibid., 76.

101 For a nuanced consideration of the National Museum of the American Indian as an ambivalent settler institution, see Miranda Brady, "Governmentality and the National Museum of the American Indian: Understanding the Indigenous Museum in a Settler Society," *Social Identities* 14, no. 6 (2008): 763–73.

102 Robin Wall Kimmerer, *Braiding Sweetgrass: Indigenous Wisdom, Scientific Knowledge, and the Teachings of Plants* (Minneapolis: Milkweed Editions, 2013) ix. Further citations are given parenthetically as *BrS*.

103 Cariou, "Sweetgrass Stories," 345.

104 Achille Mbembe, "Necropolitics," trans. Libby Meintjes, *Public Culture* 15, no. 1 (2003): 11–40, 40.

105 Cariou, "Sweetgrass Stories," 345.

106 See David Harvey, "The Body as an Accumulation Strategy," in *Spaces of Hope* (Berkeley: University of California Press, 2000), 115.

107 Whyte, "Settler Colonialism," 133–34.

EPILOGUE

1 Peter Sloterdijk, *Terror from the Air*, trans. Amy Patton and Steve Corcoran (Los Angeles: Semiotext(e), 2009).

2 Val Plumwood, "Shadow Places and the Politics of Dwelling," *Australian Humanities Review* 44 (March 2008), http://australianhumanitiesreview.org.

3 See pp. XXX, XXX.

4 Indra Sinha, *Animal's People* (New York: Simon & Schuster, 2007), 360–61.

5 Ibid., 361.

6 The Yes Men, "Exxon's Climate-Victim Candles" (2008), https://theyesmen.org.

7 Neil Smith, "Contours of a Spatialized Politics: Homeless Vehicles and the Production of Geographical Scale," *Social Text* 33 (1992): 65.

8 Orlando Patterson, *Rituals of Blood: Consequences of Slavery in Two American Centuries* (New York: Perseus, 1998), 201.

9 Erica Fretwell, *Sensory Experiments: Psychophysics and the Aesthetics of Feeling in Nineteenth-Century America* (Durham, NC: Duke University Press, forthcoming).

10 Kyla Wazana Tompkins, *Racial Indigestion: Eating Bodies in the 19th Century* (New York: New York University Press, 2012), 11.

11 Ibid., 92.

12 Kathryn Yusoff, *A Billion Black Anthropocenes or None* (Minneapolis: University of Minnesota Press, 2019).

INDEX

Page numbers in *italics* indicate figures.

Aamjiwnaang, 157

Adey, Peter, 8, 60

"The Adventure of the Creeping Man"
(Doyle), 31

"The Adventure of the Retired Colourman" (Doyle), 31

"The Adventure of the Three Gables"
(Doyle), 32

Aeolian harp, 220n29

aer nullius, 155, 239n18

aesthetics, 18–22, 183, 202; medium, 99–
100; of proximity, 153; of smells, 155;
tenets of, 64; values of, 94

affect, 17, 21

African Americans, 36–37

Ahuja, Neel, 140–41, 147, 149

airborne chemicals/toxins, 4, 7, 19, 28, 41–
42, 45, 58–59, 67, 70, 72, 89, 118

airborne materials, 4, 9, 62, 68, 85–86, 90

air canisters, 103

air conditioning, 7–9, 22; from below, 194;
decolonial, 182–92; health conditions
from, 12; in museums, 145; principle
of, 70–71; Sloterdijk framing, 194;
structural inequities in, 39; toxic
atmospheres and, 196–97; Wendt and,
166, 173

air pollution, 79–80, 108; Aamjiwnaang
band experiencing, 157; causes of,
170; disease and death from, 11–12; in
extractive zone, 161; in Hong Kong, 57;
minorities and, 223n84; from petroleum plants, 157–58; smellscapes with,
160; U.S. borders and, 22

air quality, 61–62, 88

Air Strikes around the World (Gong), 150

Akeley, Carl, 92

Akua (god), 180

Alaimo, Stacy, 10, 44, 48, 86, 209n29

Albrecht, Glenn, 240n28

Alien Capital (Day), 117

Alien Land Laws, 137

Aliso Canyon methane leak, 13

ambient smells, 39, 44–45

amino acids, 46

Anaya, Rudolfo, 30

Anderson, Ben, 8

Anderson, Jeffrey, 214n23

Andrade, Carlos, 182

Animacies (Chen), 131

animalistic behavior, 69

Animal's People (Sinha), 196, 200

Anishinaabeg, 184

anosmia, 7, 91, 145

anthropocene, 9–10, 20, 31, 93, 99–100

antiblack climate, 72

antiblackness, 72, 159, 199

anti-crowd weapon, 158–59

anxiety (concerning risk), 34, 44, 69, 72,
80–81, 158

architecture, of museums, 90–91

Arnold, Amanda, 142

aromachology, 154

art conservation, 90–91

art galleries, 103–6
art objects, 90–91
"The Art of the Scent" exhibition, 227n30
art studio, 56–57
Asia, 112–15, 129–32, 148–49
"Asiatic coolieism," 126
Asiatic subjects, 83, 112, 115–19, 127–31, 148
atmo-orientalism, 25, 83, 115–18; coastal
    fisheries and, 120–21; genealogy of,
    119–32, 150–51; Yi and, 141–42
atmospheres, 89, 102; air conditioning
    manipulating, 7–8; alienation, 173;
    captivity, 9; Chinese immunity to
    noxious, 122; climate-controlled, 84,
    90; colonial, 25, 153–62; conviviality,
    140–50; deodorizing detective and, 30,
    37; disparities, 4, 7, 11, 14, 25, 55, 70, 83,
    88, 99, 153, 200; exposure of bodies
    to, 43–44; intoxication in, 40; MCS
    and substances in, 52; microclimatic
    splintering of, 60; olfactory aesthet-
    ics, 21–22; olfactory art toxicity from,
    97–98; perception and empathy from,
    140–41; pressures, 39; race studies and,
    151; racialization and colonization in,
    24–25; in racial violence, 12; risks and,
    14; slow violence, 81, 194–95, 200–201;
    toxicity of, 40, 196–97; turn of, 7–12;
    violence, 54–55
Atmospheric Reformulation (Raspet), 102
atmoterrorism, 70–84
The Autobiography of an Ex-Colored Man
    (Johnson, J.), 199
"Away Down in Jamaica" (Eaton), 135, 137

Babilon, Daniela, 18
Bacigalupi, Paolo, 34
bacteria, 142–43, 146
bacterial artwork, 104
Ball, Molly, 69
Barad, Karen, 21
Barker, John, 214n23
basket weaving, 188, 190

Beck, Ulrich, 3, 56, 85, 158
Belgian fries, 110, 230n84
Bell, Alan, 49–50, 52
Bell, Iris, 46
Benckiser, Reckitt, 98
Berkson, Jacob, 47
Berlant, Lauren, 110
Berrigan, Caitlin, 100
Bhaumik, Sita Kuratomi, 95, 150
Bhopal catastrophe, 196–97
The Big Sleep (Chandler), 38, 215n31
biochemical processes, 143, 160
biofiction, 145
biological odors, 115
biopolitics of senses, 149, 158, 237n126
biosocial ferment, 104–5
The Birth and Death of the Miracle Man
    and Other Stories (Wendt), 162
Black Anthropocenes, 199–200
Black bodies, smells of, 33
Black Hole of Calcutta, 119, 124
Black Lives Matter, 12
Black Sun (Hirst), 95
Bloem, Frank, 97
Blood Shot (Paretsky), 41–42
Blue Vinyl (Helfand and Gold), 34
Body, Laura, 3–4
Boneshaker (Priest), 129–30
Borsato, Diane, 237n128
botanical knowledge, 2–3
Braiding Sweetgrass (Kimmerer), 186–92
brain fog, 80
Braun, Bruce, 139
breath, 10–11, 81–83, 157–58
breathability, 130–31
breathers, 8, 10, 12, 21, 24, 52, 100–101,
    200–202, 228n58
Brennan, Teresa, 17
Brown, Bill, 63
Brown, JoAnne, 61
Bryan, William, 171
Buell, Lawrence, 57, 70
Bul, Lee, 150, 238n134

Bullard, Robert, 223n84
Burk, Karl-Heinz, 96
Burr, Chandler, 227n30
Burton, Johanna, 142, 145
"By Any Other Name" (Robinson), 27–28

The Call of the Wild (London), 61
Camus, Albert, 163
A Canary's Tale (Berkson), 47
Canetti, Elias, 10
capitalism, 116–18, 138
Capitalocene, 9
carbon emissions, 233n63
carbonic acid, 119–20, 125
Cariou, Warren, 19, 160–61, 183
Carlisle, Janice, 18
Carlisle Indian Industrial School, 188–89
Casmier, Stephen, 18
Castronovo, Russ, 63
caustic odors, 48
ceramic dust, 85–86
Chadwick, Edwin, 14, 61
Chandler, Raymond, 24, 38
"Chants of Dawn" (Trask), 180
Chapman, Mary, 138
characterization and olfaction, 72–73
chemicals, 197, 200; airborne, 41–42, 59;
    biochemical processes with, 143, 160;
    clouds of, 222n74; odorant molecules
    characteristics of, 5–6; office build-
    ings with harmful, 67; senses, 17, 50;
    signature of, 102; toxic, 201. *See also*
    multiple chemical sensitivity
Chen, Mel, 44–45, 63, 106, 131
Chiang, Connie, 120–21
Chicago, Judy, 95
China, 25, 122, 233n63, 235n86
"Chinamen," 124, 126, 130–31
Chinatown, 119–21, 123–25, 132, 135–37, 145
Chinatown (film), 30
"Chinatown Declared a Nuisance!" (pam-
    phlet), 123
"The Chinatown Foray" (art), 237n128

Chinese Characteristics (Smith, A.), 125
Chinese immigrants, 117–20, 122–26, 130–
    31, 138–40
The Chinese in America (Gibson), 122–23
Chinese restaurant, 234n65
chlorine gas, 129
cholera morbus epidemic, 62
Choy, Timothy, 57
Christian church, 168
Christianson, Scott, 71
chronic illness, 77–78
Chun Afong, 127
"Chun Ah Chun" (London), 127
Church, Frederic Edwin, 92
Civello, Paul, 84
civil disobedience, 120
civilization, 3, 16, 154
civil unrest, 120, 159
Classen, Constance, 117, 134
cleaning products, 102
climate-controlled atmosphere, 84, 90
Cole, Thomas, 92
collective continuance, 191
colonial atmospherics, 25, 153–62
colonialism, 154, 163–71, 173
colonization: atmospheric manipulation
    and, 24–25; olfactory language to,
    177–78; racialized settlers from, 179;
    smellscapes manipulated by, 25–26. *See
    also* decolonization
"The Color of Violence" (Trask), 169
"Comin Home" (Trask), 177, 179
communicable disease, 106
Contagion (Soderbergh), 105
contagions, 104
conviviality, 117, 141, 150
Cooper, James Fenimore, 32
Corbin, Alain, 19, 61–62, 115
Crane, Stephen, 58, 62, 71
crime scene, 35–36, 42
crime stories, 38
Critique of Judgment (Kant), 6, 15
cross-cultural olfaction, 96

cross-racial scent, 144–45
Cuba, 108–11
cubic air ordinance, 119–21
cultural genocide, 188
cultural otherness, 115
cultural pollution, 163–64
Cypria fragment, 98

Dakota Access Pipeline, 158
Danino, Tal, 104
"Dark Time" (Trask), 177
Davis, Rebecca Harding, 61
Day, Iyko, 117
death, 11–12, 173–74
debilitation, 9, 11–13, 22, 24, 27, 39, 41, 43, 45–47, 59, 61–63, 69, 78–83, 150–51, 158–59, 173, 197
Decolonial AestheSis, 152
decoloniality, 152–53, 182–92
decolonization: air conditioning and, 182–92; multisensory approach to, 177; olfactory, 180–81; of smells, 153
De Cupere, Peter, 24, 87, 94, 100–101; *The Deflowering* by, 95; dystopian scents of, 110–11; olfactory artwork of, 106–7; *The Smell of a Stranger* by, 108–11, *109*, 195; *Smoke Cloud* by, *107*, 107–9
dehumanized economism, 117–18
DeLillo, Don, 84
deodorization: Asiatic populations odors and, 112; of Chinatown, 135–36; in civilizing process, 154; detective fiction and, 29–33; differential, 7, 13–15, 23, 29, 84, 195; discursive, 150–51; Indigenous practices of, 168–69; miasmas and initiatives of, 19; of Oceanic culture, 155; olfactory detective work of, 48; racial characteristic in, 4, 14–15; racial differences and, 4; unpleasant odors masked by, 15; Western ideologies of, 169–70
deodorizing detective, 24, 29–33, 37, 42
description, 62

detection, 29, 34, 42, 48–49, 54–55; environmental, 24, 29, 34–44
detective fiction, 28–33, 38
determinism, discourses of, 57
Devil's Root, 33
"dialectical odour," 104
Diaz, Vicente, 19, 154–55
differential deodorization, 7, 13–15, 29, 33, 54, 60, 71, 84, 108, 174, 179, 201; industrial history with, 23; olfactory activism in, 195
diffusion, 68–69
dioramas, 92, 146–49, *148*
disability, 12, 46, 80, 158
discursive deodorization, 150–51
diseases, 63; air pollution causing, 11–12; Chinatown's outbreak of, 123–24; communicable, 106; germ theory of, 14, 119; miasmas with transmission of, 61; from paints, 217n2; unhealthy air and, 100–101
disparities, 13; atmospheric, 4, 7, 11, 14, 25, 55, 70, 83, 88, 99, 153, 200; environmental, 19; geographic, 17; health, 25; racial, 41, 71, 146
"Dispossessions of Empire" (Trask), 179
distribution of the sensible, 20, 22, 28, 152, 183
Dodd, George, 18
"A Double-Barreled Detective Story" (Twain), 32
Doyle, Arthur Conan, 30–32
Dreiser, Theodore, 58
Drobnick, Jim, 19, 60, 90–91, 95, 99–100; "dialectical odour" from, 104; scents in atmospheres from, 102
drones, Shoko, 159
drug-sniffing dogs, 33, 50
Dudley, Donald L., 46
Duffield, George, 136
Dupin, C. Auguste, 29, 33
dysplacement, 157–58, 172–73, 240n28
dystopian scents, 110–11

ea, 172

Earthly Remains (Leon), 34

Eaton, Edith Maude, 25; "Away Down in Jamaica" by, 135, 137; Chinatown odor's from, 145; on Chinese immigrants, 140; "Its Wavering Image" by, 136; *Mrs. Spring Fragrance* by, 132–37, *133*; "Spring Impressions" by, 136; "Sweet Sin" by, 235n81; "Tian Shan's Kindred Spirit" by, 137–38; "Wing Sing of Los Angeles on His Travels" by, 138

ecological-othering, 92–93

economic abstraction, 117–18

ego, self-reflective, 99

Eight Mile, 13

ekphrasis. *See* description

Elias, Norbert, 154

environment: air influences from, 57–58; art galleries externalities of, 103; of Chinese immigrants, 125–26; detection of, 24, 29, 34–44; detectives detecting risks of, 54–55; discourses of determinism on, 57; disparities in, 19; ecological-othering of, 92–93; hyperosmic detectives and, 42; justice for, 59, 70–84; olfactory art's awareness of, 94–95; orientalism, 115; pesticide inhalation and, 76; racism, 41; risk, 99–111, 131–32; scented, 16–17, 99–100; smell sensitivity and, 44–45; toxicity of, 111–12, 115; violence, 82; wilderness and, 92–93

environmental justice narratives, 58–59, 70, 83

erotic imagery, 181

ethics, olfactory, 194

Everett, Percival, 34

executions, humane, 71

"An Experiment in Misery" (Crane), 61

extractive zone, 161

Fanon, Frantz, 80–81, 141, 169

farm workers, 75–76

Faulstich, Paul, 175

feminine power (*mana wahine*), 175

feminism, 95, 143

Fetterley, Judith, 132

Feuer-Cotter, Julia, 160–61

Fifteenth Ward Smelling Committee, 61

Fillion, Barnabé, 144

The First Born (Powers, F.), 127

Fisher, Rudolph, 24, 30, 35–38, 54

fisheries, 120–21

Fleissner, Jennifer, 57, 67

floral iconography, 134

Flower Missions, 134

Floyd, H. Hugh, 44, 48, 51

Foams (Sloterdijk), 7

folk medicine, 36–37, 83

food production, 108–9

Force Majeure (Yi), 146, *147*

formaldehyde, 49

Fort Harrison, 139

The Foul and the Fragrant (Corbin), 19

Fox, Josh, 34

fragrance-free advocacy, 26, 193–94, 201

"A Fragrance of Devouring" (Trask), 177, 179

Fraire, Josie Valadez, 185

Franco, Dean, 82

freeway construction, 78–79

Fretwell, Erica, 18, 127, 199

Freud, Sigmund, 16

Friedman, Emily, 18

Friedrich, Caspar David, 92

From a Native Daughter (Trask), 169–70

"From Ka'a'awa to Rarotonga" (Trask), 181

Fu Manchu, 129

fumigation techniques, 164, 185–86

Furton, Kenneth, 144

Fusco, Katherine, 64

Gagosian Gallery, 104, 142

Gain (Powers, R.), 1–4

Garner, Eric, 12

gas chamber, 71
gas chromatography technology, 96
gaseous fumes, 80
Gasland (Fox), 34
gas leak, 13, 56–57
gas warfare, 129
Gauguin, Paul, 171
Gene Thin Elk, 185
genocide, cultural, 188
geography, 17, 35, 100, 146; atmospheric, 28, 151; of risk, 8
geothermal wells, 175–77
germ theory, 14, 61, 119
Gibson, Otis, 122–23
Gilman, Charlotte Perkins, 127
Glow, Beatrice, 100, 150
god (*Akua*), 180
GO-EXPO (oil industry conference), 197–98
Gold, Daniel, 34
Goltzenleuchter, Brian, 94
Gómez-Barris, Macarena, 152, 161
Gong, Yuan, 150
Grabbing at Newer Vegetables (Yi), 105, *105*
Graham, Mark, 94
The Grapes of Wrath (Steinbeck), 71, 84
grease, rancid, 74, 208n11
Greenberg, Clement, 90
greenhouse gases, 10
Guha, Ramachandra, 92
Gulf War Syndrome, 52

habituation, 66
Hall, Edward Twitchell, 22
Halperin, Victor, 129
Hammett, Dashiell, 38
Hansen, Terri Crawford, 53–54
Haraway, Donna, 92, 146–47
hard-boiled crime fiction, 38–39, 54, 59, 84
Harlem, 37–40, 73–74
Harrison, Jill, 75
Harrison, William Henry, 139
Hartmann, Sadakichi, 150

Haug, Helgard, 96, 100
Hau'ofa, Epeli, 155
"Hawai'I" (Trask), 174
Hawaiian cosmogony, 171
Hawaiian Dictionary (Pukui and Elbert), 172
Hawaiian graves, 242n77
Hawaiian language, 243n79
Headspace (gas chromatography technology), 96
healing medicines, 183, 189
health: from air conditioning, 12; disparities, 25; from foul smells, 66–67; pesticides influencing, 75; public, 126; racial disparities of, 69; risks and smells of, 14; volatile organic compounds influencing, 51
The "Heathen Chinee" at Home and Abroad (Trumble), 124
The Heat's On (Himes), 39–40
Heim, Otto, 157
Helfand, Judith, 34
hierochloe odorata (sweetgrass), 186–87
High John the Conqueror Root, 37
Hi'iaka (forest deity), 175
Himes, Chester, 24, 39–40, 52
Hirst, Damien, 95
Holt, John Dominis, 156–57
The Homeric Hymn to Demeter, 98
hoodoo (conjure), 36–37, 83, 194, 201
horned toad powder, 214n23
The Hound of the Baskervilles (Doyle), 31
Howard, June, 64
Hutchinson, Woods, 124–25
hygiene, 61, 126, 168
hyperosmia, 24, 27–28, 31–32, 39; detectives, 29, 42; MCS risks and, 44–55; as psychosomatic condition, 46; synthetic scent toxicity and, 51
hypo-osmic characters, 55

IAO. *See* Institute for Art and Olfaction
ICOM. *See* International Council of Museums

Ideal-I, 99
I/Eye, 99
IFF. *See* International Flavors and Fragrances
Iheka, Cajetan, 153
IIC. *See* International Institute for the Conservation of Museum Objects
illness narratives, 3, 18, 43–44
immersive toxicology, 32
Immigrant Caucus (Yi), *144*, 145–47
The Importance of Being (exhibition), 107
Indigenous people, 151, 156, 168–69
Indigenous smellscapes, 156, 239n19
Indigenous ways, 185
industrial capitalism, 116–17
industry, 23, 28
infrastructure, smell of, 38
Ingold, Tim, 8
The Insidious Dr. Fu-Manchu (Rohmer), 127–29, *128*
Institute for Art and Olfaction (IAO), 96
International Council of Museums (ICOM), 89–90
International Flavors and Fragrances (IFF), 96
International Institute for the Conservation of Museum Objects (IIC), 90
Interstate and Defense Highways Act (1956), 78
"In the Depths of a Coal Mine" (Crane), 62
intoxicants, 50
intoxication, 43–44, 54, 69; atmospheric, 40; olfactory, 29–30; trans-corporeal, 22–23
"Its Wavering Image" (Eaton), 136
"I Will Be Our Saviour from the Bad Smell" (Wendt), 162, 164–69, *165*

Jackson, Deborah, 157
Jameson, Fredric, 209n29, 220n34
Jenner, Mark, 13
Jerng, Mark, 118

Jessica Silverman Gallery, 101
Jim Crow era, 74
"John Archer's Nose" (Fisher), 35, 37, 201
Johnson, Alison, 52
Johnson, Glenn, 223n84
Johnson, Hazel, 41
Johnson, James Weldon, 199
Johnson, Lutie, 72–73
Jon, Gee, 71, 221n61
Jones, Caroline, 14, 16, 34, 90, 99, 105
The Jungle (Sinclair), 62

Kaktovik community, 160
Kānaka Maoli, 156, 169–72, 175, 180–83
Kanatsiohareke land, 187–88, 190
Kant, Immanuel, 6, 15, 64, 194
Kasaipwalova, John, 164
Kauanui, J. Kēhaulani, 154
Kettler, Andrew, 117, 154
Kiechle, Melanie, 19, 134
Kim, Jina, 12, 80, 82
Kimmerer, Robin Wall, 25, 153, 182, 186–91
Kriskovets, Yulia, 107
Kroll-Smith, Steve, 44, 48, 51
Kumulipo (Hawaiian cosmogony), 171

laborers, exploitation of, 148–49
Lacan, Jacques, 99
Lai, Larissa, 150
Lament in the Night (Nagahara), 84
language: Hawaiian, 243n79; olfactory, 177–78; smell approached through, 18, 21
"The Language of the Stones" (Trumpeter), 58
Lanser, Susan, 127
Latour, Bruno, 18, 58, 92
Lawson, Lynn, 49
Leaves of the Banyan Tree (Wendt), 162
Lee, Rachel, 143, 146
Lentricchia, Frank, 84
Leon, Donna, 34
Lessy, Rose Ellen, 62

"Life in the Iron Mills" (Davis, R.), 61
Life is Cheap (Yi), 143, 149–50, 195
Lifestyle Wars (Yi), 147–49, *148*
Light in the Crevice Never Seen (Trask), 172–77
limbic system, 5, 11, 47, 64, 93
Litvinenko, Artyom, 30, 42
London, Jack, 58, 63, 127
London Fog, 31
Looby, Christopher, 18
Love Canal, 5
Luciano, Dana, 21
Lukács, Georg, 58
lungs, 50, 61, 76, 79, 173
lycanthropy-mathesis (nervous disease), 63
Lye, Colleen, 117, 126

Maggie (Crane), 71
maile vine, 171
Majestic Splendor (Bul), 150
malodorant, 25, 159
Manalansan, Martin, 113
mana wahine (feminine power), 175
Marchand, Ernest, 62
Marchetti, Gina, 64
Marez, Curtis, 75
Martin, G. Neil, 5
Martineau, Jarrett, 152
Marusek, Sarah, 30
material ambiguity, 21, 28
Matthews, Bonnye, 45, 47, 51
Mawani, Renisa, 116, 141
Maxwell, Catherine, 18
McAllister, Nia, 87–89
McBean, Michael, 100
McCann, Sean, 38
McCarthy, Cormac, 84
McCormack, Derek, 8, 10
McCormick, Gail, 45
McDougall, Brandy Nālani, 154, 162, 175, 178, 181
MCDXCII (Bhaumik), 95
McLean, Kate, 113

MCS. *See* multiple chemical sensitivity
"MCS: Trial by Science" (Dudley), 46
medical mysteries, 49–50
memory, 5, 7, 61, 81, 95–96, 127
Menstruation Bathroom (Chicago), 95
mercaptan, 13
Merck Manual, 46
miasma theory, 228n59; Asiatic, 117–32; deodorization initiatives and, 19; disease transmission in, 61; noxious, 4; olfactory regulation and, 14; structural inequities in, 33; unhealthy air in, 100–101
Michaels, Walter Benn, 64
microclimatic splintering, 60
Micro-encapsulated Surface Coating (Raspet), 101–3
Mignolo, Walter, 152
migraines, 79–80
migrant experiences, 113
Milton, 161
minorities, air pollution and, 223n84
"Missionary Graveyard" (Trask), 173–74
molecular intimacies of empire, 118
"Monterey-by-the-Smell" (Chiang), 120
Moran of the Lady Letty (Norris), 126
Morton, Timothy, 11
Mother Earth, 191
Moya, Paula, 82
Mrs. Spring Fragrance (Eaton), 132–37, *133*
multiple chemical sensitivity (MCS), 23–24, 28; atmospheric substances with, 52; hyperosmia and risks of, 44–55; illness stories from, 44; medical mysteries in, 49–50; Native Americans with, 53; olfactory system reactions in, 47; sense of smell with, 45; working-class populations and, 52–53
"Murders in the Rue Morgue" (Poe), 29
Murphy, Michelle, 66–67, 156
The Museum Environment (Thomson), 91
Museum of Modern Art, 89

Museum of the African Diaspora, 87
museums, 86–91, 145
Muskie, Edmund, 27
"My Experience with Chemical Sensitivity" (Matthews), 47

Nagahara, Shoson, 84
Narcissus, 98–99, 134
Nash, Linda, 75
Native Americans, 3–4, 53–54, 185–88, 190
Native Balm Soap, 2–3, 6
Native Son (Wright), 71
Natural History of Hawaii (Bryan), 171
naturalism, 58; air quality in, 61–62; discourses of determinism of, 70; humanity's alienation from, 93; neo-naturalism, 59, 70, 84
nature, 57, 140
naturecultures, 146
negative air machines, 103
Neocleous, Mark, 29
neologism, 60
neo-naturalism, 59, 70, 84
nervous disease (*lycanthropy-mathesis*), 63
Neurontin, 50
New York's Smelliest Blocks map (McLean), 113, *114*
Nieuwenhuis, Marijn, 159
Night Is a Sharkskin Drum (Trask), 177–82, 191
Nixon, Rob, 12, 93, 110
Noa Noa (Gauguin), 171
Nordau, Max, 15, 62, 65
Norris, Frank, 58, 126; toposmia from, 66; *Vandover and the Brute* by, 24, 56, 60–69, 83
"Notes from a Human Canary" (Lawson), 49
noxious miasmas, 4
noxious odors, 27–28, 171, 234n65

Obama, Barack, 108–9
Obeah, 135–36

Occupational Safety and Health Administration (OSHA), 111
Oceania, 166–68, 170
Oceanic culture, 155, 164–66
Oceanic seafaring, 239n11
Oceti Sakowin camp, 158
odorant molecules, 1–2, 5–6
odors, 13, 36, 115–18; from airborne materials, 68; bodies and poor hygiene with, 168; caustic, 48; of Chinatown, 121, 123, 145; climate-controlled atmosphere and, 84; deodorization masking unpleasant, 15; fumigation spray for, 164; hyperosmic sensitivity to, 31–32; Indigenous people and, 151; from industry, 28; malodorant as, 159; noxious, 27–28, 171, 234n65; poor hygiene causing, 61; of poverty, 39; rancid grease, 74, 208n11; from smoke, 68–69; stench of, 40; suffocation from, 73–74
office buildings, chemicals in, 67
oil industry conference, 197–98
oil paintings, 91
olfaction: character development and, 72–73; cross-cultural, 96; detective fiction tool of, 32–33; flowerbeds in, 134; perfume and, 31, 65; racialization and, 24–25; social intervention in, 142; trans-corporeal and, 93–99, 152–53
olfactory: activism, 195; aesthetics, 18–22, 183, 202; artists, 87, 97; capacities, 42, 220n33; characterization, 72–73; decolonization, 180–81; detective, 48; ecocriticism, 20–26; ekphrasis, 62; ethics, 194; fatigue, 66; fiction, 74; intoxication, 29–30; knowledge, 16, 239n11; language, 177–78; nerves, 123; racialization, 74, 115, 117–18; regulation, 14; representation, 41; sensitivity, 6, 50–51; signals, 46; smells characterization and, 5–6; stimuli, 208n5; surveillance, 36; system, 47; turn, 95

olfactory art: atmospheric toxicity in, 97–98; of De Cupere, 106–7; defining, 227n31; Drobnick as curator of, 100; environmental awareness in, 94–95; environmental risk and, 99–111; environmental toxicity and, 111–12; in museums, 86–87; scent fabrication services and, 96–97, 99; in U.S., 22–23; in white cube art gallery, 101
On Being Hawaiian (Holt), 156
Opium Wars, 121–22
organic materials, 45, 51, 163
organophosphates, 3, 4
OSHA. See Occupational Safety and Health Administration
Osman, Ashraf, 95
osmophobic (smell-fearing), 16
oxytocin, 191

Pader, Ellen, 120
paints, disease from, 217n2
pandemic, 105
Papahānaumoku (Earth Mother), 173, 175
Paradise Lost (Milton), 161
Paretsky, Sara, 24, 41–42
peaceful violence, 169
peculiar odor, 36
Pele (volcano deity), 175, 178, 182
Pellow, David, 41
Penn, Ivan, 13
The People of the Abyss (London), 63
perfume, 31, 37, 40, 47, 51, 53, 82, 94–96, 113, 118, 127, 135, 144, 163–64, 179; industry, 18; olfaction and, 31, 65
Perfume (Süskind), 11
perfumed handkerchief, 15–20
personal care products, 52, 99
pesticides, 75–78, 196, 222n74
petrochemical industry, 200
petroleum plants, 157–58
Petry, Ann, 24, 59, 70, 71–74
Pfaelzer, Jean, 120

Philippopoulos-Mihalopoulos, Andreas, 8–9
The Plague (Camus), 163
Plan B (Himes), 39
Plumwood, Val, 10, 195
Poe, Edgar Allan, 29
poems, by Trask, 171–82
Poisoned (Bell, A.), 49–50
poison gas, 123, 129, 196
Polanski, Roman, 30
Porteous, J. Douglas, 17, 60
Porter, Tom, 188
poverty, odors of, 39
Povinelli, Elizabeth, 154
Powers, Francis, 127
Powers, Richard, 1–2
Pratt, Richard Henry, 189
Priest, Cherie, 129–30
Pryse, Marjorie, 132
psychosomatic condition, 46
Puar, Jasbir, 12, 150
public health discourses, 61, 80, 118–20, 125–26
purity, 4, 13, 54, 57, 91, 94, 103–4, 140
"The Purloined Letter" (Poe), 29
"Putting Down Roots" (Kimmerer), 187, 190

quarantine, 104–5
Quarantine Authority, 80

race: atmospheres and, 151; bodies and, 32; breath and uneven impositions of, 82–83; China and inequality of, 235n86; colonization and settlers of, 179; degeneration, 69; in deodorization, 4, 14–15; disparities of, 41, 71, 146; health disparities by, 69; olfactory surveillance and implications of, 36; purity of, 139; toxicity and, 78
racial atmospheres, 9, 25, 116, 141

racialization, 24–25, 131
racism: air pollution and, 223n84; in atmo-orientalism, 115–16; atmosphere of, 4, 9; atmospheric violence in, 12; environmental, 41; museums and, 87–88
"Radical American Environmentalism and Wilderness Preservation" (Guha), 92
Ramazzini, Bernardino, 217n2
Rancière, Jacques, 20
Raspet, Sean, 24, 87, 96, 144; *Atmospheric Reformulation* by, *102*; *Microencapsulated Surface Coating* by, 101–3; scent fabrication company of, 104
Raux, Boris, 24, 97–98
Ravat, Klara, 97
Ray, Sarah Jaquette, 14, 92, 161
redistribution of the sensible, 20, 28, 201
reflexive modernization, 56, 98
regionalism, 132
reservations (Native American), 53
Residuals exhibition (Raspet), 101, 111
respiratory conditions, 52, 81, 83
"Returning" (Trask), 181
Revolt of the Zombies (Halperin), 129
Reyes, Barbara Jane, 180
rhizomatous tuber, 2
Rindisbacher, Hans, 18
risks: atmospheres and, 14; corporations disclosing, 3; detectives detecting, 54–55; environmental, 99–111, 131–32; geography of, 8; health, 14; MCS, 44–55; pesticide, 77–78; smells with perceptions of, 17–18
Ritskes, Eric, 152
The Road (McCarthy), 84
Robbins, Bruce, 38
Robinson, Spider, 27–28
Rodriguez, Eloy, 76
Rohmer, Sax, 127–29, *128*
romantic anti-capitalism, 138
root (*Utilis clarea*), 2

roots, evil-smelling, 36–37
Rosoff, Nancy, 185
Roy, Deboleena, 106
Roy, Kahu Mikahala, 171
rubbish odors, 115–16
Rubio, Fernando Domínguez, 89–90
"Ruins of a Great House" (Walcott), 241n56
Russell, Thomas, 221n61

sacrifice zones, 88
sage, smudging of, 184, 189
Salt Fish Girl (Lai), 150
sandalwood, 170
San Francisco Museum of Modern Art (SFMOMA), 87
sanitary laws, 119–20
sardine processing, 121
"Satan Rouses His Legions on the Shores of Syncrude Tailings Pond #4"(Cariou), 161
scented environments, 16–17, 99–100
scents, 102, 183–84; cross-racial, 144–45; culture, 107; dystopian, 110–11; fabrication services, 96–97, 99, 104; hearts of men and, 11; of pesticides, 76–77; of scentlessness, 3; spiritual associations of, 154
Second Hawaiian Renaissance, 156
segregation, 33
self-experimentation, 49
self-preservation, 5
Sennett, Richard, 165
sensory aesthetics, 19–20
sensory deprivation, 165
sensual enjoyment, 6
sensus communis (shared sensory order), 20
"A Sermon on National Development, Education, and the Rot in the South Pacific" (Wendt), 166
Servin, Jacques, 197
settler atmospherics, 158–59, 192

"Settler Atmospherics" (Simmons), 158
settler colonialism, 54, 139, 153, 178; breath in, 158; Indigenous ways eliminated by, 185
SFMOMA. *See* San Francisco Museum of Modern Art
shadow smells, 195–96, 198, 200
Shah, Nayan, 119
Shalhoub-Kevorkian, Nadera, 159
Sharrad, Paul, 163
Sherlock Holmes, 30–33
Shigenobu, Fusako, 141–42
Shiner, Larry, 107
ships, foul air of, 65–66
Shoko drone, 159
sick buildings, 52, 67
The Sign of the Four (Doyle), 30
Silva, Noenoe, 181
Simmons, Kristen, 158
Sinclair, Upton, 62
Sing, Hugh, 221n61
Sinha, Indra, 196–97, 201
Sister Carrie (Dreiser), 62, 220n29
Skunk Water, 158–59
Sloterdijk, Peter, 7–8, 70, 82, 88–91; air conditioning framed by, 194; gas warfare from, 129
slow violence, 12, 41; of airborne chemicals, 59; atmospheric, 81, 194–95, 200–201; in respiratory ailments, 83
Smell Detectives (Kiechle), 19
smelling committee, 125
The Smell of a Stranger (De Cupere), 108–11, *109*, 195
Smell of Change (Feuer-Cotter), 160–61
smells, 5–6, 15–18, 21, 44–46, 155; Asian culinary, 113; of black bodies, 33; of Chinese immigrants, 122–23; crime scene encountering, 35–36; of death, 173–74; debilitating power of, 159; decolonization of, 153; from gas leaks, 56; health conditions from foul, 66–67; health risks detected by, 14; of

infrastructure, 38; interpretations of, 35; mapping of, 100; odorant molecules in, 1–2; of organic materials, 163; postmodern aesthetic values of, 94; shadow, 195–96, 198, 200; shared sensory order of, 20; of sovereignty, 169–82; toxicity's potential in, 96; toxins and sense of, 49; Trask decolonizing, 182; urban, 69; usefulness of, 209n29; Viramontes compelled by, 74–75; Western aesthetics view of, 23; of yellowish-green cloud, 129. *See also* odors; olfaction; scents
smellscapes: with air pollution, 160; colonial, 153–62; colonization manipulating, 25–26; Indigenous, 156, 239n19; spatial experience of, 17; *Vandover and the Brute* and, 60–69; in Western modernity, 155–56
smell-walks, 83
"Smiling Corpses" (Trask), 178
Smith, Arthur Henderson, 125
Smith, Mark, 33, 74
Smoke Cloud (De Cupere), *107*, 107–9
smokestacks, 68–69
smudging, 184–86; as healing ceremony, 182–83; healing medicines and, 189
The Sniffer (Livinenko), 42–43
"Sniffing Oceania's Behind" (Diaz), 155
soap manufacturing, 1–2
social intervention, 88, 142
Soderbergh, Steven, 105
solastalgia, 240n28
sovereignty, 169–82
Spatial Justice (Philippopoulos-Mihalopoulos), 8
spiritual products industry, 37
spirit world, 184
"Spring Impressions" (Eaton), 136
squid drying, 120–21
Steinbeck, John, 84
sterilization, 125
Stink! (Whelan), 34

stink bomb, 196–98, 201
stink-tank, 161
Stoler, Ann Laura, 118
Stout, Arthur B., 136
The Street (Petry), 72–73, 83
structural inequities, 33, 39, 126
A Study in Scarlet (Doyle), 30
suffocation, 81, 119
Sui Sin Far. *See* Eaton, Edith Maude
Sunflower Seeds (Weiwei), 85–86, 111
Süskind, Patrick, 11
sweetgrass, 183–84, 186–91
"Sweet Sin" (Eaton), 235n81
The Swimming Pool (Raux), 97, 97–99
synthetic fragrances/scent, 51, 87, 96, 97, 160, 194
Sze, Julie, 69, 131

"Tarhands" (Cariou), 160–61
tar sands, 160–61
Taylor, Jesse Oak, 8, 21, 31, 33
temporal dispersion, 110
Their Dogs Came with Them (Viramontes), 78–81
Thiebaud, Wayne, 87
Thomson, Garry, 91
"Tian Shan's Kindred Spirit" (Eaton), 137–38
To Curry Favor (Bhaumik), 95, 150
Todd, Zoe, 239n18
"To Hear the Mornings" (Trask), 180
Tolaas, Sissel, 96, 100
Tomkins, Silvan, 17
Tompkins, Kyla, 116, 199
toposmia, 60, 66, 100
"Towards a New Oceania" (Wendt), 162, 164, 166
toxicity, 32, 50–53, 78; acceptable levels of, 111–12; air as medium for, 94; airborne chemicals for, 41–42, 59; in air quality, 88; of atmospheres, 40, 97–98, 196–97; chemicals, 201; of environment, 111–12, 115; exposure, 68; masculinity, 142;

smell's potential for, 96; spills, 198; of tar sands, 160–61
toxins, 6, 49
Tracy, Sarah, 17
trans-corporeality, 21–23, 59; bad air and, 67; breath and, 10–11; discursive deodorization and, 150–51; olfaction and, 93–99, 152–53
transformative material exchanges, 93
transportation infrastructure, 78–79
Trask, Haunani-Kay, 25, 153, 162; air's significance from, 172; *From a Native Daughter* by, 169–70; Hawaiian language and, 243n79; *Light in the Crevice Never Seen* by, 172–77; *Night Is a Sharkskin Drum* by, 177–82, 191; poems by, 171–82; smell decolonized by, 182
Tremblay, Jean-Thomas, 80–81
"A Trip to Japan in Sixteen Minutes" (Hartmann), 150
tropical fever, 136
Trumble, Alfred, 124–25
Trumpeter, Kevin, 58, 63
Twain, Mark, 32, 170

U-deur (Haug), 100
uncertainty, 66–67
"uncivilized" body odors, 117–18
Under the Feet of Jesus (Viramontes), 75, 77–78, 201
United Nations Educational Scientific and Cultural Organization (UNESCO), 89
United States (U.S.), 22–23, 108–11, 194
United States Exploring Expedition (1838–42), 1
urban communities, 27–28, 124–25
urban smells, 69
U.S. *See* United States
Utilis clarea (root), 2–3

Vandover and the Brute (Norris), 24, 56, 60–69, 83
Van-Van Oil, 37

Vázquez, David, 161
Vazquez, Rolando, 152
Vedenetra, Hermitra Elantra, 45
ventilation, 65
Verbeek, Caro, 227n31
violence, 12, 54–55, 82, 138–40, 169. *See also* slow violence
Viramontes, Helena María, 24, 59, 70–72, 74, 224n86; environmental violence from, 82; *Under the Feet of Jesus* by, 75, 77–78, 201; gaseous fumes and, 80; *Their Dogs Came with Them* by, 78–81; transportation infrastructure from, 78–79
visual arts, 21
Vivoleum, 197–98

Walcott, Derek, 241n56
Wald, Sarah, 161
warfare, gas, 129
The Water Knife (Bacigalupi), 34
Watershed (Everett), 34
Wat Mongkolratanaram Buddhist temple, 132
Watts, Reggie, 198–99
Watts, Vanessa, 184–85, 186
weapons, anti-crowd, 158–59
"We Cannot Breathe" (Penn), 13
Weiwei, Ai, 85–86, 111
Wendt, Albert, 25, 153; *The Birth and Death of the Miracle Man and Other Stories* by, 162; "I Will Be Our Saviour from the Bad Smell" by, 162, 165, 167; *Leaves of the Banyan Tree* by, 162; "A Sermon on National Development, Education, and the Rot in the South Pacific" by, 166; "Towards a New Oceania" by, 162, 164, 166

Western aesthetics, 23
Western culture, 109, 131
Western ideologies, 169–70
Western modernity, 155–56, 168
Wharton, Edith, 62
Whelan, Jon, 34
white cube art gallery, 24, 84, 91, 101, 112
White Noise (DeLillo), 84
Whyte, Kyle Powys, 184
wihkaskwa, scent of, 183
wiingasshk (sweetgrass), 187
wildness, 92–93
Wilson, Richard, 95
"Wing Sing of Los Angeles on His Travels" (Eaton), 138
Wolff, Shepard, 197–98
working-class populations, 52–53

Ybarra, Priscilla Solis, 161, 169
yellowish-green cloud/haze, 129, 131
yellow miasmas, 117–32
Yellow Peril, 126–27
"The Yellow Wallpaper" (Gilman), 127
the Yes Men, 197–201
Yi, Anicka, 24–25, 87, 101, 140–42; biopolitics of senses from, 237n126; *Force Majeure* by, 146, 147; *Grabbing at Newer Vegetables* by, 105, 105; *Immigrant Caucus* by, 144, 145–47; *Life is Cheap* by, 143, 149–50, 195; *Lifestyle Wars* diorama by, 148
You Can Call Me F (exhibition), 104–6
Yusoff, Kathryn, 199

Ziser, Michael, 131
Zitkala-Ša (Gertrude Simmons Bonnin), 156
zombification gas, 129–30

ABOUT THE AUTHOR

Hsuan L. Hsu is Professor of English at Concordia University in Montreal and the author of *Geography and the Production of Space in Nineteenth-Century American Literature* and *Sitting in Darkness: Mark Twain's Asia and Comparative Racialization*. He received his PhD in English from UC Berkeley in 2004.